Asia in the
Global Economy

Finance, Trade and Investment

Asia in the Global Economy

Finance, Trade and Investment

Ramkishen S Rajan

George Mason University, USA

Sunil Rongala

Research Manager, An international professional services organization, India

World Scientific

NEW JERSEY · LONDON · SINGAPORE · BEIJING · SHANGHAI · HONG KONG · TAIPEI · CHENNAI

Published by

World Scientific Publishing Co. Pte. Ltd.

5 Toh Tuck Link, Singapore 596224

USA office: 27 Warren Street, Suite 401-402, Hackensack, NJ 07601

UK office: 57 Shelton Street, Covent Garden, London WC2H 9HE

Library of Congress Cataloging-in-Publication Data
Rajan, Ramkishen S.
   Asia in the global economy : finance, trade and investment / Ramkishen S. Rajan, Sunil Rongala.
      p. cm.
   ISBN-13: 978-981-270-573-0
   ISBN-10: 981-270-573-2
   1. Finance--Asia. 2. Asia--Foreign economic relations. 3. Asia--Commerce. 4. Asia--Economic
conditions. 5. International economic relations. I. Rongala, Sunil. II. Title.
   HG187.A2R36 2008
   337.5--dc22

                                                                    2007045602

British Library Cataloguing-in-Publication Data
A catalogue record for this book is available from the British Library.

Printed in Singapore.

Dedicated to

Harminder (Rajan)

and

Jyothsna and Agastya (Rongala)

Preface and Acknowledgments

A common complaint against many economists is that their musings and writings can only be understood by other economists. Not surprisingly, books or articles on contemporary international economic issues that are easily accessible to non-economists appear to be hard to come by despite there being a seemingly significant appetite for them by students (in applied economics, public policy, international affairs, and international business and commerce), as well as by policy-makers, practitioners, and interested observers.

This volume consists of 20 chapters divided into four sections on various dimensions of international economic policy with specific (though not exclusive) focus on Asia. Chapters 1–5 in Sec. 1 on "Monetary and Exchange Rate Issues" deal with topics on exchange rate regimes, reserve buildup in Asia, and global macroeconomic imbalances. Chapters 6–10 in Sec. 2 on "Financial Liberalization, Financial Crisis, and Financing of Development" discuss topics relating to bank liberalization, international capital flows in Asian economies as well as sources of development finance. Chapters 11–15 in Sec. 3 on "Trade, Investment, and the Rise of China and India" explores topics on foreign direct investment (FDI) flows, production networks, manufacturing and outsourcing, and infrastructure financing in Asia, paying particular attention to the economic rise of China and India. Chapters 16–20 on "Economic Regionalism in Asia", highlight various dimensions of trade, financial, and monetary integration in Asia. While the various chapters are interconnected, each essay can be read quite independently of one another. We have endeavored to provide a number of key references in each chapter in order to document the arguments made, and also in case interested readers want to follow up on the issues discussed.

Given the rapidly changing dynamics in the world economy and especially in Asia, it is inevitable that any volume on international economic policy runs the risk of becoming "old news" quite quickly. Nonetheless, we believe the strength of the essays in this volume is the quality of the overall economic analysis; we are confident it will stand the test of time. In any event, many of the issues explored are more structural and long-term in nature and that should further allay fears of relevance or lack thereof. Similarly, since the book is meant as a general and easy read, the individual chapters are short and — as much as possible — sharp.

Some of the chapters in this volume are an outgrowth of op-eds initially written by the first author (Ramkishen Rajan) for the *Business Times* in Singapore and the *Economic and Political Weekly* in India. Vikram Khanna, Associate Editor of the *Business Times* in Singapore has been extremely supportive of and instrumental in the first author writing a regular column in the *Business Times*. The first author would like to acknowledge his support and encouragement. The first author would also like to acknowledge the late Krishna Raj, Editor of *Economic and Political Weekly (EPW)* as well as his Deputy Editor at that time, Padma Prakash. Both urged the first author to contribute regularly to *EPW* and they always made sure that the articles were carried promptly in the periodical. Krishna Raj's sudden passing has been a great loss. While Padma Prakash has since moved from *EPW*, we are happy to note that she has started a new on-line magazine *eSocialScience* (http://www.esocialsciences.com). We have no doubt that this venture will be successful and look forward to helping make it so.

The first author would like to acknowledge the support of his colleagues and resources provided by his current place of employment, the School of Public Policy at George Mason University (SPP-GMU) in Virginia, USA as well as ongoing conversations and insights on policy issues by Mukul Asher of the National University of Singapore. The second author (Sunil Rongala) would like to acknowledge the first author for getting him involved in this project. He would also like to acknowledge his former employer, the Murugappa Group in Chennai, India for giving their acquiescence to his participating in this project. Both authors would like to acknowledge their teacher and mentor, Thomas Willett, at Claremont Graduate University in Claremont, California.

A few essays have been co-authored with colleagues and former students of the first author. We would like to thank in particular Rahul Sen, Sadhana Srivastava, Surabhi Jain, and Jose Kiran. In addition, assistance from Jose Kiran, Alice Ouyang, and Sadhana Srivastava, and especially Nicola Virgill was instrumental in helping us compile and organize this volume. We appreciate their assistance. We would also like to acknowledge the continuing support extended to us by WSPC. Chan Yi Shen, Venkatesh Sandhya, Kim Tan, and their colleagues at WSPC have been highly professional and personable and a pleasure to work with.

Lastly, but most importantly, our family members (partners, parents, and siblings) have remained unstinting in their support of our respective careers and have provided us the stability necessary to remain focused on our writings.

Ramkishen S. Rajan
Virginia, USA
and
Sunil Rongala
Chennai, India

July 2007

Contents

Preface and Acknowledgments   vii

Section 1: Monetary and Exchange Rates Issues   1

  1. Asia's Embarrassment of Riches: A Story of   3
      Prudence, Global Imbalances, and Some Good
      Old Fashioned Mercantilism
  2. The Known Unknown: The Whopping US Current   15
      Account Deficit and Its Implications
        (*With Surabhi Jain*)
  3. Will the US Dollar Remain "Top Dog"?:   25
      The Billion Dollar Question
        (*With Jose Kiran*)
  4. A Central Banker's Holy Grail: Inflation-Targeting   37
      Frameworks with Reference to Asia
        (*With Tony Cavoli*)
  5. Singapore's Currency Baskets and the Mantra   51
      of Competitiveness: The Importance of Real
      Exchange Rates

Section 2: Financial Liberalization, Financial Crises   63
           and the Financing of Development

  6. Barbarians at the Gates: Foreign Bank Entry in Asia   65
  7. The Tobin Tax: A Panacea for Financial Crises?   77
  8. International Capital Flows to Asia: The Never-Ending   87
      Magic Spigot?
  9. Using Reserves to Finance Infrastructure in India: 99
      Will It Clear the Gridlock?
 10. The Goldmine of Development Finance: 111
      Reassessing the Importance of Migrants'
      Remittances

Section 3: Trade, Investment and the Rise of China   **123**
                  and India

11. The "Do's and Don'ts" of Attracting Foreign   125
      Direct Investment.
12. Chips from East Asia, Hardware from Southeast   139
      Asia, and Assembled in China: Production
      Sharing and Trade in Asia
13. All Paths Lead to India: Do Other Asian   149
      Countries Pose a Challenge to Its
      Dominance in Services Outsourcing?
          (With Sadhana Srivastava)
14. The Rise of the Indian Manufacturing Sector: 159
      A True Underdog Story
15. Will the Big Tiger Leave Any Crumbs for the   175
      Little Dragons? China vs. Southeast Asia

Section 4: Economic Regionalism in Asia   **191**

16. Embracing One's Neighbor: Redefining the   193
      Importance of India to ASEAN
17. Going It Alone: Singapore's Trade Strategy   203
          (With Rahul Sen)
18. ASEAN Economic Integration: Taking Care   217
      of Business
19. Uncooperative Cooperation: The Saga of   229
      Economic Cooperation in South Asia
20. Monetary and Financial Cooperation in Asia: 243
      More than Just Buzzwords?

Unless stated explicitly, dollars ($) in the book refer to US dollars ($).

Section 1

Monetary and Exchange Rates Issues

Chapter 1

Asia's Embarrassment of Riches: A Story of Prudence, Global Imbalances, and Some Good Old Fashioned Mercantilism*

Introduction

Asia has had an insatiable appetite for foreign exchange reserves and the proof is that its share of global reserves rose from about 46 percent in January 1995 to 67 percent by August 2005. Central banks in Asia alone accounted for three quarters of the total global reserve buildup between 2002 and 2005.[1] The combined foreign exchange reserves of China, Japan, South Korea, Hong Kong, Taiwan, India, Malaysia, and Singapore stood at approximately around $860 billion at the start of 2000, surging to $2.6 trillion by the end of 2005. By the end of 2006, the combined reserves of these countries had increased to almost $3 trillion (Fig. 1). China's foreign exchange reserves alone stood at over $1 trillion in December 2006 (Fig. 2).

Given that most Asian central banks are obstructing the tendency of their currencies to appreciate against the US dollar (some more than others), an interesting dynamic appears to be taking hold in China and other reserve-rich economies like India and Korea. Large reserves are viewed by the market as an indication that the domestic currency has to appreciate at some point of time. They also tend to be taken to indicate strong "fundamentals", hence leading to upgrading of the country's credit ratings. This expectation of future capital gains and lower risk perceptions motivates large-scale capital inflows. This in turn adds to the country's stock of reserves as central banks mop up excess US dollars to keep the bilateral exchange rate stable in nominal terms. Thus,

---

* This chapter draws on Rajan, RS. Asia's embarrassment mountain of riches (27 April 2005), *Business Times* (Singapore) and Rajan, RS. US deficit a ticking time-bomb (28 January 2005), *Business Times* (Singapore).
[1] See European Central Bank (2006) The Accumulation of Foreign Reserves. *Occasional Paper No. 43.* http://www.ecb.int/pub/pdf/scpops/ecbocp43.pdf [February 2006].

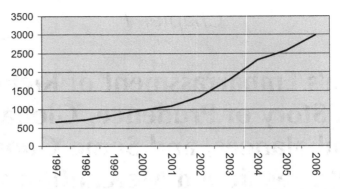

Fig. 1.   Foreign exchange reserve buildup in Asia (US$ millions) (1997–2006).
Source: Bloomberg.

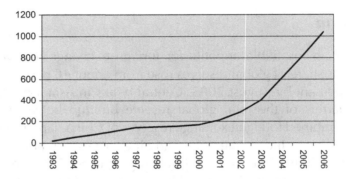

Fig. 2.   Foreign exchange reserve buildup in China (US$ millions) (1993–2006).
Source: Bloomberg.

reserve growth in China in 2003 was primarily due to large surpluses in the
capital account as well as in the errors and omissions section of the balance of
payments account (which reflects net nonofficial capital flows) (Fig. 3).[2]

---

[2] The Chinese government finally loosened its strict US dollar peg and allowed for a small revaluation from
8.28 to 8.11 CNY per US dollar in 21 July 2005 and simultaneously announced that the currency would be
pegged to a basket of currencies. Interestingly, China has since experienced a sharp increase in its trade surplus relative to the capital account despite expectations of continued upward pressure on the CNY (i.e., one
logically would have expected to see an intensification of speculative inflows). On the one hand, the decline
in the capital account surplus was partly policy-induced. The government has been promoting outward investments by Chinese corporates and domestic institutional investors and has loosened a number of restrictions
on capital outflows to ease some appreciation pressures from huge reserves accumulation, while simultaneously tightening some restrictions on capital inflows such as imposing a quota in July 2004 on offshore borrowing by foreign banks operating in China. On the other hand, the sharp increase in the country's current account
balance is somewhat harder to rationalize. It has been suggested by some observers that the current account
surplus has been partly driven by over-invoicing of exports and under-invoicing of imports. See Ouyang, A,
RS Rajan and TD Willett (2006). China as a reserve sink: The evidence from offset and sterilization coefficients,
Working Paper No. 10/2007, Hong Kong Institute for Monetary Research, May. Also see Prasad, E and SJ Wei
(2005). Understanding the structure of cross-border capital flows: The case of China, mimeo, IMF (December).

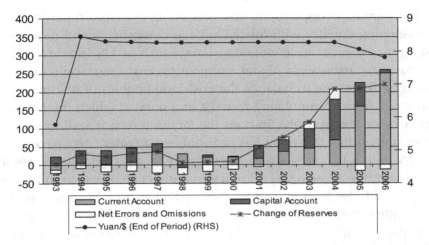

Fig. 3. Trends in China's balance of payments transactions (US$ billions) (1993–2006). *Source*: IFS, the SAFE web site, Bloomberg, and TEJ Great China Database.

Prudence Motive for Reasons Reserve Build-Up — The Limits

The initial motivation behind the rapid stockpiling of Asian reserves was understandable — following the crisis of 1997–1998, there was a belief that reserves were needed for precautionary or insurance motives. These motives encompass both crisis management and crisis prevention objectives. The former refers to the role of reserves in reducing the extent of exchange rate (and output) adjustment if a crisis does happen. This in turn could refer either to the ability to finance underlying payments imbalances, or to provide liquidity in the face of negative external shocks. Crisis prevention refers broadly to a reduction in the incidence of a crisis. The argument here is simply that, other things equal, high reserves may be viewed as a sign of strength or increased creditworthiness of an economy, thus reducing the chances of a run against the currency. Indeed, many studies have confirmed that low short-term debt to foreign exchange reserves and/or money supply ratios have consistently stood out as being quite robust predictors of a crisis.[3]

However, the prudence rationale for amassing a war chest of reserves begets the question as to *"how much is enough?"* Apart from potentially inflationary consequences of reserve buildup (or carry costs of sterilized intervention),

---

[3] See Bussiere, M and C Mulder (1999). External vulnerability in emerging market economies: How high liquidity can offset weak fundamentals and the effects of contagion, *IMF Working Paper No. 99/88*; Dadush, U, D Dasgupta and D Ratha (2000). The role of short-term debt in recent crises, *Finance and Development* 37, 54–57 and World Bank (2000). *Global Economic Prospects and the Developing Countries*. New York: Oxford University Press.

there is a significant opportunity cost of holding reserves. In particular, why is a developing country with relatively large domestic capital requirements investing its resources in low-yielding assets such as US Treasury securities when domestic assets yield higher marginal returns? One would expect that a central bank looking to balance the costs and benefits of holding reserves would desist from accumulating reserves at a point at which the costs at the margin exceed the benefits. So does the fact that Asia is still accumulating reserves suggest that this point has not yet been attained? Not necessarily. If a country with a balance of payments surplus stops accumulating reserves, by definition it is allowing its currency to appreciate. Apart from prudence, reserves could also be amassed as a side effect of an exchange rate policy. Asia has attempted to maintain somewhat undervalued exchange rates with varying degrees of flexibility as an integral part of an export-led growth strategy (mercantilism).[4] In particular, Asian central banks have intervened in the foreign exchange market to sell their currencies — and, in return, have accumulated international reserves — in an attempt to minimize the appreciation of their currencies against the US dollar.

Another point of view regarding the US current account deficit (CAD) is based on the financial account side of the ledger. The argument here goes something as follows. The US CAD is nothing but a reflection of a desire by non-residents to hold US assets. A large part of this demand in turn arises from Asian central banks' holdings of foreign reserves, much of which is denominated in US dollars. In other words, the US financial account surplus is viewed as driving the country's CAD rather than merely being a function of it. To be sure, Asian central banks hold about two thirds of global reserves, about three quarters of which is denominated in liquid US dollar assets (usually US Treasuries). The large and rising reserve holdings by Asian countries is presumed to be a consequence of undervalued exchange rates as their monetary authorities have attempted to keep their respective currencies stable in the face of significant buying pressure by selling their currencies.

Taking this line of reasoning even further, the current global macroeconomic situation whereby the US current account deficit is partly financed by the reserves accumulated by Asian countries which have maintained undervalued exchange rates might be viewed a perfectly normal state of affairs. Why?

Proponents of such a view point to the Bretton Woods system of fixed exchange rates that was initiated in 1944 with an agreement between the war-ravaged Western European countries and the United States that the

---

[4] This issue (of mercantilism versus precaution) is explored in more detail by Aizenman, J and J Lee (2005). International reserves: Precautionary vs mercantilist views, theory and evidence, *Working Paper No. WP/05/198*, IMF and Aizenman, J and J Lee (2006). Financial versus monetary mercantilism: Long-run view of large international reserves hoarding, *Working Paper No. WP/06/280*, IMF.

latter would keep its borders open for exports from the former. Thus, while the United States acted as the "importer of last resort", the Western European countries pegged their respective currencies at undervalued levels to the US dollar to remain cost-competitive. The currency undervaluation and resulting foreign exchange market intervention allowed Western Europe to acquire reserves which were in turn used to finance the US current account deficit at a low cost. There was no immediate or obvious pressure on the United States to check its excessive spending. This system of global fixed exchange rates pegged to the US dollar lasted until 1973. Indeed, this United States–Western Europe axis between 1944 and 1973 (with Japan joining in the 1960s) seems to be bear an uncanny resemblance to the current relationship between the United States and the vendor financing by Asia leading some to suggest that a New Bretton Woods system has emerged since the 1990s.[5]

Advocates of this point of view argue that the current arrangement of international settlements ought to be able to persist for a long time to come as many developing Asian countries (China in particular, but also others in Southeast Asia, India, and Korea) are attempting to grow rapidly by exporting to the United States while maintaining an undervalued currency. In turn the Asian central banks are perfectly happy to hold US sovereign paper as a necessary condition to sustain the export-led growth. According to proponents of this view, Asia will not stop financing the United States on a large scale as that will lead to a marked rise in US long-term interest rates, which in turn might trigger a collapse in the US property and equity prices and a concomitant fall in US consumer spending on all goods and services, including those from Asia. According to this logic, the current global macroeconomic imbalances are structural and inherently stable; fears of global instability are grossly overstated.

Mercantilism or Low Domestic Demand?

While the suggestion that a New Bretton Woods system has emerged is rather intriguing, it runs into some major problems when matched against the facts.

The rapid build up in reserve in Asia really took place after the Asian crisis of 1997–1998, and escalated from 2000 onwards largely because of capital account surpluses (as foreign investors have been anticipating Asian currency revaluations and resulting capital gains). Prior to the 1997 crisis,

---

[5] The pioneers of this view are Dooley, M, D Folkerts-Landau and P Garber. See set of papers here: http://www.frbsf.org/economics/conferences/0502/. For a critical overview of this and other debates on global imbalances, see Eichengreen, B (2006). Global imbalances: The blind men and the elephant, *Issues in Economic Policy No. 1*. Washington: Brookings Institution.

many developing countries in Asia actually ran current account deficits. The conventional wisdom then was that Asian economies were growing and industrializing rapidly and needed high levels of foreign capital to spur their development, and the current account deficits would eventually be self-correcting. This was, after all, the experience of a number of other developed countries in Asia such as Singapore.

Thus, unless there has been a significant and conscious change in the growth strategies in Asia post-crisis, one would be hard pressed to argue that the ongoing imbalances are part of some sort of grand bargain or implicit global understanding, which can persist ad infinitum. More likely, at least in the case of Southeast Asia and Korea, the current account adjustments (from deficit to surplus) was forced on the region by the crisis and it has persisted partly because domestic demand — investment demand in particular — has not fully recovered from the shock of 1997–1998. As such, while many Southeast Asian countries continue to be high savers, they are not nearly as high investors as they used to be in the 1980 and 1990s. The resulting surpluses in the private sector financial balances in Asia have in turn been recycled to the US to finance their dissavings.[6]

In any event, just for argument's sake, let us accept the hypothesis of the New Bretton Woods system (at least with regard to the United States and China). Let us also ignore the fact that the original Bretton Woods system was "artificially" prolonged at least partly by a carrot-and-stick approach towards Western Europe by the United States before eventually breaking down in 1973. The conclusion that the current pattern of international settlements is stable does not automatically follow. While the official sector dominated capital flows in pre-1970s period, international private portfolio flows are much more significant nowadays. Thus, even if there was some grand Bretton Woods-type bargain between the United States and Asian central banks, there is no reason to expect private sector's assessment of relative attractiveness of US assets to be influenced by any such global understanding among national governments.

In Search of Higher Yields

It is extremely difficult to decipher the precautionary motives from the exchange rate and trade objectives. However, a good clue that many Asian central banks have satisfied their precautionary demand for reserves, despite

---

[6] For a discussion of the savings–investment trends, in Asia, see Kharas, H, RS Rajan and E Vostroknutova (2006). In *An East Asian Renaissance: Ideas for Competitive Growth*, H Kharas, and I Gill (eds.), World Bank: Washington, DC; Also see Kramer, C (2006). Asia's investment puzzle. *Finance and Development*, June.

reserves being accumulated unabated, is offered from recent actions and policy statements. Specifically, if the aim is to hold reserves for insurance purposes, the primary focus ought to be on ensuring that the reserves are invested in highly liquid and risk-free assets so that they can be utilized immediately in the event of a crisis. However, it has become commonplace to hear Asian policy-makers talk about channeling some part of their reserves to alternative higher yielding but non-liquid uses.

China was among the first country to find non-liquid uses for its reserves when it used them for recapitalizing their big banks. The People's Bank of China injected some $60 billion between 2003 and 2006 into the three biggest banks, namely, China Construction Bank, Bank of China, and Industrial and Commercial Bank of China.[7] Given the magnitude of non-performing loans (NPLs) in China's banking system, there have been indications that the Chinese may inject more of their reserves to recapitalize other state banks. It has also been suggested that China might also use some of its huge foreign exchange reserves to finance the purchase of oil imports for a strategic reserve the country is planning. Early in 2007, there was some news that China was planning to diversify its foreign reserves but there has not been any clear-cut plan on how this is to be done. Perhaps an indication of one of the possible ways that they may choose to diversify is to invest in global companies; that is if their $3 billion investment for a 9.9 percent stake in Blackstone, a top US private equity firm is any indication.[8]

Similarly, Korea has discussed the possibility of using some part of its reserves to help buildup financial infrastructure to turn Seoul into an international financial center. More recently, some Asian countries including India and Thailand have been actively exploring the possibility of earmarking some of their reserves for financing physical infrastructural projects. In fact, in the country's 2005–2006 budget, the Indian finance minister, Palaniappan Chidambaram, announced the creation of a special purpose vehicle (SPV) to channel some of its reserves to infrastructural spending on "financially viable" projects (areas specified are roads, ports, airports, and tourism).[9] However, while the idea of using low yield assets to finance something that will arguably give a higher return appears to be a good one, the idea of using reserves is not as simple as it seems. In fact, the idea of creating an SPV to use foreign reserves to finance infrastructure in India died a

---

[7] See Ma, G (2006). Sharing China's bank restructuring bill. *China & World Economy* 14(3), 19–37.

[8] If China had purchased a stake of 10 percent or over it would have been considered foreign direct investment (FDI) and the transaction would have come under the scrutiny of the Committee on Foreign Investments in the United States (CFIUS). The CFIUS could potentially have blocked the investment if it was considered detrimental to US national security (broadly defined). See http://www.treas.gov/offices/international-affairs/exon-florio/

[9] This issue is explored in Chapter 9 in this Volume.

quiet death after its announcement by the finance minister. This was partly because the foreign reserves in India are managed by the central bank while the idea of creating an SPV came from the finance ministry and this had the potential to create an image that the independence of the central bank had been compromised.

These non-liquid uses of reserves have an important bearing on exchange rate choices and strategies. The argument some make is that Asian countries might be concerned about appreciating their currencies, not because they want to consciously increase reserves, but because of concerns about the capital losses they will suffer on their US dollar reserves in local currency terms. This is a flawed argument. If the focus is purely on the precautionary demand for reserves, what matters is the US dollar value of reserves (the major intervention currency). Thus, capital gains or losses due to exchange rate changes ought not to be a significant issue (i.e., so-called paper losses without any discernible economic consequences). However, if the intention is to use some of the reserves for domestic needs (bank recapitalization or for local public works), any fall in the value of the reserve currency (i.e., US dollar) relative to the domestic currency can cause significant capital losses, as the domestic purchasing power of reserves will be eroded. This is one of the many conundrums over revaluation that is currently being faced by a number of Asian countries, including China. In other words, even if central banks are willing to eschew their mercantilist objectives, they may still be reluctant to allow their currencies to appreciate "too sharply" because of concerns about capital losses, especially if a portion of the reserves has been earmarked for other objectives (i.e., concerns about "asset dollarization").

Given these diverse and, in some cases, conflicting objectives, some countries seem to be eager to switch out of US dollar denominated assets in search of higher yields so as to minimize the capital losses. This strategy seems to be the one favored by Russia and some oil-rich Mid East countries that may be shifting more of their oil revenue windfalls (i.e., "Petrodollars") into euros given their fairly large trading links with Europe. If this becomes a generalized move against the US dollar, one would expect to see a considerable decline in the share of central bank holdings in US denominated assets. This has not yet happened. Why? Part of the reason is that many Asian countries that have much stronger trading relations with the United States or conduct a large part of their international transactions (trade, investments, foreign exchange intervention, etc.) in US dollars have thus far been quite circumspect about switching away from US dollar-denominated assets. They are also fully cognizant of the fact that any such portfolio adjustments by even one of the regional economies with large reserve holdings (Japan, China, Taiwan, Korea, India, Hong Kong, and Singapore — all which hold over US$200 billion of reserves individually) could precipitate a free fall in the value of the US dollar and push US interest rates upwards, with potential negative real sector repercussions in the United States and globally.

In view of this, while some countries have intermittently publicly suggested that they may be ready to diversify their assets on a large-scale basis, no Asian country has yet broken ranks from the implicit dollar-financing cartel. This said, some of the Asian countries have been channeling a greater share of their reserves into potentially higher-yielding US-denominated assets such as US equities and corporate bonds, while simultaneously moving a somewhat greater share of new reserve assets into non-US dollar assets (i.e., diversification at the margin). There is also an enduring concern that at some stage one or more Asian central banks with large reserve holdings may decide to diversify existing reserve stocks from US dollar denominated assets. If this happens it will add to the structural pressures on the US dollar as well as compromise the ability of the United States to finance its widening current account gap. In the absence of any signs of global macroeconomic coordination, all one can do is hope that the adjustments required to return the global economy to some sort of balance takes place in a smooth and calibrated manner.

Costs of Monetary Sterilization

Beyond the opportunity costs of reserve holdings and potential capital losses form currency changes; reserve buildup (in any currency) creates liquidity in the domestic financial system with attendant inflationary repercussions. Most Asian central banks have been aggressively sterilizing inflationary pressures via the sales of government bonds (secondary issues). Sustained contractionary open market operations (OMOs) to curb liquidity growth have depleted the stock of the government bonds. This, along with most central banks' understandable reluctance to use relatively costlier and far blunter instruments like reserve requirements. In the case of India, this implies that the sustainability of the Reserve Bank of India's (RBI) sterilization operations for neutralizing the monetary impact of its forex intervention is in some doubt. This problem has been overcome in other countries in Asia by the central banks floating their own bonds or bills (primary issues).

The RBI, however, decided against following this route for two reasons. First, if the central bank issues its own bonds it would have to bear the costs of sterilization (hence decreasing central bank capital). These quasi-fiscal costs arise if the central bank uses OMOs to offset the growth in reserves. Therefore, the central bank is effectively selling high-yielding domestic assets for low-yielding foreign ones.[10] Additionally, issuance of central bank bonds may raise the risk premium demanded on government bonds (which tend to be perceived as riskier than those issued by the central bank), hence exacerbating the costs of raising much-needed finances by the government.

Instead, the RBI launched so-called market stabilization bonds (MSBs), which are issued by the Government of India with the specific aim of absorbing the liquidity created in the financial system due to forex intervention. The proceeds of the MSBs will not add to the fiscal deficit (other than the normal fiscal costs of sterilization) as they are held in a separate non-interest bearing account called the Market Stabilization Scheme (MSS) account which is to be maintained and operated by the RBI. The government cannot spend the money available in the MSS account except to pay back maturing debt. The MSS account will help improve the transparency of the RBI's sterilization operations.

While the MSBs have alleviated the physical constraints hindering sterilization over the short and medium terms, as with its other Asian counterparts, only allowing a generalized currency appreciation can durably offset the pressure on liquidity buildup. Absent this, in the case of China, one can envisage two possible scenarios going forward. The benign scenario is one in which the consequent direct inflationary effects — which are admittedly not yet apparent with the exception of asset prices — of the domestic credit boom will erode the price competitiveness of Chinese goods, thus reducing the country's balance of payments surplus and stemming reserve inflows. In other words, while the nominal exchange rate may be rigid, the real exchange rate (nominal rate adjusted for relative prices) is self-equilibrating. A less rosy scenario is plausible in view of the fact that the surge in domestic credit is intermediated via the banking system. Given the relatively lax prudential supervision of banks and other financial institutions, and to the extent that it is generally more difficult to discriminate between good and bad risks during a boom, resources have been inefficiently allocated to relatively unproductive investment projects, including real estate, hence further fueling asset price inflation.

---

[10] One way of overcoming these costs is to try and reduce the monetary base directly by requiring banks to hold excess reserves which may generate low returns. By so doing, however, the quasi-fiscal costs are merely transformed into financial or banking costs as the domestic banks' profitability is reduced while bank management decisions (regarding asset allocation) are constrained. These costs of sterilization are clearly unsustainable over time and can even be counterproductive, as they prevent interest rates from declining, thus prolonging capital inflows. For a detailed discussion and computation of sterilization, see Ouyang, A, RS Rajan and TD Willett (2007). Managing the monetary consequences of reserve accumulation in emerging Asia, mimeo (February).

Conclusion

All in all, it is imperative for Asian currencies to introduce a greater degree of flexibility to their currencies. The move initiated by China and Malaysia in 22 July 2005 to introduce a degree of greater flexibility is a noteworthy step in the right direction. However, as long as the currencies remain anything less than flexible, one can expect, that over time, Asia will continue to buildup reserves. In order to maximize the effectiveness of holding reserves it is important to keep in mind that the management of reserves cannot be seen in isolation. It must be seen as part of an entire package of macroeconomic policies including exchange rate regimes, financial sector soundness, surveillance, and debt management. In order to minimize the net costs of reserve stockpiles, countries could always attempt to improve the risk-return performance of their respective reserve portfolios. In this regard, the gradual rebalancing of reserve holdings from US dollar denominated assets to euros and higher yielding regional currencies is an important dynamic that could have significant and long-lasting impacts on global macroeconomic imbalances and financial markets. These effects might include a sharp fall in the US dollar, a spike in US interest rates, and a possible further rise in the euro with a consequent impact on Euroland's growth.

Beyond efficient management of reserves, is there any way in which the liquidity yield from holding reserves might be generated without the need for individual countries to continue to accumulate them at such a large scale and pace so as to reduce the insurance cost? One possibility is for regional economies to benefit from scale economies by pooling some part of their reserves. An obvious starting point in this regard would be reinforce and augment the existing regional swap arrangement (Chiang Mai initiative) as well as extend it to a broader set of countries in the region with high reserve levels.[11] Intensive discussions are ongoing in policy circles in Asia on various possibilities along these lines.

---

[11] This issue is explored in Chapter 20 in this Volume.

Chapter 2

The Known Unknown: The Whopping US Current Account Deficit and Its Implications*

(With Surabhi Jain)

Introduction

What exactly is the current account, what are the components that make a current account, and why is the current account important? A good description of the current account and its components is as follows:

> "The current account measures the change over time in the sum of three separate components: the trade account, the income account, and the transfer account. The trade account measures the difference between the value of exports and imports of goods and services. A trade deficit occurs when a country imports more than it exports. The US trade deficit is by far the largest component of the US current account deficit. In fact, fluctuations in the trade deficit are the primary cause of fluctuations in the current account deficit. The income account measures the income payments made to foreigners net of income payments received from foreigners. For the United States, the income account largely reflects interest payments made by the United States on its foreign debt and interest payments received by the United States on its foreign assets. An income deficit arises when the value of income paid by the United States to foreigners exceeds the value of income received by the United States from foreigners. The transfer account measures the difference in the value of private and official transfer payments to and from other countries. The largest entry in the transfer account for the United States is foreign-aid payments."[1]

The US current account deficit (CAD) has been at the center of the debate on macroeconomic imbalances that supposedly bedevil the global

---

* This chapter draws on Rajan, RS and S Jain, Predict value of dollar? Just toss a coin (8 July 2005), *Business Times* (Singapore).

[1] See Holman, JA (2001). Is the large US account deficit sustainable. *Economic Review*, First Quarter, Federal Reserve Bank of Kansas City, pp. 5–23.

economy. No one really knows whether the US CAD is sustainable, when it will unravel, how it will unravel, or in fact, whether there will be any unraveling at all in the near future (i.e., is the CAD sustainable?). This chapter examines the dynamics of the US current account deficit, how it has evolved over time, how it is being financed (via international capital flows), and the impact on the US dollar over the last decade.

Evolution of the US CAD and the US Dollar

Having reached a situation of external balance in 1991 (coinciding with the recession in the US), the US CAD as a share of GDP remained below 2 percent until 1997. Thus, even though there was a domestic consumption and investment boom (especially in high-technology capital goods), the overall CAD as a share of GDP remained stable, as this was a period of considerable fiscal consolidation in the United States under the Clinton administration. However, the US current account balance actually began its secular deterioration from 1997 (Fig. 1).

At a superficial level, the increase in the US CAD during this period is easily explained. Initially, the US dollar experienced a generalized appreciation in 1996 against the Japanese yen and many European currencies (The Euro came into being only in 1999). This in turn contributed to a rise in "cheap" US capital and consumer imports to fuel the ongoing growth. Despite the sharp appreciation of the US dollar relative to other major currencies (for instance, the yen depreciated from around 100 per US dollar in January 1995 to almost 118 yen per US dollar by January 1997) on a trade weighted basis, the appreciation in the US dollar was limited to some extent

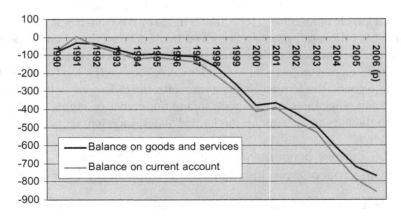

Fig. 1. US current account balance (US$ billions) (1990–2006).

Source: US Bureau of Economic Analysis.

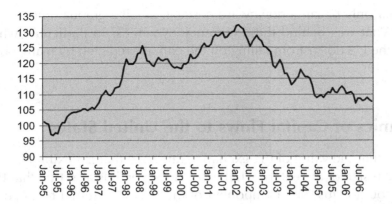

Fig. 2. The dollar trade weighted index, January 1995–December 2006 (1995 = 100).
Source: Federal Reserve Bank of Atlanta.

because many emerging Asian currencies were effectively pegged to the US dollar. Indeed, this US dollar peg and consequent appreciation of the emerging Asian currencies (against the yen) and loss of emerging Asia's export competitiveness was one of many factors behind the Asian crisis that began in mid-1997 and continued until early 1999 (Fig. 2).

The worsening of the US CAD during this period (1997 onwards) was largely a reflection of the curtailed domestic demand in Asia following the Asian crisis, which persisted till early 1999. In addition to the negative income effect that shrunk demand for United States goods to emerging Asia during this period, the sharp depreciation of the Asian currencies also led to an even more marked real exchange rate appreciation of the US dollar. To illustrate, after a period of relative stability between 1989 and 1996, while the real effective exchange rate of the dollar (the dollar trade weighted index) rose slightly, by less than 10 percent, in the two years between mid-1995 and mid-1997, it appreciated by almost 15 percent in just a single year thereafter (mid-1997 to mid-1998). While the Asian countries recovered from early 1999 onwards, the policies used by these countries to maintain undervalued currencies (partly to promote exports and also to stockpile reserves to safeguard against future crises), along with the continued robust growth in the United States, contributed to the sustained worsening of the US CAD.

It is generally believed that the real exchange rate is eventually self-equilibrating or mean-reverting over the long run. The interesting question, therefore, is why the secular deterioration of the US CAD did not lead to a correction of the real value of the US dollar. In actual fact the US dollar continued to appreciate rather than depreciate in real terms, peaking in early 2002. Thus, the US dollar appreciated by about 35 percent in real terms and about 45 percent in nominal terms between mid-1995 and early 2002. The

US dollar only began a downward descent, albeit a gradual one, from early 2002. What was behind these currency dynamics? In particular, what prevented the US dollar from falling off the cliff as predicted by many observers since 1999?

Dynamics of Capital Flows to the United States

It is true that the value of the exchange rate (one that is flexible) is dependent on the size of the external balance. However, it is also true that the current account is just one component of the overall external balance. When thinking about the exchange rate it is also important to consider the capital (financial) account. It is in this context that arguably a more useful indicator of long-term sustainability of a country's external balance is the so-called basic balance, which is the summation of the current account, net foreign direct investment (FDI), and foreign investment in US government bonds.

FDI flows averaged US$4 billion between 1985 and 1996 (0.01 percent of GDP). Net foreign direct investment inflows however surged following the Asian financial crisis, peaking in 2000 at over US$162 billion, easing off significantly since then. Net FDI flows in 2004 stood at about US$110 billion as outward FDI from the United States outpaced inward FDI to the United States. However, in 2005, net FDI became positive and it stood at around US$100 billion. The reason for this turnaround was a rapid fall in US investment abroad, which fell to negative US$12 billion in 2005 from $222 billion in 2004. However, the net FDI for 2006 again became negative and the number stood at US$65 billion (Fig. 3).

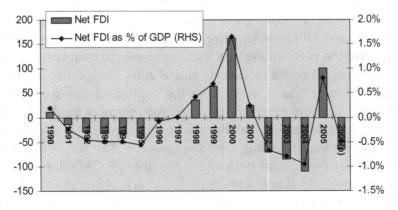

Fig. 3.   Net FDI flows to US (US$ billions) (1990–2006).

Source: US Bureau of Economic Analysis.

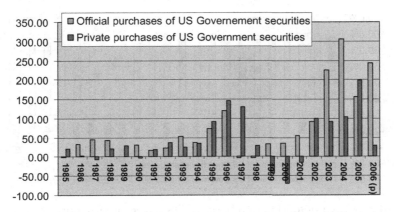

Fig. 4.   Foreign purchases of US government securities (US$ billions) (1985–2006).

Source: US Bureau of Economic Analysis.

Note: Private purchases of government securities refer to purchase of US Treasuries.

What about foreign investment in US government bonds? Purchases of US sovereign bonds can either be made by foreign governments/central banks or by other private investors looking to invest in liquid, relatively risk-free USD assets. The total official flows into US government securities averaged $40 billion over the period 1985 and 1996 and constituted a rather insignificant proportion of the total capital flows during this period (Fig. 4). However, the flows into US Treasury market have surged following the Asian crisis as foreign central banks in the Asian economies have rapidly built up their reserves. Most of the Asian reserves have been channeled into US government securities, typically US Treasuries; the proportion invested into "other securities" has remained low and dropped to 10 percent in 2004.[2] The total official foreign purchases of US government securities increased from US$30 billion in 1999 to nearly $305 billion in 2004, growing at an average annual rate of almost 60 percent compounded annually. This, however, fell to $243 billion in 2006. Private investment into government securities had been low, but rose after 1993 and peaked in 1996 at around US$150 billion. The private flows turned negative from 1999 to 2001 but have increased thereafter, averaging well over $100 billion between 2002 and 2005. However, private purchases of US Treasuries fell by a huge margin in 2006 to just $30 billion. A possible explanation for this fall is that private investors diverted their funds to other US securities where investments in 2006 were $620 billion compared to $474 billion in 2005.

---

[2] This consists of US treasury and export–import bank obligations not included elsewhere, and of debt securities of US government corporations and agencies. See Chapter 1 for a discussion of Asian reserves.

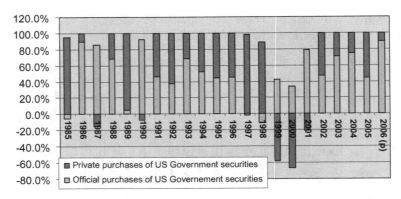

Fig. 5. Breakdown of foreign purchases of US government securities (1985–2006).

Source: US Bureau of Economic Analysis.

Note: Private purchases of government securities refer to purchase of US Treasuries.

Examining the breakdown of foreign purchases of US government securities, it is instructive to note that between 2002 and 2004 about 60 percent of US government securities were purchased by foreign central banks and 40 percent by the private sector (Fig. 5). These proportions may substantially understate the actual magnitude of foreign central bank purchases (i.e., so-called "policy buying"), as some of the central banks have regularly invested though third parties (private brokers), or may have bought US fixed income assets in the foreign secondary market.[3] Foreign purchases of US government securities are generally considered a fairly stable source of capital inflows as it reflects the demand for liquid and relatively risk-free assets. While official purchases are conducted by foreign central banks eager to channel some of their reserves into USD assets, private sector purchases are made by a number of longer-term institutional investors such as pension funds. Such investments in US government securities are considered relatively risk-free — a reflection of the role of the USD as a global reserve currency. Thus, until and unless the USD ceases being viewed as a reserve currency, one will expect foreign purchases of US government securities to persist (see Conclusion). Interestingly, while the CAD as well as the basic balance (current account balance + net FDI) has been on a secular decline since 1997, the broad basic balance (current account balance + net FDI + official and private purchases of US government securities) hovered at largely around 2 to 3 percent of GDP between 1998 and 2005 (Fig. 6). This was

---

[3] It is generally known that the Bank of Japan (BOJ) tends to make purchases directly and so their policy intervention is relatively easy to capture. In contrast, the People's Bank of China (PBOC) tends to use third parties to purchase US securities.

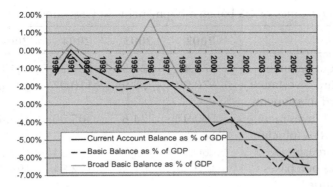

Fig. 6.   US current account and broad basic balance as percent of GDP (1990–2006). *Source*: US Bureau of Economic Analysis.

largely because of an explosive increase in the investment into US government securities. Seen in this light, the US external deficit appears far more sustainable.[4]

Intuitively, the relative stability of the broad basic balance (compared to the CAD) is understandable. For simplicity let us focus just on the United States and Asia, Just as a large part of Asia's exports have been stimulated by FDI, part of the US CAD is due to US companies investing abroad and selling the products by to the United States. The US basic balance deficit with Asia is matched by a basic balance surplus and reserve build-up in Asia. Asian reserves are in turn recycled to the US via foreign purchases of US government securities which help to ensure that US yields remain low and spur US consumption and, therefore, Asian export growth. In other words, there may be an inherent tendency for the US broad basic balance to be relatively stable in the *short run* because of this mutual co-dependence with Asia. Of course, over time, if the Asian central banks want to maintain rigid currencies but lose faith in the US dollar, the basic balance could worsen significantly, a prospect that has kept foreign exchange markets on tenterhooks in the last few years.

The other pertinent observation here is that the US central bank purchases alone cannot explain the strengthening of the US dollar until 2002. Indeed, the broad basic balance has remained in deficit since 1997, suggesting a net sale of US dollars. However, the US dollar was supported by the inflows of other types of so-called mobile capital, viz. securities and bank financing (Table 1). In fact the big — though not sufficiently recognized — story about

---

[4] However, in 2006, the broad basic balance as a percentage of GDP suddenly shot-up to 4.9 percent but that was a result of the net FDI turning negative but it does not take away from the substance of the above argument.

Table 1.   Dynamics of US balance of payments in US$ billions (2002–2006).

	2002	2003	2004	2005	2006 (p)
Current account balance	−472.45	−527.51	−665.29	−791.51	−856.66
Net FDI (inward investment less outward investment)	−70.09	−85.94	−110.97	100.68	−65.29
Foreign official investment in US securities (official)	90.97	224.87	305.00	156.45	243.79
Of which US treasury	60.47	184.93	263.34	71.75	118.34
Foreign private purchases of US Treasuries	100.40	91.46	102.94	199.49	29.42
Securities (Foreign purchases in US less US purchases abroad)	234.73	73.98	234.94	294.02	343.46
Claims reported by banks (US claims reported by US banks less US liabilities reported by US banks)	58.15	84.19	−24.88	−33.17	−41.19

Source: Bureau of Economic Analysis, US Department of Commerce and Federal Reserve Statistical Releases.
Note: p — preliminary estimate.

US capital inflows has been the sharp increase in the net purchases of US corporate and agency bonds (the latter being bonds backed by the US government) by foreign private sector. The demand by foreigners for this asset class climbed more than tenfold from a mere US$33 in 1997 to about US$300 billion in 2001. This was due partly to a decline in US purchases of foreign bonds, but more so due to an upsurge in demand by foreigners for US corporate bonds. The IMF has opined that the increased appetite for US corporate bonds is due to the relative scarcity of high-grade debt issuances. The deep and highly liquid nature of US capital markets is also no doubt an important factor motivating the strong preference for all forms of US fixed income assets including corporate and agency debt. In contrast, net equity flows which had surged in 1999–2000 have tapered off significantly following the decline in US equity markets in early 2000, and have remained moderate ever since.

Conclusion

Received wisdom is that the burgeoning US CAD is a reflection of US overspending (fiscal profligacy and low household savings), and requires some combination of a pick up in domestic demand in the rest of the world (Asia in particular), a cyclical slowdown in US demand, as well as reconfigurations of exchange rates (i.e., generalized and significant depreciation of the US dollar) to rein it in. However, in a speech delivered in 2005, the current Chairman of the Federal Reserve, Ben Bernanke, contested this view.[5] Bernanke hypothesized that the huge American CAD was not because of American profligacy but rather there was a huge savings glut in the world and they invested in American treasuries because of its safety and their trust in the economic system. Thus, rather than the US CAD being financed by international capital flows, Bernanke turned things around and suggested that there are excess savings in the rest of the world — so-called "savings glut" — that is in search for safe investment options and that in turn has contributed to the United States having to run a CAD.

To quote Bernanke:

> "I will take issue with the common view that the recent deterioration in the US current account *primarily* reflects economic policies and other economic developments within the United States itself. Although domestic developments have certainly played a role, I will argue that a satisfying explanation of the recent upward climb of the US current account deficit requires a global perspective that more fully takes into account events outside the United States. To be more specific, I will argue that over the past decade a combination of diverse forces has created a significant increase in the global supply of saving — a global saving glut — which helps to explain both the increase in the US current account deficit and the relatively low level of long-term real interest rates in the world today."[6]

Regardless of whether the US CAD is financed by or caused by international capital flows, the fact remains that the value of the US dollar is largely dependent on the magnitude of mobile capital flows, which by their very nature, tend to be variable and virtually impossible to forecast. As the adage goes, you are better off tossing a coin than trying to forecast short-term exchange rate movements with any degree of accuracy! Factors that will impact these inflows include actual yield and expected growth differentials.

---

[5] Bernanke, B (2005). The global saving Glut and the US current account deficit, speech delivered on 10 March 2005, at the Sandridge Lecture, Virginia Association of Economists, Richmond, Virginia.

[6] *The Economist* wrote the following as a reaction to Bernanke's speech:

> "All the same, these imbalances are weakening America's economy. They cannot increase indefinitely and will be hard to unwind without sending the world economy into recession. Nudging global saving and investment patterns into a healthier balance will require new thinking, both inside and outside America. Policymakers bear more responsibility for the thrift shifts, and the global imbalances, than Mr. Bernanke cares to admit." (*The Economist*, The great thrift shift, 22 September 2005).

Over the medium term, to a large extent the amount of capital inflows into US government and agency bonds depends on the extent of reserves accumulated by foreign central banks and other risk averse long term institutional investors, as well as the degree to which they will be willing to denominate their assets in US Dollars. This in turn is a function of whether the USD continues to be viewed as an international reserve currency. Whether it will be is the focus of the next chapter.

Chapter 3

Will the US Dollar Remain "Top Dog"?: The Billion Dollar Question*

(With Jose Kiran)

Introduction

Countries have been holding foreign exchange reserves since the advent of international trade. In the 19th and early 20th centuries, since "the sun never set on the British Empire", most of the holdings of foreign exchange reserves were logically in pound sterling. Britain was the world's leading trading nation and around 60 percent of the world trade was invoiced and settled in pound sterling. London was also the undisputed financial capital of the world, and, as a result, the sterling was the logical invoicing currency for debt securities and other financial instruments. Conscious efforts were also made to encourage the use of the sterling throughout the British Empire as a medium of exchange so as to simplify transactions. In addition to the sterling's roles as a vehicle and invoicing currency of choice, given that it was fully convertible, central banks used the sterling most often to intervene in foreign exchange markets. All of this led to the sterling becoming the pre-eminent reserve currency of the world. The sterling's share in foreign exchange holdings of official institutions stood at 64 percent in 1899, more than twice the total of its nearest competitors, the French franc and the Deutsche mark (Table 1), and much greater than the US dollar (USD).[1]

However, by 1919 the United States had surpassed the United Kingdom in terms of overall productive capacity, aggregate trade flows, and as a net

* This chapter draws on Rajan, RS and J Kiran (2006). Will the greenback remain the world's reserve currency? *Intereconomics*, 41(3), 124–128.
[1] For details, see Eichengreen, B (2005). Sterling's past, Dollar's future: Historical perspectives on reserve currency competition, *Working Paper No. 11336*, NBER; Eichengreen, B (1997). The euro as a reserve currency, mimeo (November); Frankel, J and M Chinn (2005). Will the euro eventually surpass the dollar as leading international reserve currency?, *Working Paper No. 11510*, NBER.

Table 1.　Shares of currencies in known official foreign exchange assets (1899–1913).

	End of 1899	End of 1913
Sterling	64	48
Francs	16	31
Marks	15	15
Other currencies	6	6

Source: Eichengreen, B (2005). Sterling's past, dollar's future: historical perspectives on reserve currency competition, *Working Paper No. 11336*, NBER.
Note: Percentages may not sum to 100 due to rounding.

international creditor.[2] In addition to the growing relative strength of the US economy, economic historians have argued that the creation of a Federal Reserve System in December 1913 and subsequent development of New York as the world's financial center provided another strong impetus for the rise of the US dollar's role as a major international currency. However, it was only after the shock of the two World Wars and the resulting devastation of the other European economies, as well as the gross mismanagement of the British economy that the United States took over the role of the world's reserve currency, thus breaking the *de facto* "sterling standard".

Rise of the US Dollar Standard

The Bretton Woods system of pegged exchange rate that was centered on the USD and which was put in place in the mid-1940s consolidated the position of the USD as the world's reserve currency in the postwar period. The USD's share of world's reserves peaked at almost 85 percent in the early 1970s. In contrast, the sterling's share continued to drop dramatically following the successive devaluations of the sterling in the 1950s and 1960s. Despite the collapse of the Bretton Woods system in 1971, the USD remained the dominant international currency, though its share in global reserves began to decline, reaching a trough of 50 percent in 1990, only to bounce back to about 60 percent since the late 1990s and well until 2005 (Table 2). This time frame also roughly coincides with the rapid accumulation of foreign reserves by Asian central banks which have chosen to maintain a large share of their massive reserves in US dollar assets.

---

[2] See Eichengreen, B (2005), *ibid.*

Table 2. Share of currencies in allocated official holdings of foreign exchange (percent) (1991–2006).

	1991	1992	1993	1994	1995	1996	1997	1998	1999	2000	2001	2002	2003	2004	2005	2006
US dollar	50.6	54.7	56.1	53.1	53.4	56.8	59.1	62.6	64.9	66.6	66.9	63.5	63.8	65.7	66.7	64.7
Pound sterling	3.4	3.2	3.1	2.8	2.8	3	3.3	3.5	3.6	3.8	4	4.4	4.4	3.4	3.6	4.4
Deutsche mark	15.9	13.7	14.2	15.3	14.7	14	13.7	13.1	—	—	—	—	—	—	—	—
French franc	2.8	2.5	2.2	2.5	2.4	1.9	1.5	1.7	—	—	—	—	—	—	—	—
Swiss franc	1.2	1	1.1	0.6	0.5	0.5	0.5	0.5	0.4	0.5	0.5	0.6	0.4	0.2	0.2	0.2
Netherlands guilder	1	0.6	0.6	0.7	0.5	0.4	0.5	0.5	—	—	—	—	—	—	—	—
Japanese yen	8.7	7.7	7.7	7.8	6.7	6	5.1	5.4	5.4	6.2	5.5	5.2	4.8	3.9	3.6	3.2
ECU	10.6	10.1	8.6	7.7	6.8	5.9	5	0.8	—	—	—	—	—	—	—	—
Unspecified currencies[1,2]	5.7	6.3	6.3	9.5	12.1	11.5	11.3	12	12.1	6.6	6.4	7.1	6.8	1.9	1.7	1.7
Euro	—	—	—	—	—	—	—	—	13.5	16.3	16.7	19.3	19.7	25	24.2	25.8

Source: IMF Currency Composition of Official Foreign Exchange Reserves (COFER) Database. http://www.imf.org/external/np/sta/cofer/eng/index.htm.

Note: (1) The residual is equal to the difference between total foreign exchange reserves of Fund member countries and the sum of the reserves held in the currencies listed in the table.

(2) The residual is equal to the difference between total foreign exchange reserves of IMF member countries and the sum of the reserves held in the currencies listed in the table.

Table 3. World's largest economies in PPP terms in 2006 (International dollars, millions).

Rank	Country	PPP GDP 2005
1	United States	13,201,819
2	China	10,048,026
3	India	4,247,361
4	Japan	4,131,195
5	Germany	2,616,044
6	United Kingdom	2,111,581
7	France	2,039,171
8	Italy	1,795,437
9	Brazil	1,708,434
10	Russian Federation	1,704,756

Available at http://siteresources.worldbank.org/DATASTATISTICS/Resources/GDP_PPP.pdf.
Source: World Bank.

Table 4. Size of US versus Europe (US$ trillions) (2003–2005).

	2003	2004	2005
United States	11.0	11.5	11.8
Eurozone (12 countries)	8.8	9.0	9.8

Source: Chinn, M and J Frankel (2005). Will the euro surpass the dollar as leading international reserve currency, mimeo (June), World Bank.

What is behind the persistent preeminence of the USD in the international monetary system and can it expected to last? First, studies have estimated that every 1 percent increase in a country's share of the world product (measured in PPP terms) is associated with a rise of 0.9–1.3 percentage points in that currency's share of central bank reserves.[3] Therefore, economic size is clearly important in determining the choice of a reserve currency. Referring to Tables 3 and 4, we note that on the basis of economic size, the United States is still the single largest economy in the world even though its relative share of the world's GDP (in Purchasing Power Parity terms) has declined somewhat over the past two decades. The United States is followed by China, Japan, and India.

However, if considered in aggregate, the eurozone with its 12 member economies becomes the world's second largest economy. If we add

---

[3] The lower figure (0.9 percentage points) is probably more appropriate as it incorporates lagged or inertial effects; See Eichengreen, B (1998). The euro as a reserve currency. *Journal of Japanese and International Economics*, 12, 483–506; Eichengreen, B and J Frankel (1996). The SDR, reserve currencies and the future of the international monetary system. In *The Future of the SDR in Light of Changes in the International Financial System*, M Mussa, J Boughton and P Isard (eds.), Washington, DC: IMF.

Denmark, Sweden, and Britain, the eurozone-15 surpasses the United States in economic size. In view of this, it is generally believed that the euro in particular, but also the yen pose the most likely near term challenges to the dominance of the USD. The Chinese renminbi and possibly the Indian rupee are viewed as much longer-term contenders to rival the USD (with a stress on the longer). This said, while the euro and the yen have remained the second and third most important reserve currencies, together they still constitute only about a quarter of the world's reserves and have hitherto failed to come anywhere close to challenging the USD.[4]

The Coming End of the USD Hegemony?

Ever since 1990, when the United States became a net external debtor (Fig. 1), nagging concerns have been expressed about the external store of value of the USD — i.e., the possibility of capital losses due to sharp or prolonged USD depreciation.[5] Other things equal, the greater the unease about

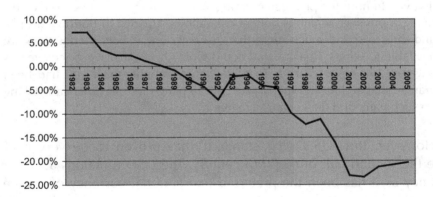

Fig. 1.   US net international investment position (market value) as a percent of GDP (1982–2005).

Source: US Bureau of Economic Analysis (BEA), Bloomberg.

---

[4] Almost all global reserves are held in five currencies, viz. the USD, the euro, the yen, the sterling, and the Swiss franc.

[5] It is unclear whether there is some upper limit to the amount of net claims that foreigners are willing to hold against the United States. The issue of sustainability of the US external debt position is an area in need of further research. For detailed computations and discussions of this issue see Gourinchas, P and H Rey (2005). From world banker to world venture capitalist: The US external adjustment and the exorbitant privilege, mimeo (May); Roubini, N and B Setser (2004). The US as a net debtor: The sustainability of the US external imbalances, mimeo (November); Also, see The passing of the buck? (2 December 2004), *The Economist.*

the prospects for the long term sustainability of the US dollar, the more rapid will be the transition away from the USD. Robert Mundell, for instance, noted in 1998:

> "It would be a mistake to ignore (the fact that) ... in the last 15 years US current account deficits have turned the US from the world's biggest creditor to its biggest debtor ... The low-saving high-debt problems will one day come home to roost ... There will come a time when the pileup of international indebtedness makes reliance on the dollar as the world's only main currency untenable ... The fact that the bulk of international reserves is held in dollars makes the currency a sitting duck in a currency crisis ... Sole reliance on the dollar as the main reserve, invoice and intervention currency presents risks that are no longer necessary."[6]

In similar vein, *The Economist* reported:

> "The dollar has been the leading international currency for as long as most people can remember. But its dominant role can no longer be taken for granted. If America keeps on spending and borrowing at its present pace, the dollar will eventually lose its mighty status in international finance. And that would hurt: the privilege of being able to print the world's reserve currency, a privilege which is now at risk, allows America to borrow cheaply, and thus to spend much more than it earns, on far better terms than are available to others. Imagine you could write checks that were accepted as payment but never cashed. That is what it amounts to. If you had been granted that ability, you might take care to hang on to it. America is taking no such care, and may come to regret it."[7]

However, the "US Dollar standard" has proven to be very resilient since the second half of the 20th century. The USD functions as a reserve currency as it has been the preferred international currency of choice for invoicing of transactions, currency peg, and a medium of exchange.[8] The military and geopolitical clout of the United States (particularly critical in this day and age of global terrorism) and the deeply entrenched network externalities that is enjoyed by the incumbent will work in tandem to ensure that the USD will remain the dominant reserve currency for a long time to come. This point has some empirical validation. A study of the currency

---

[6] Mundell, R. The case for the Euro — I and II (24 and 25 March 1998), *Wall Street Journal.*
[7] See The disappearing dollar (2 December 2004), *The Economist.*
[8] For an elaboration of the functions of an international currency, see Pollard, PS (2001). The creation of the euro and the role of the dollar in international markets, *Federal Reserve Bank of St. Louis Review,* September/October, pp.17–36; Also see Frankel, J and M Chinn (2005). *op. cit.*

composition of global reserves in the 1970s, 1980s, and 1990s arrives at the following conclusion:

> "We do not detect radical shifts in the currency composition of reserves over time. The choice of reserve asset by developing countries continues to be influenced by a dense web of exchange rate, financial, and commercial links with the reserve-currency countries, which itself continues to develop gradually over time. To be sure, there are ongoing changes in these relationships and policies ... (b)ut these are evolutionary processes, which again suggests that the currency composition of reserves will change gradually, not discontinuously. There are plenty of potential sources of instability affecting exchange rates and the international monetary system. But ... instability in the demand for reserves seems unlikely to be one of them."[9]

While there may be some concern about the store of value function of the USD over time, the US economy will have to significantly underperform the rest of the world on a sustained basis for it to lose its global dollar hegemony. Indeed, given the desire by central banks and other investors for greater yield on their reserves, it is possible that they will choose to shift more of their assets into longer yielding US assets rather than into other currencies. As such, while accepting the possibility of capital losses (in the event of a longer term decline in the USD), investors are at least being partly compensated for taking on greater liquidity risk by extending the duration of their portfolios. As noted by an analyst from Morgan Stanley:

> "(A)s central banks shift from a traditional liquidity management posture to a return-enhancing investment strategy, reserve diversification ... does not necessarily mean USD selling or USD weakness ... The US corporate bond market accounts for close to three times the corporate bond market in euroland, and 3.5 times as big as in Japan. In fact, this market is bigger than the other corporate bond markets combined. Similarly, the total market cap of the US equity market is dominant, 2.5–3 times bigger than the markets in euroland or Japan. Therefore, as central banks diversify across assets, there is a greater justification to increase their exposure to USD risky assets ... Thus, if central banks diversify ... it is far from clear it will be USD-negative."[10]

---

[9] Eichengreen, B and D Mathieson (2000). The currency composition of foreign exchange reserves: Retrospect and prospect, *Working Paper No. 00/131*, IMF, p. 17; Also see Frankel, J and M Chinn (2005). *op. cit.*

[10] Jen, S (2005). USD: Is reserve diversification negative for the dollar?, *Global Economic Forum*, Morgan Stanley (September 16).

Possible Rivals to the US Dollar Standard

In the heyday of the Japanese economy in the 1970s and 1980s, the yen's share of global reserves peaked at almost 9 percent of global reserves in 1991 and there was a concomitant decline of the USD's share from 55 percent in 1987 to 50 percent in 1991 (due also to the intensification of the European monetary integration). However, the main factors hindering the yen's global use at that time were a conscious policy on non-internationalization of the yen and Japan's underdeveloped financial markets. While the Japanese have been keen on promoting the international use of the yen since the mid and late 1990s, the economy stagnated and its financial sector became burdened by inefficiencies and non-performing loans (following the burst of the asset bubble). In addition, Japan's bank based financial system has precluded the country from developing as deep and liquid financial and capital markets as available in the United States or Western Europe. Thus, despite Japan's size and its rapid rate of growth pre 1990s, the yen has failed to become a significant competitor to the USD. The yen's share has in fact declined since the 1990s, falling to less than 5 percent in 2003.

In contrast to Japan, Europe's financial markets have depth and liquidity (which has been further enhanced with the advent of the euro in 1999),[11] and many European policy-makers have been keen on promoting the euro as an alternative to the USD since its inception. Prior to the launch of the euro and ever since then, a number of observers have argued that it would challenge the USD's hegemony.[12] In contrast, however, Barry Eichengreen noted as far back as 1997:

> "(I)ncumbency is a strong advantage in the competition for reserve-currency status. Both historical and econometric evidence point in this direction. The dollar being the reigning champion, it accounts for a larger share of global foreign exchange reserves than suggested by a simple comparison of US and EU GDP's, and it should do so for some time to come. A more institutionally-oriented analysis reinforces the point. Reserve currencies are those which are issued by the governments of countries that are international financial centers. The United States gained its status as a financial center and the dollar its reserve-currency role only once the country acquired a central bank ready and willing to engage in day-to-day liquidity management and prepared to mount lender-of-last-resort operations. The Maastricht Treaty does not foresee the European Central Bank as assuming comparable responsibilities. This will

---

[11] For an analysis of the impact of the euro on European financial markets, see Galati, G and K Tsatsaronis (2001). The impact of the euro on Europe's financial markets, *Working Paper No. 100*, BIS.

[12] For a balanced discussion on the challenge posed by the euro to the USD, see Portes, R and H Rey (1998). The emergence of the euro as an international currency. *Economic Policy*, 26, 306–332.

tend to slow the development of the eurozone as an international financial center and, by implication, limit the euro's reserve-currency role."[13]

A number of other factors have further held back the rise of the euro as a dominant reserve currency. First, there has been a lack of economic dynamism in the eurozone compared to the United States and there remains a need for significant structural adjustments in many of the major Western European countries. Second, there are widening yield differentials between the United States and the eurozone (though this is only a transitory factor).[14] Third and more recently, the dissatisfaction by many European citizens with the eurozone (as evidenced by the rejection of the EU constitution by France and Netherlands' in 2005) has been a further setback to the euro challenging the USD. In relation to this, there remain persistent concerns that the lack of forward movement in political union in Europe has implied that the euro is a "currency without a state". For instance, an analyst from Morgan Stanley has observed:

"Europe's widening political fractures and economic divergences raise the specter of an EMU break-up over the next five to ten years. I don't believe (and I certainly don't hope) that this is the *likely* outcome, but the break-up risk is larger than generally perceived. In my view, the lingering risk of an unraveling of the euro project implies that the euro will not be able to rival the dollar as a reserve currency, despite the dollar's own problems."[15]

So, in the short and medium terms, while the euro is closer to challenging the USD as the world's dominant reserve currency than is the yen, it is unlikely that Asian and other central banks will be willing to shift a significant share of their USD denominated reserve portfolios into these currencies. There has been speculation that the one country that could possibly challenge the USD is the Chinese renminbi given that China is likely to become the world's largest economy and trader within the next half century. For instance, one observer has noted:

"Whatever China does, it will reveal the emergence of a wide and significant renminbi-bloc. Asia is not a dollar, or yen-bloc but a renminbi-bloc. China's likely status as the world's largest economy and trader well before 2050

---

[13] Eichengreen, B (1997). *op. cit.*, pp. 23–24.

[14] In others words, there is a need to distinguish the role of the USD as a funding (reserve) currency from its role in terms of providing relatively higher yields. The former is structural in nature while the latter is transitory. See Jen, S (2005). USD: From a funding to a high-yield currency, *Global Economic Forum*, Morgan Stanley (September 30).

[15] Felms, J (2005). Global: Pondering the composition of central bank reserves (Part 1), *Global Economic Forum*, Morgan Stanley (October 18); Also see Bergsten, F (2005). The euro and the world economy, mimeo (April).

marks it out as the most likely usurper of the dollar's status as the financial world's numeraire."[16]

While this is an interesting point of view, the acute weaknesses of the Chinese financial system and shallowness of its financial markets, the non-convertibility of its currency, and the persistent restraints on the capital account, makes the possibility of the Chinese renminbi as a challenger to the USD extremely remote anytime in the near future.[17] Similar concerns rule out the currency of the other Asian giant, India, for the time being. While India's financial system is far stronger than that of China and arguably has better respect for property rights, India lags China in terms of trade and investment linkages with the rest of the world.

Conclusion

Given the absence of credible rivals, it is very likely that America's "exorbitant privilege" of being Asia's and the world's reserve currency will be sustained for some time to come, serious consideration should be given to *The Economist's* warning:

> "In 1913, at the height of its empire, Britain was the world's biggest creditor. Within 40 years, after two costly world wars and economic mismanagement, it became a net debtor and the dollar usurped sterling's role. Dislodging an incumbent currency can take years. Sterling maintained a central international role for at least half a century after America's GDP overtook Britain's at the end of the 19th century. But it did eventually lose that status. If America continues on its current profligate path, the dollar is likely to suffer a similar fate. But in future no one currency, such as the euro, is likely to take over. Instead, the world might drift towards a multiple reserve-currency system shared among the dollar, the euro and the yen (or indeed the yuan at some time in the future). That still implies a big drop in the long-term share of dollar assets in central banks' vaults and private portfolios. A slow, steady shift out of dollars could perhaps be handled. But if America continues to show such neglect of its own currency, then a fast-falling dollar and rising American interest rates would result. It will be how far and how fast the dollar falls that determines the future for America's economy and the world's."[18]

More realistically, while the USD may remain the dominant reserve currency, its share of global reserves may see a rather gradual but distinct decline over time. The world is likely to gradually shift to a multiple reserve-currency

---

[16] Persuad, A and S Spratt (2004). The new renminbi bloc, mimeo (June).

[17] This point has been emphasized by Eichengreen, B (2005), *op. cit.*

[18] See The passing of the buck? (2 December 2004) *The Economist op. cit.*

system involving the USD, euro and one or more Asian currencies. This shift is more likely to occur if:

(a) European countries are able to overcome their continuing structural impediments facing their economies and that the institutional commitment to the eurozone is renewed and some key players such as UK (with its large financial markets) join the eurozone.[19]
(b) The Japanese economy is also successfully restructured and it returns to a path of sustained robust growth.
(c) Some important commodities such as oil are increasingly invoiced in currencies other than USD, and the surpluse or major oil exporting countries or "Petrodollars" are consequently converted to "Petroeuros".[20]
(d) Asian countries enhance regional financial and monetary cooperation,[21] including take further steps toward strengthening the Asian Bond Fund initiatives (where Asian bonds are issued in local currencies).[22]
(e) Asian and other currencies continue to move away from pegging to the USD.[23]
(f) There is a sustained downturn in the US economy.

---

[19] This point has been emphasized in the empirical analysis by Frankel, J and M Chinn (2005), *op. cit.*

[20] While the run up in oil prices until 2006 has lead to increased savings by oil exporting countries, their share of global reserves (relative to Asia) has declined significantly since the 1980s (though some non-OPEC member countries like Russia have seen a significant rise). This having been said, a significant shift into euros by oil exporting countries could have major consequences on currency markets. There appears to be limited data, however, on the extent of recycling of oil revenues into USD or other assets to comment more specifically on this issue. For useful discussions of this issue, see McCaughrin, R (2005). Global: Pump pains and petrodollars, *Global Economic Forum*, Morgan Stanley (May 17); Jen, S and M Baker (2005). Redirection of petrodollars a USD negative?, *Global Economic Forum*, Morgan Stanley (May 17). http://www.morganstanley.com/GEFdata/digests/20030307-fri.html.

[21] For a detailed discussion of monetary and financial cooperation in Asia, see papers in Asian Development Bank (2004). *Monetary and Financial Cooperation in East Asia*, Palgrave-McMillan Press for the Asian Development Bank, Vols. 1 and 2.

[22] See Chapter 20 of this Volume.

[23] This point is of particular importance. While the USD's share of global reserve portfolios may be high relative to the global share of the US economy (in purchasing power parity terms), it is in line with the global share of the *de facto* Dollar zone (i.e., those countries pegged to the USD). See the BIS (2005). BIS 75th Annual Report, Basle: Bank for International Settlements. As the report notes:

> "(T)he notion can be disputed that official reserves are overweight in dollars. Excluding Japan, the dollar share of foreign exchange reserves may have been no more than 57 percent in mid-2004. (Unreported forward sales of dollars against euros could lower this figure further.) Such a share is high in relation to the share of the US economy in the world economy, but not necessarily in relation to the share of the dollar zone in the world economy. If one allocates economies, measured at purchasing power parity, to the dollar, euro or yen zones according to the behavior of their currencies ..., the dollar zone produces an estimated 59 percent of global output... This is almost identical to the current dollar share of reserves outside Japan...In sum, the case for a portfolio imbalance, including in official portfolios, seems weaker than much commentary would suggest. There remains, however, a pending problem. The dollar zone has been shrinking, and any acceleration of this could eventually give rise to a portfolio imbalance in both the private and official sectors." (p. 96)

Chapter 4

A Central Banker's Holy Grail: Inflation-Targeting Frameworks with Reference to Asia*

(With Tony Cavoli)

Introduction

What exactly is inflation targeting? While definitions vary in the literature, the following definition is consistent with the consensus — Inflation targeting is a monetary policy strategy that encompasses five main elements[1]:

(1) The public announcement of medium-term numerical targets for inflation.
(2) An institutional commitment to price stability as the primary goal of monetary policy, to which other goals are subordinated.
(3) An information inclusive strategy in which many variables, and not just monetary aggregates or the exchange rate, are used for deciding the setting of policy instruments.
(4) Increased transparency of the monetary policy strategy through communication with the public and the markets about the plans, objectives, and decisions of the monetary authorities.
(5) Increased accountability of the central bank for attaining its inflation objectives.

The list should clarify one crucial point about inflation targeting, viz. it entails much more than a public announcement of numerical targets for inflation for the year ahead. This is important in the context of emerging

---

* This chapter draws on Cavoli, T and RS Rajan (2007). Inflation targeting arrangements in Asia: Exploring the role of the exchange rate. *Briefing Notes in Economics*, forthcoming, and expands on some of the arguments initially outlined in Rajan, RS (2004). Inflation targeting frameworks in Asia. *Business Times* (Singapore), 24 March.
[1] Mishkin, F (2000). Inflation targeting in emerging market countries. *American Economic Review*, 9, 106–107. Also see Eichengreen, B (2001). Can emerging markets float? Should they inflation target? mimeo (April), p. 4.

economies. Notwithstanding the fact that many central banks routinely reported numerical inflation targets or objectives as part of their governments' economic plans for the coming year, their monetary policy strategies cannot be characterized as inflation targeting, which requires the other four elements for it to be sustainable over the medium term.

The IMF writes that explicit inflation targets play two key roles in the effort to reduce and control inflation[2]:

- By communicating to the public the objective that monetary policy seeks to achieve, they act as a coordination device in wage and price setting processes and in forming the public's inflation expectations.
- They provide a transparent guide to the management of monetary policy, whose commitment and credibility can then be evaluated on the basis of whether policy actions are taken to achieve the targets.

The idea of having an inflation target is not a new one (Table 1). The first country to start inflation targeting was New Zealand, which did so in the April of 1988. Section 8 of the Reserve Bank of New Zealand Act 1989 says its main function is "to formulate and implement monetary policy directed to the economic objective of achieving and maintaining stability in the general level of prices".[3] Section 9 of the act requires that the finance minister and the governor of the Reserve Bank of New Zealand negotiate and set out "Policy Targets Agreement" that specifies inflation targets. Countries such as Canada started targeting inflation in 1991, while the Bank of England adopted an inflation-targeting framework in the October of 1992. While the US Federal Reserve does not explicitly have an inflation target, it follows a monetary policy that is directed at having a low rate of inflation.

Buoyed by the apparent success of inflation targeting (IT) in industrial countries in the early to mid-1990s in terms of bringing down rates of inflation (see Figs. 1–3), it has been advocated by the IMF and others as a viable policy option for emerging economies in Asia and elsewhere.[4] Since the Asian financial debacle of 1997–1998, four of the five crisis-hit countries — Korea, Indonesia, Thailand, and the Philippines — have instituted monetary policy arrangements fashioned around an inflation objective.[5] Each of these

---

[2] The two key roles are direct quotes from the *IMF Survey* published on 11 November 1996.

[3] See http://www.rbnz.govt.nz/about/acct.pdf.

[4] For a discussion of inflation targeting during IMF structural adjustment programs, see Blejer, MI, AM Leone, P Rabanal and G Schwartz (2001). Inflation targeting in the context of IMF-supported adjustment programs. *Working Paper No. 01/31*, IMF.

[5] Malaysia shifted to a rigid US dollar peg in September 1998 but moved to a rather non-transparent managed float in July 2005.

Table 1. Inflation-targeting start dates for some central banks.

	Start of inflation-targeting
Australia	September 1994
Brazil	June 1999
Canada	February 1991
Chile	January 1991
Colombia	September 1999
Czech Rep	January 1998
Hungary	July 2001
Iceland	March 2001
Israel	January 1992
South Korea	April 1998
Mexico	January 1999
New Zealand	April 1988
Norway	March 2001
Peru	January 2002
Philippines	January 2002
Poland	October 1998
South Africa	February 2000
Sweden	January 1993
Switzerland	January 2000
Thailand	May 2000
United Kingdom	October 1992

Source: Fracasso A, H Genberg and C Wyplosz (2003). How do central banks write? Evaluation of inflation targeting central banks. *Geneva Reports on the World Economy Special Report 2*. London: Center for Economic Policy Research.

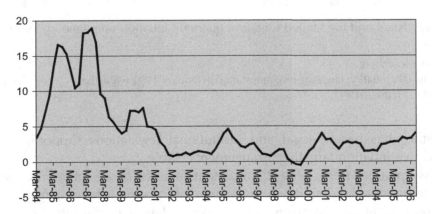

Fig. 1. New Zealand quarterly inflation rate (January 1984–June 2006).

Source: Bloomberg.

Note: New Zealand's inflation-targeting program started in April 1988.

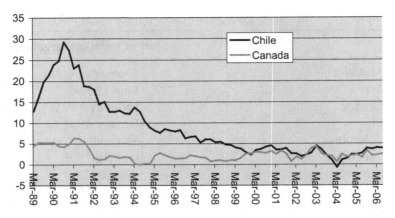

Fig. 2. Chile and Canada quarterly inflation rate (January 1989–June 2006).

Source: Bloomberg.

Note: Chile's inflation targeting program started in January 1991 while Canada's started in February 1991.

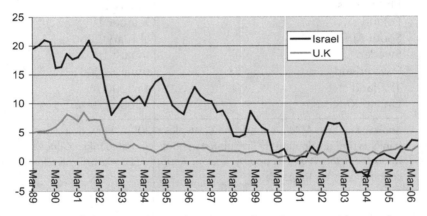

Fig. 3. Israel and the United Kingdom quarterly inflation rate (January 1989–June 2006).

Source: Bloomberg.

Note: Israel's inflation targeting program started in January 1992 while that of United Kingdom started in October 1992.

countries has passed legal and institutional legislations supporting their respective inflation-targeting arrangements (Table 2).[6]

As apparent from Table 2, important features of an inflation-targeting regime include the definition of what type of inflation is being targeting, the inflation target range, the use of exclusion clauses or caveats (i.e., under

---

[6] The revised Bank of Korea Act was passed in December 1997 (and revised in April 1998), the new bank of Indonesia Act was passed in May 1999, and the Bank of Thailand Act was passed in May 2000 (Table 1).

Table 2. Highlights of inflation-targeting regimes in selected Asian economies (as of July 2005).

Country	Date of initiation of inflation-targeting regime	Target price index	Target rate	Target horizon	Escape clauses	Accountability	Target set by	Publication and accountability
Indonesia	May 1999	Headline CPI	5%–6%	3 years	None	None, but parliament can request reports at any time	Government in consultation with central bank	Quarterly Inflation report, Annual report to public
Philippines	December 2001	Headline CPI. Also monitors core CPI (excluding agricultural products and petroleum products)	4%–6%	2 years	Yes, in the event of oil price shocks, food supply shocks	Public explanation of the nature of the breach and steps to address	Government in consultation with central bank	Quarterly inflation report, publication of monetary policy meetings
Thailand	April 2000	Core CPI (excluding fresh food and energy)	0%–3.5%	Indefinite	None	Public explanation of breach and steps taken to address it	Central bank in consultation with Government	Inflation report, inflation forecasts, and publication of models used
Korea	January 1998	Core CPI (excluding non-cereal agricultural products and petroleum products)	2.5%–3.5% 2.5%	1 year Indefinite	Changes caused by major force	None	Central bank in consultation with Government	Inflation report and submission to parliament, publication of monetary policy meetings

Source: Compiled by authors from the Bank of Korea, Bank Indonesia, Bank of Thailand, Bangko Sentral ng Pilipinas web site.

what circumstances the central bank is able to overshoot its target), and the target horizon. All of this information need to be publicly available and fully transparent.

Inflation targeting is conducted in conjunction with a monetary policy rule (MPR). In general terms the MPR is one element of a strategy employed by the central bank as part of its overall monetary policy. The MPR specifies how the instrument of monetary policy is to be changed given the characteristics of the macroeconomy and the policy objectives of the central bank. The MPR implicitly assumes that the instrument of monetary policy will always react strongly to inflation (or some forecast of future inflation). MPRs and inflation targets do not necessarily mean the same thing. The two are different elements of a general monetary policy strategy. The MPR provides a guide to the policy-maker as to how to manipulate the instrument of monetary policy and the inflation target simply makes a statement about the purpose for which the instrument is ultimately being used.

What is an Inflation-Targeting Arrangement?

An immediate lesson that many observers appear to have drawn from recent financial crises in emerging market economies in the 1990s is that the only viable exchange rate option boils down to the one between flexibility, on the one hand, and "credible pegging", on the other. According to this view, emerging economies have to gravitate to these two extremes. Any currency arrangement that lies in between these polar extremes or corners (i.e., those in the "middle") is viewed as being inherently unstable and crisis-prone. However, the former First Deputy Managing Director of the IMF, Stanley Fischer has acknowledged that there are many instances where intermediate regimes might well be "more appropriate" than corner solutions.[7] He notes that the supposed bipolar view of exchange rates ought to be presented as a choice between a hard peg versus a "more flexible regime" rather than a flexible exchange rate regime *per se.*[8] The latter option implies the absence

---

[7] Fischer, S (2001). Exchange rate regimes: Is the bipolar view correct? *Journal of Economic Perspectives,* 15, 3–24. Also see Frankel J (1999). No single currency regime is right for all countries or at all times. *Essays in International Economics No. 215.* Princeton University: International Economics Section; and Willett, TD (2002). Fear of floating needn't imply fixed rates: Feasible options for intermediate exchange rate regimes. mimeo (May).

[8] As Fischer (*ibid.*) notes:

"Proponents of what is now known as the bipolar view — myself included — probably have exaggerated their point for dramatic effect. The right statement is that *for countries open to international capital flows:* (i) pegs are not sustainable unless they are very hard indeed; but (ii) that a wide variety of flexible rate arrangements are possible; and (iii) that it is to be expected that policy in most countries will not be indifferent to exchange rate movements.

of any explicit exchange rate target, i.e., intervention should not be framed primarily in terms of defending a particular exchange rate target (pegged rate). Such targets inevitably tempt speculators by offering them the infamous one-way option which basically implies that if speculators think that the peg is unviable, they will short-sell the currency knowing that there is only one direction or one way the currency can or will move.

Thus, exchange rate and monetary policy strategies must involve a "fairly high" element of flexibility rather than a single-minded defense of a particular rate. One way this flexibility might be achieved is via a band-basket-crawl or BBC regime, whereby a country loosely targets its trade-weighted or effective exchange rate. Singapore is a well-known and successful practitioner of a BBC-type regime in Asia and more recently China is said to have adopted such a regime (or at least is moving to be one). Another possible manner of introducing greater exchange rate flexibility is for a country to adopt an open economy inflation-targeting arrangement.[9]

The Role of Exchange Rates Under Inflation Targeting

Conventionally an inflation-targeting regime ought to be accompanied by a flexible exchange rate, with the interest rate used as the monetary policy instrument. It is generally recognized that for small and open economies in Asia and elsewhere, fluctuations in the exchange rate can have significant and direct impact on the domestic economy. In particular, assuming a high degree of pass-through from exchange rate changes into domestic inflation, it has sometimes been argued that exchange rate fluctuations ought to be explicitly incorporated in any MPR.[10] However, there are two significant concerns about doing so.

To put the point graphically, if exchange rate arrangements lie along a line connecting free floating on the left with currency boards, dollarization or currency union on the right, the intent was not to remove everything but the corners, but rather to pronounce as unsustainable a segment of that line representing a variety of soft pegging exchange rate arrangements. This formulation accommodates all three of the above positions. For countries open to capital flows, it leaves open a wide range of arrangements running from free floating to a variety of crawling bands with wide ranges, and then very hard pegs sustained by a highly credible policy commitment, notably currency boards and the abandonment of a national currency."

[9] The topic of currency basket arrangements for Asia has been extensively dealt with elsewhere. For instance, see Bird, G and RS Rajan (2002). Optimal currency baskets and the third currency phenomenon: Exchange rate policy in Southeast Asia. *Journal of International Development*, 14, 1053–1073; and Rajan, RS (2002). Exchange rate policy options for post-crisis Southeast Asia: Is there a case for currency baskets? *The World Economy*, 25, 137–163.

[10] This assumption itself can be contested. For instance, see Ghosh, A and RS Rajan (2007). Exchange rate pass-through in Asia: What does the literature tell us? forthcoming in *Asia Pacific Economic Literature*.

First, an attempt to control the inflationary effects of exchange rate changes effectively implies raising interest rates during periods of exchange rate weakness and vice versa during periods of exchange rate strength. The concern is that responding too heavily and frequently to currency movements in the short-term could risk transforming the flexible inflation target to a *de facto* soft currency peg which in turn tends to be crisis-prone. This observation may be especially pertinent to some Asian economies where there are concerns of a reversion to exchange rate based monetary policy regimes.[11] Second, insofar as interest rate changes have a lagged effect on the economy on the one hand, and pass-through from exchange rates tends to be fairly immediate on the other, the central bank will have to forecast short-term exchange rate movements. This is near impossible to be done on a consistent basis.

One way to partially overcome the problem of exchange rate fluctuations on domestic inflation is for the central bank to focus on "core" rather than "headline" inflation (the former being headline inflation minus food and energy prices).[12] Referring to Table 2, one sees that a number of the Asian central banks pursuing inflation-targeting regimes are in fact targeting core inflation. The benefit of doing so is that any exchange rate fluctuations that directly impact the imported price of foodstuffs and energy will be excluded. While targeting of core inflation does not completely offset the impact of exchange rate fluctuations on all domestic prices (as a country could be importing other goods and there could be a seeping through of non-core price inflation into overall inflation), it has been seen as a way of addressing the exchange rate debate for small and open economies.[13]

While targeting core inflation helps to loosen the tie between exchange rates and domestic monetary policy, there is a more basic concern with exchange rate movements on the monetary transmission mechanism, viz. what if pass-through is incomplete such that nominal exchange rate changes do not immediately translate into real exchange rate changes? If this happens, it implies that the real exchange rate will not revert to its original value (i.e., purchasing power parity will not hold), which in turn could impact domestic output, growth, and inflation over time. In other words, a flexible exchange rate could lead to persistent exchange rate misalignment that

---

[11] This issue is the focus of Cavoli, T and RS Rajan (2005). Have exchange rate regimes in Asia become more flexible post-crisis? Revisiting the evidence. mimeo (November).

[12] For a more detailed discussion of general issues on core inflation in the context of the Philippines and other Asian countries, see Monetary Stability Sector, Bangko Sentral ng Pilipinas (2005). "Frequently Asked Questions on Core Inflation", www.bsp.gov.ph/downloads/2005/faq/inflation.pdf.

[13] While core inflation has the advantage of stripping out components that may cause idiosyncratic price changes arising from supply shocks, a problem targeting core inflation is that it is much harder to communicate the logic of this target to the general public. The public is generally not aware of the meaning of core inflation, and if there is a wide gap between core and headline inflation, the central bank's anti-inflationary credibility might be affected.

could be sustained over prolonged periods. Insofar as these exchange rate misalignments have sustained impact on the real sector, ought not the central bank to explicitly incorporate exchange rate misalignments in their policy rule, even if the focus is on core inflation? While there may be a logic for this in principle, in practice such a policy is hard to implement effectively as it basically requires that the central bank be able to estimate equilibrium real exchange rates, something which is not easy to do so, especially given that the equilibrium real exchange rate could fluctuate over time.[14] Does this imply a complete neglect of persistent exchange rate or other asset price fluctuations under an inflation-targeting regime?[15]

Strict versus Flexible Targeting

There is a school of thought that argues that as long as the country's inflation outlook remains consistent with the medium-term inflation target range (i.e., the policy reference period), the central bank has space to use its judgment to judiciously meet other objectives and respond effectively to various shocks and "obvious" asset price misalignments in the interim.[16] This suggests a degree of discretion in being able to prick "asset price bubbles" including exchange rate and housing ones (or better still, be pre-emptive so as to prevent bubbles from forming in the first instance). However, multiple targeting (over and above inflation and output) is not without its drawbacks.

First, multiplicity of objectives/flexibility in implementing the inflation target invariably complicates the communication strategy of the central bank's monetary policy. As Fredric Mishkin notes:

> "The KISS principle ("Keep It Simple Stupid") suggests that monetary policy should be articulated in as simple way as possible. The beauty of inflation target

---

[14] For instance, for a fast growing open economy, the productivity growth in the tradable sector generally outpaces the nontradable sector (so-called "Balassa-Samuelson effect") thus suggesting an appreciation of the country's equilibrium real exchange rate. For discussion of the concept of equilibrium real exchange rates, see the collection of papers Hinkle, LE and PJ Montiel (eds.) (1999). *Exchange Rate Misalignment.* Oxford: Oxford University Press and the World Bank.

[15] For elaborate discussion on the role of exchange rates in inflation targeting arrangements, see Eichengreen, B (2001), *op. cit.*; Sgherri, S (2005). Explicit and implicit targets in open economies? *Working Paper No. 05/176*, IMF; and Taylor, J (2001). The role of the exchange rate in monetary-policy rules. *American Economic Review*, 91, 263–267. For a more formal analysis of the role of exchange rates in central bank's objective function, see Hammermann, F (2003). Comparing monetary policy strategies: Towards a generalized reaction function. *Working Paper No. 1170*, Kiel Institute for World Economics, and these issues are explored more formally in Cavoli, T and RS Rajan (2005). Inflation targeting and monetary policy rules for Asia: With particular reference to Thailand. mimeo (October).

[16] One might call this the "Australian view" of inflation targeting. See Debelle, G (2001). The case for inflation targeting in East Asian countries. *Future Directions for Monetary Policies in East Asia*. Sydney: Reserve Bank of Australia.

regimes is that by focusing on one objective — inflation — communication is fairly straightforward."[17]

Second, when monetary authorities explain their monetary policy actions by referring to the need to ensure output or exchange rate stability, "the political debate about monetary policy is likely to focus on short-run issues",[18] be it job creation, exchange rate stability, or even asset price stability. This, in turn, may "obscure the transparency of monetary policy and make it less likely that the public will support a monetary policy that focuses on long-run considerations"[19] and may worsen the output–inflation trade-off.

Another area of debate pertains to the role of asset prices in the inflation-targeting processes. It is important to keep in mind that there is a significant difference between keeping an eye on asset price changes as offering information about the underlying economy compared to explicitly targeting them. The former is rather uncontroversial; the latter is not.[20] There is a concern that central banks are not able to estimate bubbles or misalignments (would not they be rich if they could?), and there could also be instances where various asset prices give conflicting signals.[21] Ben Bernanke, Chairman of the Federal Reserve, has argued strongly against the central bank attempting to respond to asset price bubbles. As he notes:

> "If we could accurately and painlessly rid asset markets of bubbles, of course we would want to do so. But as a practical matter, this is easier said than

---

[17] Mishkin, F (2002). The role of output stabilization in the conduct of monetary policy. *Working Paper No. 9291*, NBER, p. 14.

[18] *Ibid.*, p. 11.

[19] *Ibid.*, p. 14.

[20] Similarly, many central banks in Asia and elsewhere also keep an eye on the so-called "Monetary Conditions Index" or MCI which is a weighted average of interest rate and exchange rate and this is not controversial. If they attempt to explicitly target the MCI it would be much more controversial. For discussion of the MCI in the context of Hong Kong, see Hong Kong Monetary Authority (HKMA) (2000). A monetary conditions index for Hong Kong. *Quarterly Bulletin*, 11/2000, 56–70.

[21] Also see Bean, C (2003). Asset prices, finances imbalances and monetary policy: Are inflation targets enough? *Working Paper No.140*, Bank for International Settlements. This said, not everyone is convinced by such concerns and offer the counterargument that monetary policy needs to be cautious but not "paralyzed". For instance, a recent prominent paper concluded: "(W)e are not persuaded that one should ignore asset price misalignments simply because they are difficult to measure. The standard response to noisy data is to use econometric methods to extract the signal. This is common practice in the use of statistics in a policymaking environment. If central bankers threw out all data that was poorly measured, there would be very little information left on which to base their decisions". See Cecchetti, S, H Genberg and S Wadhwani (2002). Asset prices in a flexible inflation targeting framework. Paper presented at the *Conference on Asset Price Bubbles: Implications for Monetary, Regulatory, and International Policies*, p. 19, Federal Reserve Bank of Chicago and the World Bank (Chicago: April 22–24).

done, particularly if we intend to use monetary policy as the instrument, for two main reasons. First, the Fed cannot reliably identify bubbles in asset prices. Second, even if it could identify bubbles, monetary policy is far too blunt a tool for effective use against them.... (A)s a society, we would like to find ways to mitigate the potential instabilities associated with asset-price booms and busts. Monetary policy is not a useful tool for achieving this objective, however. Even putting aside the great difficulty of identifying bubbles in asset prices, monetary policy cannot be directed finely enough to guide asset prices without risking severe collateral damage to the economy. A far better approach, I believe, is to use micro-level policies to reduce the incidence of bubbles and to protect the financial system against their effects. I have already mentioned a variety of possible measures, including supervisory action to ensure capital adequacy in the banking system, stress testing of portfolios, increased transparency in accounting and disclosure practices, improved financial literacy, greater care in the process of financial liberalization, and a willingness to play the role of lender of last resort when needed."[22]

Even if there is a case for the central bank to respond to signs of obvious bubbles, it probably cannot be incorporated in an explicit rule. If monetary authorities choose to respond to such misalignments infrequently they should do so on a discretionary basis. This leads us to the next issue as to whether an inflation-targeting arrangement errs on the side of policy rigidity and discipline or discretion and flexibility? While the exact balance between flexibility and rigidity will no doubt vary between countries (and possibly over time within a country), broad rules of thumb suggest: (a) the less credible the central bank (i.e., poorer its inflation-fighting track record); (b) the less its technical ability; and (c) the lower its political independence, the more advisable it is to pre-commit to a "strict" or "hard" inflation target (i.e., preference for a rule over discretion).

In the final analysis, regardless of the extent of flexibility or discretion that is pursued, it is imperative that the central bank pursuing an inflation-targeting regime communicates effectively to the public the lexicographic ordering of its objectives and the time frame over which the central bank is committed to returning inflation to target. The central bank needs to be publicly committed to relinquish all other goals in order to meet the inflation target.

---

[22] Bernanke, B (2002). Asset-price "bubbles" and monetary policy. Speech before the New York Chapter of the National Association for Business Economics, New York (15 October), pp. 3 and 8. Also see Bernanke, B and M Gertler (2001). Should central banks respond to movements in asset prices. *American Economic Review*, 91, 253–257.

Conclusion

Ben Bernanke, in a speech made in 2003 on inflation targeting, concludes:

> "Inflation targeting, at least in its best-practice form, consists of two parts: a policy framework of constrained discretion and a communication strategy that attempts to focus expectations and explain the policy framework to the public. Together, these two elements promote both price stability and well-anchored inflation expectations; the latter in turn facilitates more effective stabilization of output and employment. Thus, a well-conceived and well-executed strategy of inflation targeting can deliver good results with respect to output and employment as well as inflation."[23]

The inflation targeters in Asia have thus far not faced significant trade-offs between inflation and other objectives in view of the fact that the global economic environment has, until recently, been non-inflationary. In other words, given that inflation has never really threatened to overshoot its predetermined band, many of the Asian central banks have been largely free to use monetary policy to attain other goals such as smoothing exchange rate changes. It would appear though that there is an asymmetry in the way that many Asian central banks treat exchange rate movements. Specifically, they have not always altered interest rates in response to upward (buying) pressure on their currencies, preferring to intervene in the foreign exchange market, but they are more willing to hike interest rates in the midst of downward (selling) pressure on their currencies. This in turn inevitably has led to a rapid stockpiling of international reserves which has had to be sterilized so as to prevent a domestic monetary overhang and overheating, including the creation of asset bubbles in the housing and equity markets.

Monetary sterilization makes good sense when the balance of payments pressures are considered to be temporary. However, when these pressures are sustained, the carry costs of this reserve accumulation can become fairly high, as they have in a number of countries.[24] There are also questions about the success of such sustained (as opposed to temporary) sterilization efforts.

Of course, the pressure on the balance of payments and thus the exchange rate can always be reduced to some extent by allowing interest rates to decline, though this would compromise the domestic inflationary objective. Thus, a bona fide inflation-targeting central bank should appropriately respond by allowing the currencies to appreciate vis-à-vis major

---

[23] Bernanke, B (2003). A perspective on inflation targeting. Speech delivered at the *Annual Washington Policy Conference of the National Association of Business Economists* (Washington, DC: 25 March 2003).

[24] As discussed in Chapter 1.

currencies including the US dollar to lessen the pressures on reserve buildup. This would be the policy that the Australian and New Zealand central banks would generally adopt (both being credible inflation targeters with flexible exchange rates).

Among the Asian economies, Korea and Thailand stand out as having done just that. The Korean won appreciated from 1,040 per US dollar in July 2005 to about 920 won per US dollar by early December 2006, while the Thai baht appreciated vis-à-vis 42 baht per US dollar in July 2005 to almost 35 baht in early December 2006. The trend appreciation despite some valid concerns of its potential negative repercussions on the exportables sector seemed to underscore the commitment of both central banks to their inflation-targeting frameworks. Things changed quite dramatically on 19 December 2006 when the Bank of Thailand attempted to impose Chilean type of controls so as to curb capital inflows. While the policy was quickly reversed in the face of massive sell-off of the Thai equity and currency markets, the action betrayed an unwillingness of the Bank of Thailand to fully commit to its new monetary framework.

Of course, an alternative route to alleviate the pressure on the currency might have been to ease any remaining restrictions on capital outflows and effectively allow domestic residents to hold more foreign assets (rather than the central bank having to do so via foreign exchange intervention). China and India have been doing exactly this, albeit gradually.

Chapter 5

Singapore's Currency Baskets and the Mantra of Competitiveness: The Importance of Real Exchange Rates*

Introduction

Governments in Asia and elsewhere are preoccupied with the question of what needs to be done to remain competitive in the global economy. However "competitiveness of nations" is one of those terms that everyone thinks they understand but few are able to define with any degree of precision. In Asia, Singapore is probably exceptional in the degree of attention and emphasis paid to these indices. The website of the Ministry of Trade and Industry of Singapore makes the following statement "Competitiveness of the Economy: Maintaining international competitiveness is a fundamental tenet of Singapore's economic philosophy and Singapore has constantly ranked high against the world's most competitive nations".[1]

While it is fairly clear what it means for a particular business to be globally competitive, what about an entire nation that is made up of a myriad of firms, industries, sectors, products, and factors? Indeed, in a well-known article, Paul Krugman has observed:

> "concerns about competitiveness are, as an empirical matter, almost completely unfounded ... and the obsession with competitiveness is not only wrong but dangerous, skewing domestic policies and threatening the international economic system ... Thinking in terms of competitiveness leads, directly and indirectly, to bad economic policies on a wide range of issues, domestic and foreign ..."[2]

---

* This chapter draws on Rajan, RS (2004). Competitiveness in the global economy with reference to Singapore. *IPS Policy Brief*, No. 1, 1 April; Rajan, RS (2004). Merits of a currency basket arrangements. (4 May) *Business Times*; and Cavoli, T and RS Rajan (2006). A basket case, *Wall Street Journal Asia*, 27 March.

[1] http://www.mti.gov.sg.

[2] Krugman, PR (1994). Competitiveness: A dangerous obsession. *Foreign Affairs,* March/April, 1–17.

Policy-makers and the popular press often make frequent reference to the well-known indices of competitiveness such as the ones by the World Economic Forum (WEF) or the Swiss-based International Management Development (IMD). These two institutions bring out a competitiveness index every year which ranks countries from most to least competitive. Asian countries like Singapore are probably exceptional in the degree of attention they pay to these indices. While the indices may act as useful benchmarks in certain areas, their analytical basis as proxies for national competitiveness is open to question.

Competitiveness Indices

IMD, a business school in Switzerland, comes out annually with the *World Competitiveness Yearbook* where they rank countries on "competitiveness". The United States has consistently topped their rankings from 2001 to 2005. The rankings of select countries are shown in Table 1. The IMD methodology essentially takes four main factors (economic performance, government

Table 1.   Competitiveness rankings of select countries based on IMD rankings.

	2001	2002	2003	2004	2005
USA	1	1	1	1	1
Hong Kong	4	13	10	6	2
Singapore	3	8	4	2	3
Canada	9	7	6	3	5
Finland	5	3	3	8	6
Denmark	15	6	5	7	7
Switzerland	8	5	9	14	8
Australia	12	10	7	4	9
Taiwan	16	20	17	12	11
Japan	23	27	25	23	21
United Kingdom	17	16	19	22	22
Germany	13	17	20	21	23
Thailand	34	31	30	29	27
Malaysia	28	24	21	16	28
Korea	29	29	37	35	29
France	25	25	23	30	30
China Mainland	26	28	29	24	31
India	42	41	50	34	39
Philippines	39	40	49	52	49
Indonesia	46	47	57	58	59

Source: *World Competitiveness Yearbook*, IMD (www.imd.ch/wcy).

efficiency, business efficiency, and infrastructure) and scores them. These four factors each have five different subfactors. For example, the subfactors in infrastructure are basic infrastructure, technological infrastructure, scientific infrastructure, health infrastructure, and education.[3]

The other well-known competitiveness index is brought out annually by the World Economic Forum in a publication called *The Global Competitiveness Report*. The methodology for constructing the index rests on nine "pillars", viz. institutions, infrastructure, macroeconomy, health and primary education, higher education and training, market efficiency, technological readiness, business sophistication, and innovation. All these nine factors have subfactors to them. Table 2 shows the ranking of some countries in the index. *The Global Competitiveness Report* writes:

"The selection of these pillars as well as the factors that enter each of them is based on the latest theoretical and empirical research. It is important

Table 2. Global competitiveness rankings.

	2005	2006
Switzerland	4	1
Finland	2	2
Denmark	3	4
Singapore	5	5
United States	1	6
Japan	10	7
Germany	6	8
United Kingdom	9	10
Hong Kong SAR	14	11
Taiwan	8	13
Canada	13	16
France	12	18
Australia	18	19
Korea, Rep.	19	24
Malaysia	25	26
Thailand	33	35
India	45	43
Indonesia	69	50
China	48	54
Philippines	73	71

Source: World Economic Forum.

[3] The full IMD methodology is available at: http://www.imd.ch/research/centers/wcc/research_methodology.cfm

to note that none of these factors alone can ensure competitiveness. The value of increased spending in education will be undermined if rigidities in the labor market and other institutional weaknesses make it difficult for new graduates to gain access to suitable employment opportunities. ... Innovation or the adoption of new technologies or upgrading management practices will most likely not receive broad-based support in the business community, if protection of the domestic market ensures that the returns to seeking rents are higher than those for new investments."[4]

Table 3 shows the ambiguity regarding competitiveness. It compares the rankings for countries in 2005 between the IMD rankings and the WEF rankings. While both indices use different methodologies, there ought to be some

Table 3.   Comparative competitiveness rankings for 2005.

	WEF competitiveness rankings for 2005	IMD competitiveness rankings for 2005
Australia	18	9
Canada	13	5
China	48	31
Denmark	3	7
Finland	2	6
France	12	30
Germany	6	23
Hong Kong SAR	14	2
India	45	39
Indonesia	69	59
Japan	10	21
Korea, Rep.	19	29
Malaysia	25	28
Philippines	73	49
Singapore	5	3
Switzerland	4	8
Taiwan	8	11
Thailand	33	27
United Kingdom	9	22
United States	1	1

Source: IMD and World Economic Forum.

---

[4] See World Economic Forum (2006). *Global Competitiveness Report 2006*, p. 5. http://www.weforum.org/pdf/Global_Competitiveness_Reports/Reports/gcr_2006/chapter_1_1.pdf.

degree of closeness in the country rankings since both attempt to measure competitiveness of countries and rank countries accordingly. Somewhat surprisingly this is not the case. For example, the WEF ranks the United Kingdom as the ninth most competitive country, while the IMD ranks it at 22. The WEF ranks China at 6, while the IMD ranks it at 23. Hong Kong is ranked at 14 by the WEF while it is ranked at 2 by IMD. The list goes on and on. The two rankings give quite different relative rankings of many countries. Despite the attention paid to them, it is debatable as to whether a high or low ranking in these indices actually really mean very much. Many economists have expressed deep skepticism of the analytical bases of the two competitiveness rankings.[5]

Real Exchange Rates and Currency Basket Regimes

When a macroeconomist thinks about economic competitiveness at a macro or national level, the focus is usually on the trade-weighted or real effective exchange rate (REER). This in turn refers to the nominal effective or trade-weighted exchange rate (NEER) adjusted for relative prices between foreign and domestic prices. To put this in more concrete terms, assume that the exchange rate is measured in terms of foreign currency per, for example, Singapore dollar. The REER is then simply the NEER multiplied by the aggregate price index in Singapore divided by a trade-weighted foreign price index. A rise in the REER would thus imply a real appreciation of the Singapore dollar. This rise in the real value of the Singapore dollar, especially if it takes place suddenly, might be taken as an indication of loss of price or economic competitiveness of Singapore goods and services in global markets (as they become more expensive in foreign currency terms).[6] (Figures 1–3 show the REER for nine Asian countries from January 2000 to December 2006 using monthly data.)

---

[5] For instance, see Lall, S (2003). Assessing industrial competitiveness: How does Singapore fare. In *Sustaining Competitiveness in the New Global Economy: The Experience of Singapore*, Rajan, RS (ed.), pp. 63–90. Aldershot: Edward Elgar.

[6] In fact the real exchange rate can be divided into three parts, viz. (a) the relative foreign currency price of Singapore's tradables with those of the rest of the world; (b) the relative price of tradables and nontradables in Singapore; (c) and the relative price of tradables and nontradables in the rest of the world. For a small open economy like Singapore, we might realistically assume that it has little to no impact on the relative price of tradables and nontradables in the rest of the world, and also that the share of tradables in the overall economy is fairly large. Under these assumptions, the change in the real exchange rate is largely a reflection of relative tradable prices in foreign currency terms. For a discussion of different measures of the real exchange rate, see Chinn, M (2004). Measuring real effective exchange rates. In *Exchange Rate Regimes in East Asia*, G de Brouwer and M Kawai (eds.), pp. 268–301. London and New York: Routledge.

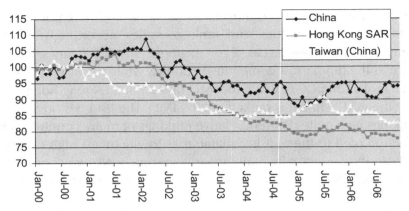

Fig. 1.   Real effective exchange rate for China, Hong Kong, and Taiwan (2000 = 100) (January 2000–December 2006).

Source: Bank of International Settlements.

Note: Rise implies real depreciation.

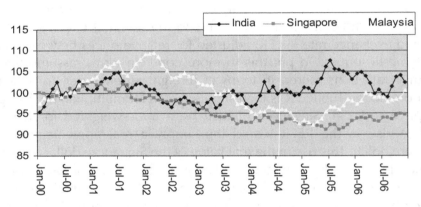

Fig. 2.   Real effective exchange rate for India, Malaysia, and Singapore (2000 = 100) (January 2000–December 2006).

Source: Bank of International Settlements.

Note: Rise implies real depreciation.

Accordingly, steps to regain economic competitiveness in the short-run center on either the NEER or domestic prices/costs or both. In most countries nominal costs and prices tend to be fairly rigid downward, leaving the nominal exchange rate as the sole short-term instrument to regain economic competitiveness. This, however, is not true in Singapore, where there is a debate as to whether a downward adjustment of the REER in the context of a downturn ought to be engineered via a nominal depreciation of the Singapore dollar or through a reduction in domestic unit business costs.

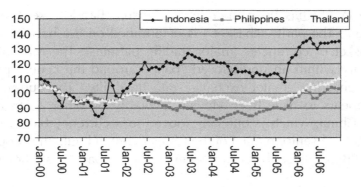

Fig. 3. Real effective exchange rate for Indonesia, Philippines, and Thailand (2000 = 100) (January 2000–December 2006).

Source: Bank of International Settlements.

Note: Rise implies real depreciation.

Given the importance of a trade-weighted exchange rate, many central banks pay particular attention to the NEER. For example, the former governor of the Reserve Bank of India (RBI), Bimal Jalan, wrote:

> "From a competitive point of view and also in the medium term perspective, it is the REER, which should be monitored as it reflects changes in the external value of a currency in relation to its trading partners in real terms. However, it is no good for monitoring short term and day-to-day movements as "nominal" rates are the ones which are most sensitive of capital flows. Thus, in the short run, there is no option but to monitor the nominal rate."[7]

Some countries like Singapore have actually chosen to manage exchange rate changes against a composite bundle of currencies (i.e., stabilizing the "effective" exchange rate) as a means of buffering themselves against outside exchange rate shocks (such as G-3 currency variations) and neutralizing this source of instability.[8] In particular, since 1981, the Monetary Authority of

---

[7] Jalan, B (2002). *India's Economy in the New Millennium: Selected Essays*. India: UBS Publishers and Distributors.

[8] The issue of stability noted above can also be contested. If anything, the East Asian financial crisis demonstrated the deficiencies of pegging to a single reference unit such as the US dollar. Thus, if a country like Thailand had given greater weight to the yen in its currency management pre-crisis, there would not have been as large a real exchange rate overvaluation of the baht following the sharp nominal appreciation of the US dollar relative to the yen between June 1995 to April 1997 (from 85 to 125 yen/US$). Pegging against the US dollar was, in hind-sight, clearly sub-optimal, whereas pegging against a more diversified composite basket of currencies would have enabled the regional countries to better deal with the so-called "third currency phenomenon" (i.e., yen–US$ and euro–US$ fluctuations) which contributed in part to the crisis. See Bird, G and RS Rajan (2002). Optimal currency baskets and the third currency phenomenon: Exchange rate policy in Southeast Asia. *Journal of International Development*, 14, 1053–1073.

Singapore (MAS) has been operating a flexible Band-Basket-Crawl (BBC) arrangement. The parity ("basket") is determined on the basis of an undisclosed basket of currencies (major trading partners). The MAS allows the SGD to vary within an undisclosed "band" around the central parity as a means of ensuring greater exchange rate flexibility.[9] The currency basket regime appears to have been viewed favorably by other Asian countries, including China, which is officially moved to a currency basket regime in July 21, 2005. A senior official of the China's central bank, the People's Bank of China (PBOC), describes China's new currency basket as follows:

> "The countries and regions and their currencies that take a comparatively major position in China's foreign economic activities concerning foreign trade, foreign debt and foreign direct investment will be taken into account when the center bank adjusts the exchange rate of the Chinese yuan.... They will constitute the basket of the currencies and be weighted accordingly...The United Stated, European Union, Japan and the Republic of Korea are China's most important trade partners, so their currencies naturally become the main currencies in the basket.... Singapore, Britain, Malaysia, Russia, Australia, Thailand, and Canada also have important roles in China's foreign trade, so their currencies are important for the RMB exchange rate as well."[10]

Abstracting from the details regarding the computation of optimal weights for the currency *basket*, there are other important issues that need to be sorted out such as whether there should be a band around the peg (Singapore's band is estimated at ±1.5–2.0 percent); whether the bands should be "soft" such that the central bank may or may not intervene if the currency threatens to fall outside the predetermined band (i.e., no absolute commitment); and whether the government should make explicit the values of the bands, or this should be left more ambiguous as in the case of Singapore.

At a general level, more flexibility (i.e., wider and relatively soft bands) is preferable to less. Irrevocably fixing a composite peg may lead to problems in just the same way as it would be for fixing a single currency peg. More flexible exchange rates act as a safety valve by providing a less costly mechanism for relative prices to adjust in response to shocks, as opposed to the slow and often costly reductions that occur under fixed rates through deflation and productivity increases vis-à-vis trade partners. Nonetheless, it could

---

[9] See Khor, HE, E Robinson and J Lee (2004). Managed floating and intermediate exchange rate systems: The Singapore Experience. *Staff Paper No. 37*, Monetary Authority of Singapore (MAS). The MAS reviews both the band and parity from time-to-time and makes alterations according to changing market circumstances if necessary.

[10] For instance, see http://english.sina.com/business/1/2005/0811/42039.html.

well be that a country that is initially concerned about exchange rate variability may want to start by shifting from a US dollar peg to a fairly rigid and transparent peg consisting of a composite basket of currencies. However, once the country's monetary authority becomes more comfortable with the basket regime and builds up credibility in managing the new currency arrangement, and agents get used to the exchange rate variability and realize the need to buy cover against currency fluctuations, there could be a movement toward wider pegs that allow for more policy discretion *a la* Singapore. This policy discretion in Singapore is an important dimension of its BBC.

A Study of Policy Discretion in Singapore

There are two ways of operating a BBC arrangement. One way is to operate a largely mechanical regime, whereby the central bank tries to keep the effective rate more or less within a band. Another way of operating a basket peg would be for the central bank to have a more activist-/forward-looking orientation. In other words, the BBC arrangement is thus viewed as a means to an end; the monetary authority maintains an implicit or explicit monetary policy rule (MPR), whereby it varies the effective exchange rate on the basis of its forecasted inflation and output gaps.

Recent studies have confirmed that the MAS has been consciously and successfully been using the exchange rate as a countercyclical tool.[11] While the MAS has been consciously using the exchange rate as a countercyclical tool, the real effective value of the Singapore Dollar appears to have been broadly aligned with alternative estimates of the long run equilibrium rate based on the underlying macroeconomic fundamentals.[12] However, one cannot be sure whether this alignment is due to a conscious exchange rate policy of the MAS to return the nominal effective exchange rate (NEER) to its "neutral" level over the duration of the business cycle,[13] or a consequence of the fairly high domestic wage and price flexibility in Singapore which leads to a reversion of the REER to its longer run equilibrium value.

---

[11] See Khor *et al.*, *op. cit.*, Cavoli, T and RS Rajan (2007). Managing in the middle: Characterizing Singapore's exchange rate policy. mimeo (April); and Parrado, E (2004). Singapore's unique monetary policy; How does it work? *Working Paper No. 04/10*, IMF.

[12] Khor *et al.*, *op. cit.*; MacDonald, R (2004). The long-run real effective exchange rate of Singapore — A behavioural approach. *Staff Paper No. 36*, Monetary Authority of Singapore (MAS); and Rajan, RS and R Siregar (2002). The choice of exchange rate regime: Currency board (Hong Kong) or monitoring band (Singapore)? *Australian Economic Papers*, 41, 538–556.

[13] For instance, the MAS explicitly states that "the exchange rate policy band is periodically reviewed to ensure that it remains consistent with the underlying fundamentals of the economy" (Khor *et al.*, *op. cit.*, p. 3).

Available data suggests that the MAS has historically pursued an asymmetric policy. Periods of overheating have been confronted with a NEER appreciation (which is indirectly deflationary). Periods of economic downturn have generally been dealt via domestic cost reductions (which is directly deflationary) rather than through a nominal depreciation (which is expansionary). Hence, it is not surprising that Singapore's prices relative to those of its trading partners have experienced a long-term downward trend (Fig. 1). This is taken as evidence by some that domestic macroeconomic policy has imparted a strong deflationary bias over time, and may have skewed aggregate demand too heavily to external demand (net exports) at the expense of internal demand (consumption).

There are sensible reasons for limiting the use of the NEER as a policy instrument. The most cited rationale is that the high import content of manufactured goods implies that, other things being equal, a nominal depreciation may not translate into a significant real depreciation, as domestic prices may rise as well. Certainly, repeated use of exchange rate depreciations by itself to boost competitiveness quickly loses effectiveness as costs and prices rise in anticipation of — or simultaneously with — a currency depreciation. Given the high stock of non-inflation indexed wealth that households and firms in Singapore have accumulated, concerns about keeping a tight lid on inflation are understandable.

A secondary reason why NEER depreciation is used sparingly in Singapore as a policy instrument to regain economic competitiveness is the desire to promote a greater degree of internal price flexibility in the downward direction. Nominal exchange rate rigidity may force domestic prices to become increasingly flexible, thereby reducing the need for significant nominal exchange rate variations. While this may be true in the Singapore context, it has certainly not been the case in some other countries like Argentina in the late 1990s which had to forsake its US dollar-based currency board arrangement (CBA) in the face of a deep domestic recession (an inevitable outcome of inflexible factor markets).

Singapore is also better able than most other countries to pursue a policy of price deflation during a period of economic downturn as it has a certain supply side or income tools readily available to it, such as its national pension fund, the Central Provident Fund (CPF). The cordial tripartite alliance between government, management, and labor has further contributed to keeping wages in Singapore fairly flexible. Apart from keeping wage costs in check, the government could also try to curb land costs, transportation, and other transaction costs and corporate related taxes. However, the problem with such a deflationary strategy is twofold.

First, there is obviously a trough or limit to which a lid can be kept on cost pressures. For instance, in the case of corporate or income tax cuts, the goal of fiscal sustainability may be compromised. In the case of cuts in the employer CPF contribution, this could compromise the savings-for-retirement objective. In the case of land costs there is a limit to how much they can be reduced in a land-scarce city (though alteration in the current market structure of land ownership — a virtual government monopoly — can reduce costs further). In addition, too steep a decline in land prices may trigger asset price deflation with adverse consequences for aggregate demand and short-term growth. More generally, the repeated and aggressive use of deflationary instruments tends to exacerbate the sense of economic insecurity of the general populace. It is almost inevitable that as individuals face greater market risks — which are at least partly an outcome of increasing globalization of economic activities — there will be a yearning for economic security which the government will need to respond to. In the absence of a comprehensive social safety net, some have argued that Singapore might be better off relying relatively more on expansionary policies (fiscal and exchange rate) during periods of downturn, their limitations notwithstanding.

Second, no matter how successful one may be in keeping costs down, an established fact of the new global economy is that newer and more cost-effective countries and regions continuously emerge (regions in China, India, and Vietnam among others).

Conclusion

Sustaining competitiveness over the medium and longer terms requires that focus be squarely on enhancing physical and human capital stock (including via greater levels of foreign direct investment and attracting more and highly skilled migrants), using labor-saving technologies more intensively, and augmenting the stock of directly applicable/commercial R&D to boost both technological progress and technological effort. In addition, while it is conventionally assumed that inputs are automatically used efficiently, it is increasingly recognized that government policy and entrepreneurship are key factors determining the effectiveness with which available resources are utilized. Indeed, one could even think of these as being separate factor inputs. Accordingly, there is renewed interest in countries in Asia in finding ways of nurturing local entrepreneurship and examining the appropriate role of government and government-linked companies.[14]

---

[14] Some of the structural issues facing Singapore economic competitiveness have been explored in Rajan, RS (ed.), *op. cit.*

In the final analysis, it is vital to keep in mind that national economic competitiveness is important, not for its own sake, but because it is a prerequisite for rapid and sustained growth. This in turn is essential for enhancing a society's overall quality of life. It is therefore important that there be a constant and active debate on how best this shared objective can be reached.

Section 2

Financial Liberalization, Financial Crises and the Financing of Development

Chapter 6

Barbarians at the Gates: Foreign Bank Entry in Asia*

Introduction

Banking and currency crises co-exisiting has been found to be the norm during the late 1980s and early 1990s. Most frequently banking crises appear to have taken the lead, and these twin crises seem to be far more pervasive in developing economies than the developed ones. Banking crises themselves seem to be more likely following financial liberalization, with sharp increases in domestic (bank) lending acting as significant predictors of currency crises.[1] The IMF has suggested that the greater frequency of banking crises world-wide since the 1980s is "possibly related to the financial sector liberalization that occurred in many countries during this period".[2]

Until the mid-1990s, Asia's banking system remained heavily regulated and barriers to foreign bank entry remained prohibitively high. However, in the aftermath of the East Asian crisis of 1997–1998, financial sector restructuring has been an essential element in structural adjustment programs in Indonesia, Korea, Thailand, and the Philippines.[3] Broadly, governments in the crisis-hit regional economies have attempted to restructure their financial systems by closing down commercial banks and finance companies, merging

---

* This chapter draws on Rajan, RS, Who's afraid of bank liberalization? (30 January 2005), *Business Times* (Singapore).
[1] See Kaminsky, G and C Reinhart (1999). The twin crises: The causes of banking and balance-of-payments problems. *American Economic Review*, 89, 473–500; Glick, R and M Hutchison (1999). Banking and currency crises: How common are twins?, *Working Paper No. PB99-07*, Center for Pacific Basin Monetary and Economic Studies, Federal Reserve Bank of San Francisco, (December); Table 1 in Eichengreen, B and C Arteta (2000). Banking crises in emerging markets: presumptions and evidence, mimeo (August) succinctly summarizes the principal empirical studies on banking crises. Their comprehensive empirical investigation finds rapid domestic credit growth to be one of the few robust causes of banking crises.
[2] International Monetary Fund (IMF) (1998). *World Economic Outlook 1998*, Washington, DC: IMF (May), p.115.
[3] For a detailed discussion of the restructuring of East Asia's financial sectors post-crisis, see Lindgren, CJ, TJT Baliño, C Enoch, AM Gulde, M Quintyn and L Teo (2000). *Financial Sector Crisis and Restructuring Lessons from Asia*, Washington, DC: IMF. For a more succinct overview, see Rajan, RS and G Bird (2002). Still the weakest link: The domestic financial system and post-crisis recovery in east Asia. *Development Policy Review*, 19, 355–366.

some existing institutions and nationalizing others, injecting public funds to recapitalized viable banks, putting in place systematic asset resolution strategies, as well as easing regulatory impediments to foreign bank entry.

While the liberalization of entry norms for foreign banks has borne fruit, most of Asia continues to lag other emerging markets in Central or Eastern Europe and Latin America (Tables 1 and 2).[4] For instance, a recent report by the Committee on the Global Financial System (CGFS) made the following observation:

> "One of the features that differentiates Asia from other emerging market economies is the limited degree of foreign participation in the domestic banking sector ... (T)he share of foreign bank assets in Asia, at about 10 percent, is far smaller than 33 percent in Latin America and over 50 percent in Eastern Europe. In Latin America and Eastern Europe, a series of "mega" takeovers have led to a significant foreign bank presence in many countries, frequently with a large portion of the banking system owned by foreign institutions. The average size of cross-border financial sector M&A deals during the last five years was around US$40 million in Asia, considerably smaller than that of around US$187 million in Latin America. This mostly reflects the fact that in Asia, many takeovers were either purchases of small financial institutions or acquisitions of minority stakes, with the exception of Thailand."[5]

The slow penetration of banks into Asia is no accident. Regulation in Asia by and large still remains stacked against foreign banks with limits being placed on their ownership levels. However, that is changing with countries such as Korea lifting ceilings while India increased foreign bank holdings in commercial banks to 75 percent and is planning to lift all restrictions by 2010.

Economic Motivations Behind Foreign Bank Entry

Asia is becoming a rich region and many Asian economies can boast of the fastest pace of growth in the world. The consulting firm, Boston Consulting Group (BCG), reported that the total assets under management of high net worth individuals in Asia was US$6.2 trillion in 2003.[6] Banks have a tendency to follow the money and it is in Asia where the money is. Thus, there is a

---

[4] For a discussion on the difficulties of measuring the degree of internationalization of the financial sector, see Reserve Bank of Australia (2003). Foreign Participation in East Asia's Banking Sector, Mimeo (June).

[5] The Committee on the Global Financial System is a central bank forum established by the Governors of the G10 central banks to monitor and examine broad issues relating to financial markets and systems. See CGFS (2003). Financial sector FDI in Asia brief overview, mimeo (March 6), pp. 1–2. Also see *The Economist* (8 February 2003) for a general survey of Asian financial systems post-crisis.

[6] The information contained in the Boston Consulting Group (BCG) report was from *The Economist* (2004). Private banking in Asia: Striking it rich, June 10.

Table 1. Some features of bank systems in emerging market economies.

Country	Bank assets (percent of GDP)	Five largest banks' share of deposits (percent)	Share of bank assets owned by:		Index of bank restrictions	Number of foreign bank licenses:	
			Government (percent)	Foreigners (percent)		Requested	Denied
East Asia							
Korea	98.0	47.5	29.7	0.0	2.3	0.0	0.0
Thailand	117.0	74.8	30.7	7.2	2.3	0.0	0.0
Malaysia	166.0	30.0	0.0	18.0	2.5	0.0	0.0
Indonesia	101.0	52.9	44.0	7.0	3.5	5.0	3.0
Philippines	91.0	45.6	12.1	12.8	1.8	23.0	10.0
Latin America							
Argentina	54.0	48.0	30.0	49.0	1.8	8.0	0.0
Brazil	55.0	57.6	51.5	16.7	2.5	12.0	9.0
Chile	97.0	59.4	11.7	32.0	2.8	0.0	0.0
Mexico	30.0	80.0	25.0	19.9	3.0	0.0	0.0
Peru	36.0	81.2	2.5	40.4	2.0	1.0	0.0
Venezuela	6.0	63.8	4.9	33.7	2.5	3.0	1.0

(Continued)

Table 1. *(Continued)*

Country	Bank assets (percent of GDP)	Five largest banks' share of deposits (percent)	Share of bank assets owned by:		Index of bank restrictions	Number of foreign bank licenses:	
			Government (percent)	Foreigners (percent)		Requested	Denied
Eastern Europe							
Czech Republic	125.0	74.0	19.0	26.0	2.0	0.0	0.0
Poland	54.0	57.2	43.7	26.4	2.5	12.0	0.0
Russia	16.0	80.0	68.0	9.0	2.0	0.0	0.0
Estonia	59.0	95.0	0.0	85.0	2.0	0.0	0.0
Bulgaria	20.4	63.0	17.6	73.3	—	3.0	0.0
Hungary	50.0	—	2.5	62.0	2.3	1.0	0.0
Slovakia	61.6	71.3	25.8	56.7	—	4.0	2.0

Source: Reserve Bank of Australia (2003). Foreign Participation in East Asia's Banking Sector, mimeo (June).

Notes: (1) Data are shown for the latest year available, which are mainly 2001.

(2) The index ranges between 0 and 4. The higher the index value, the more restrictive the country's banking sector.

(3) Based on the number of applications over the previous five years.

Table 2.   Foreign bank penetration in developing countries.

	Foreign Bank Assets in total bank assets	Number of foreign banks in total number of banks	Share south foreign banks assets in total foreign assets	Share south foreign banks in total foreign banks
East Asia & Pacific	0.02	0.25	0.06	0.2
Europe & Central Asia	0.47	0.38	0.02	0.15
Latin America & Caribbean	0.41	0.43	0.05	0.27
Middle East & North Africa	0.11	0.26	0.09	0.29
South Asia	0.03	0.07	0.2	0.18
Sub-Saharan Africa	0.14	0.38	0.17	0.49

Source: van Horen, N, Foreign Banking in Developing Countries; Origin Matters (May 2006). Available at SSRN: http://ssrn.com/abstract=904659.

Notes: (a) A foreign bank is defined to have at least 50 percent foreign ownership.

(b) Figures reported are ratios of number of foreign banks to total number of banks (in 2005) and foreign bank assets to total bank assets (average over 2000–2004) in each country, and the ratios of the number of south foreign banks in total number of foreign banks and south foreign bank assets to total foreign bank assets in each country. Income and region classifications follow World Bank definitions as published in Global Development Finance (2006), New York: Oxford University Press.

(c) South foreign bank is a foreign bank headquartered in a developing country.

great interest by foreign banks to enter Asia. But what is the rationale behind the growing enthusiasm by emerging economies in Asia and elsewhere toward permitting the entry of foreign banks?

A common view is that this was a policy imposed on the regional economies by the IMF and its largest shareholder as a condition of the 1997–1998 IMF-led bailouts.[7] While this perception may be valid, it is instructive that even countries relatively unimpacted by the regional financial crisis such as Singapore have been taking steps to promote the internationalization of their banking sectors, as are India and China, albeit less aggressively. No doubt a proximate cause has been the World Trade Organization (WTO) Agreement in trade in financial services which requires gradual easing of restrictions on foreign banks.[8] However, there is also a realization among

---

[7] For a descriptive overview of the policies towards FDI in the financial sector in ASEAN, see Chua, HB (2003). *FDI in the Financial Sector: The Experience of ASEAN Countries over the Last Decade*, mimeo (March).

[8] For a discussion on financial services and the WTO, see Mattoo, A (2000). Financial services and the WTO: Liberalization commitments of the developing and transition economies. *The World Economy*, 23, 351–386; Crawford, A (2004). The WTO negotiations on financial services: Current issues and future directions, *Discussion Papers No. 172*, UNCTAD; Tamirisa, N, P Sorsa, G Bannister, B McDonald and J Wieczorek (2000). Trade policy in financial services, *Working Paper No. 00/31*, IMF.

policymakers in Asia and elsewhere that a policy of easing barriers on foreign bank entry may in and of itself be in the best interest of their economies. Why?

Apart from helping recapitalize the banking systems (particularly important in the immediate aftermath of a financial crisis), it is becoming increasingly apparent that foreign competition brings with it additional benefits that may not be likely in the case of domestic competition.

First, there is a growing body of empirical evidence of the benefits of foreign bank entry in emerging economies by way of reductions in cost structures, improvements in operational efficiency, introduction and application of new technologies and banking products, marketing skills and management and corporate governance structures. These static and dynamic pro-competitive gains brought about by free trade in financial services are not dissimilar to those arising from trade in merchandise goods.[9] The big difference between the trade in goods and services is that the latter usually requires the right of establishment of foreign suppliers.

Second, a banking system with an internationally diversified asset base is more likely to be stable and less crisis-prone. In addition, the domestic branches of foreign banks may be able to obtain financing from the foreign head office which could act as a private lender of last resort during a period of financial stress.[10] This said, it is important to ensure that foreign investments do not largely originate from a single home country as this might increase rather than decrease instability. Diversification of exposure is the key to enhancing financial stability.[11]

Third, a more competitive financial sector in turn should improve the effectiveness of monetary policy transmission as well as help mitigate the effects of booms and busts.[12]

Fourth, bank internationalization may create domestic pressures for local banking authorities in the host countries to enhance and eventually harmonize regulatory and supervisory procedures and standards and the overall financial infrastructure to international best practice levels.[13]

---

[9] For instance, see Levine, R (1996). Foreign banks, financial development, and economic growth. In *International Financial Markets: Harmonisation versus Competition*, C Barfield (ed.), Washington, DC: AEI Press; Claessens, S and T Glaessner (1998). Internationalization of financial services in Asia, *Policy Research Working Paper No. 1911*, World Bank (April); Claessens, S, A Demirgüç-Kunt and H Huizinga (1998). How does foreign entry affect the domestic banking market? *Policy Research Working Paper No. 1918*, World Bank (June); Also see Tamirisa, N and P Sorsa IMF (2000). *International Capital Markets*, Washington, DC: IMF, Chapter 6 and references cited within.

[10] Claessens and Glaessner, *op. cit.*

[11] In view of this, trade agreements which give preferential access to foreign banks from only one or two countries should be eschewed in favor of a more broad-based liberalization on a multilateral basis.

[12] This issue is elaborated upon in Bird, G and RS Rajan (2002). Banks, financial liberalization and financial crises in emerging markets. *The World Economy*, 24, 889–910.

[13] Kono, M and L Schuknecht (1999). Financial services trade, capital flows, and financial services. *Staff Working Paper ERAD No. 98-12*, WTO.

Fifth, entry of foreign banks ought to reduce the extent of "non-commercial" or "connected" lending, as these banks are not as politically connected as the homegrown institutions and therefore less susceptible to political patronage.[14]

Sixth, foreign banks could enhance the quality of human capital in the domestic banking system by importing high-skilled personnel to work in the local host subsidiary as well as via knowledge spillovers to local employees.

Seventh, opening up of the domestic banking sector to foreign participation might also encourage some of the local banks to venture overseas to compensate for the loss of domestic revenue sources or more generally because they have learnt from the experiences of their foreign competitors who have entered the local market. Thus, as Singapore's domestic banking system has become more internationalized since 1997–1998, local banks in Singapore have both consolidated their operations while also aggressively expanded their operations overseas and been active participants in cross-border mergers and takeovers. Singapore banks, for instance, have purchased significant stakes in banks in India, Hong Kong, Thailand, the Philippines, and Indonesia, just to name a few.[15]

The Fear Behind Foreign Bank Entry

Notwithstanding the foregoing, as with any liberalization initiative, there are those who are strongly opposed to it, and have raised questions about whether foreign ownership in the banking sector "is appropriate". This is especially true in Asia, which, as noted has lagged behind Latin America in the pace of liberalization.

Broadly, the economic justifications for continued protection of the domestic banking system boil down to the usual "infant industry" and "strategic" industry arguments. The first essentially argues that time is needed for domestic bank consolidation if local banks are to be able to compete effectively against multinational foreign banks which have much larger and more diversified capital bases. The second maintains that the financial sector, with its intricate linkages to the rest of the economy, is "too important to be left in the hands of foreigners".

While the infant industry argument has merit in theory, as is usually the case, the problem in practice is that most infants take too long to grow up, and many a times they grow old rather than grow up. The other problem with

---

[14] Kroszner, R (1998). On the political economy of banking and financial regulatory reform in emerging markets. *Research in Financial Services*, 10, 33–51.

[15] For discussions of the overseas expansion of Singapore's largest domestic banks, see Tschoegl, AE (2001). The international expansion of singapore's largest banks, *Working Paper No. 01-20*, the Wharton School, University of Pennsylvania and IMF (2005). "Singapore: Selected Issues", *Country Report No. 05/140*, IMF, pp. 9–15.

infant industries is since they form a dependency on the state to protect them all the time from threats, it makes them become fairly inefficient and it is usually the consumer who usually gets the raw deal at the end.

With regard to the strategic industry argument, one could turn it on its head and suggest that, in view of the importance of the banking and overall financial sector to the rest of the economy and society, everything possible must be done to ensure it is as efficient as possible, and that includes welcoming foreign bank participation. In any event, as with most other industries, the infant and strategic industry arguments appear more valid as grounds for moderating the pace and possibly even the extent of foreign bank entry, rather than opposing the policy in its entirety.

A common criticism of foreign bank entry, or more broadly, internationalization of the financial sector, is that it could make the country prone to international capital booms and reversals. For instance, consider the following statement made by a Leftist party in India to protest a proposal that would enhance the FDI cap in the banking sector in India:

> "Deregulation of the banking sector, which is a vital component of financial liberalization, greatly enhances the scope of speculative activities and exposes the financial system to the risks associated with volatile capital flows. This lesson was painfully learnt by several developing countries through the decade of the nineties. Far from contributing positively to economic growth, asset creation, and employment generation, financial liberalization has precipitated crises in several countries."[16]

However, many casual observers of financial liberalization fail to make a distinction between "capital account deregulation", on the one hand, and "internationalization of the financial sector", on the other. The latter is broadly defined as the elimination of barriers to entry and discriminatory treatment of foreign competition and cross-border provision of financial services. The nexus between international capital flows and financial services may be succinctly and effectively captured in Table 3. Cell I on the uppermost left-hand corner refers to the case of financial autarky, i.e., neither the financial services trade nor an open capital account. Cell IV on the bottom right-hand side denotes the case of "complete" international financial liberalization, i.e., liberal capital account and bank internationalization. The remaining two cells may be broadly classified as "partial international financial liberalization". Specifically, Cell II involves the case of bank internationalization with capital restrictions; while Cell III is the case of capital account deregulation but with restrictions on trade in banking services maintained. Of course, in reality,

---

[16] The full letter is available at http://www.cpim.org/upa/2005_fdi_banking.htm.

Table 3.   Domestic versus international capital flows and bank internationalization.

	Loan provided by domestic supplier	Loan provided by foreign supplier
Loan involves domestic capital only	Cell I: Neither financial services trade nor international capital flows.	Cell II: Financial services trade only.
Loan involves international capital only	Cell III: International capital flows only.	Cell IV: Financial services trade and international capital flows.

Source: Kono, M and L Schuknecht (1999). Financial services trade, capital flows, and financial services. *Staff Working Paper ERAD No. 98-12*, WTO.

matters are not nearly as simple; the two elements of international financial liberalization are closely intertwined and cannot be cleanly separated. Nonetheless, the assumption of total separability is useful conceptually.[17]

The General Agreement on Trade in Services (GATS) recognizes the right of countries to maintain sovereignty over prudential and related regulations of all financial firms resident in the country. However, studies suggest that the introduction of foreign banks into developing countries will create domestic pressure for local banking authorities in the host countries to enhance and eventually harmonize regulatory and supervisory procedures and standards to international levels, particularly with regard to risk management practices.[18]

Indeed, there is some evidence to suggest that the positive benefits of foreign bank entry (in terms of improving banking system competitiveness) are dependent on the sequence of liberalization. Those economies that liberalized their stock markets prior to foreign bank liberalization more likely benefited from the pro-competitiveness effects of bank liberalization, while those that liberalized capital account prior to foreign bank entry were less likely to experience the efficiency gains from liberalization.[19]

---

[17] There is evidence that the former inevitably leads to *de facto* weakening of capital controls. For some evidence of this in the case of China, see Liu, LG (2005). The impact of financial services trade liberalization in China, mimeo (September).

[18] For a discussion of the nexus between foreign bank entry and capital account regulation, see Kono and Schuknecht, *op. cit.* and Tamirisa, NT (1999). Trade in financial services and capital movements, *Working Paper No. 99/89*, IMF. The latter study finds that while financial service liberalization in general has insignificant effects on capital inflows, different modes of entry and different types of financial services (e.g., banks versus insurance) could have differential effects on capital flows.

[19] Bayraktar, N and Y Wang (2004). Foreign bank entry, performance if domestic banks and the sequence of financial liberalization, mimeo (August).

Conclusion: Timing and Pace of Foreign Bank Entry

Heather Montgomery (2003) writes:

> "This increase in foreign participation in the banking sector should be welcomed by policymakers. The presence of foreign banks will likely improve the financial infrastructure, including accounting and transparency, by stimulating the establishment and strengthening of rating agencies, auditors, credit bureaus. Foreign banks effectively "import" financial system supervision and supervisory skills from home country regulators, and these skills may spill over to the host country. In addition, foreign banks can help improve financial services within a country both by offering services directly and through increased competition with domestic banks. Increased competition from foreign entrants stimulates the efficiency of both foreign and domestic players in the market."[20]

From the regulators perspective, any form of financial services liberalization requires that the institutional and regulatory environment be fortified before and during the process of liberalization. Liberalization in a weak or ineffective regulatory and supervisory environment can be calamitous. This was made abundantly clear by the East Asian crisis of 1997–1998 which was partly caused by the ill-timed and ill-sequenced liberalization of the financial sector. This is an important reason to favor introducing competition in a phased and nuanced manner.

There are other reasons for a gradual as opposed to "cold turkey" or "big bang" approach to bank internationalization. The long sheltered and coddled local banking sector usually needs some "breathing space" and lead time to prepare for the impending competition. This in turn necessitates a broad consolidation of many of the hitherto relatively weak and small banks and nonbank financial institutions via mergers or takeovers. Absent this, apart from outright closures of some smaller and inefficient banks, remaining domestic banks may opt for increasingly risky and speculative investments to compensate for declining market shares, lower profit margins and eroding franchise values. If such "gambling for redemption" occurs, an increase in bad loans due to risky investments will partially offset the efficiency gains associated with greater international competition. In addition, foreign banks may, in some instances, be in a position to engage in "cherry picking", i.e., being able to choose clients/debtors of highest quality and leaving the domestic banks with lower quality (default-prone) borrowers. There is some evidence that this has been happening in some Asian countries like Korea.[21]

---

[20] See Montgomery, H (2003). The role of foreign banks in post-crisis Asia: The importance of method of entry, *ADB Institute Research Paper Series No. 51*, January.

[21] Kim, HE and BY Lee (2004). The effects of foreign bank entry on the performance of private domestic banks in Korea, mimeo (March).

This said, the danger of a gradualist approach to internationalization is that it may eventually "run out of steam" as opponents of the program will have more opportunities to block it. Lest there be any wavering of commitment by Asian policy makers to bank internationalization, it is imperative to keep in mind that what matters for growth and welfare is the availability of high quality products and services at internationally competitive prices, not who provides them. It warrants repeating that the need for efficiency in banking services is paramount as it is a key input in all other sectors of the economy. This point needs to be reinforced in Asia where, despite noteworthy steps having been taken to lower barriers and encourage foreign participation in their domestic banking sectors, the region's banking sectors remains somewhat less internationalized than their counterparts in Latin American and Eastern Europe. Indeed, many Asian countries, especially China and India, are only at the early stages of internationalizing their banking and financial systems.

As long as the internationalization of the banking sector is properly managed, fears that no domestic financial institutions may survive following foreign bank entry are exaggerated. Indeed, cross-country evidence suggests that the first mover and informational or familiarity advantages enjoyed by domestic banks for some business like consumer lending and deposit taking tends to limit the extent of inroads that foreign banks can make, at least in the short run. Experience from other regions suggests that domestic financial institutions will continue to play a crucial role in the financial system.

Chapter 7

The Tobin Tax: A Panacea for Financial Crises?*

Introduction

On the 19th of December 2006 the government of Thailand imposed a number of measures to limit the extent of short-term capital inflows, including a 30 percent unremunerated reserve requirement (URR) on foreign investments in securities and other assets and an additional 10 percent principle deduction on overseas investments that were withdrawn within a year. The Bangkok stock exchange index fell by almost 15 percent on that day (Fig. 1). The fall in the market was the biggest in 16 years and wiped over $22 billion in market capitalization. The market did recover somewhat the next day, but that was only after the Thai government capitulated and withdrew the tax as well as rolled-back some of the other restrictions on capital flows.

The imposition of a tax on capital flows by Thailand was not something novel, nor was it the first country to do so. What was somewhat different about Thailand's capital controls was that while a number of emerging countries impose such a tax, they are usually meant to act as a disincentive to foreign investors to pull out money within a short time frame to prevent sharp declines in domestic asset prices including exchange rates.[1] Thailand, on the other hand, imposed this control to prevent money from entering the country on the argument that the Thai baht had appreciated too much and it could harm exports. As Fig. 2 makes apparent, the baht had risen by almost 20 percent in 17 months between June 2005 and December 2006.

The Thai episode brought back into the limelight a tax known as the "Tobin Tax". The Tobin tax is named after noted economist and Nobel laureate James Tobin who proposed a tax on international foreign exchange

---

* This chapter draws on Rajan, RS (2002). The Tobin tax: A global tax for global purposes?, *Economic and Political Weekly*, 37(11), 1024–1026.
[1] A well known example in this regard is Malaysia in September 1998. See Rajan, RS and G Bird (2000). Restraining international capital flows: What does it mean? *Global Economic Quarterly*, 1, 57–80.

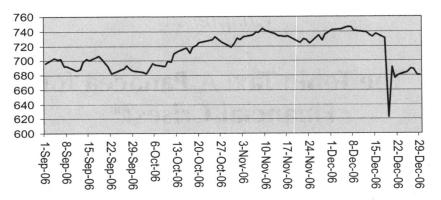

Fig. 1.   Thailand SET index (1 September 2006–31 December 2006).

Source: Bloomberg.

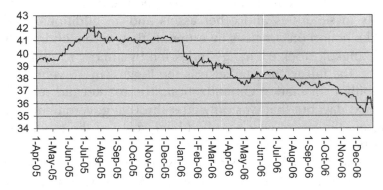

Fig. 2.   US dollar vs. Thai baht exchange rate — (1 April 2005–31 December 2006).

Source: Bloomberg.

(forex) activities. The objective of the tax was to deter speculators who were undermining the ability of central banks to follow appropriate monetary policies. The Tobin tax is essentially a permanent, uniform, ad-valorem transactions tax on international forex flows. The burden of a Tobin tax is claimed to be inversely proportional to the length of the transaction, i.e., the shorter the holding period, the heavier the burden of tax. For instance, a Tobin tax of 0.25 percent implies that a twice daily round-trip carries an annualized rate of 365 percent; while in contrast, a round-trip made twice a year, carries a rate of 1 percent. Accordingly, and considering that 80 percent of forex turnover involves round-trips of a week or less, it has been argued that the Tobin tax ought to help reduce exchange rate volatility and consequently curtail the intensity of "boom-bust" cycles due to international capital flows.

Open Capital Accounts, Financial Crises and Safeguards

A notable aspect of the 1990s was the accelerated progress toward the liberalization and integration of global financial markets, a process that began in earnest in the 1980s. The potential benefits of an open capital account, assuming that the necessary pre-conditions are met, include:[2]

- static resource allocation gains through international specialization in the production of financial services and appropriate portfolio diversification internationally;[3]
- dynamic or "x-efficiency" gains through the introduction of competition in the financial sector;
- gains from inter-temporal trade through access to global financial markets; and
- absence of rent-seeking costs and other costs of capital restraints.

There is another oft-noted benefit of an open capital account, viz. it helps impose market discipline on policy-makers by ensuring that profligate policies, such as unsustainable fiscal imbalances or excessive monetary growth, trigger capital outflows and a financial crisis. Thus, a policy-maker looking to avoid a crisis situation is forced to ensure a degree of policy discipline in the running of the economy. While this market disciplining benefit of an open capital account is compelling, it has proved to be a double-edged sword.

There is a clear evidence that financial markets tend to react too late, and when they do react they have a propensity to over-react with calamitous effects on the real economy and society at large.[4] Of even more concern is that recent events suggest an economy may suffer from such bouts of crisis and instability even when macroeconomic imbalances are not necessarily "unsustainable". To be sure, there is a class of models that allows for multiple equilibria and shows how currency runs may

---

[2] For elaborations of these benefits, see Mathieson, D and L Rojas-Suarez (1993). Liberalization of the capital account: Experiences and issues, *Occasional Paper No. 103*, IMF; Obstfeld, M (1998). The global capital market: Benefactor or menace? *Journal of Economic Perspectives*, 12, 9–30; Prasad, E, K Rogoff, SJ Wei and MA Kose (2003). Effects if financial globalisation on developing countries: Some empirical evidence, *Economic and Political Weekly*, 4319–4330.

[3] The nexus between capital account deregulation and financial efficiency is admittedly not automatic.

[4] See Willett, TD (2000). International financial markets as sources of crises or discipline: The too much too late hypothesis. *Princeton Essays in International Economics No. 218*, International Economics Section, Princeton University.

be "self-fulfilling".[5] The focus of these models is on the trade-off faced by policymakers between the benefits of retaining a pegged exchange rate, on the one hand, and the costs of doing so, on the other. This set of models stresses that while speculative attacks are not inevitable (based on underlying bad fundamentals), neither are they altogether arbitrary or random (i.e., unanchored by fundamentals). Rather, there must exist some weaknesses in the economic fundamentals of the country for an attack to occur as the credibility of the fixed exchange rate regime is less than perfect.[6]

In view of this failure to distinguish between potential efficiency gains of capital account deregulation, on the one hand, and the possibility of crisis with consequent negative real sector effects on the other, much of the cross-country empirical literature has failed to find a robust relationship between capital account liberalization and growth.[7] One recent study, that is careful to make this distinction, does find that while capital account deregulation could lead to instances of crises which depress growth, it does also have a positive impact on resource allocation and efficiency.[8] The authors conclude:

> "Our results suggest that the net effect is context specific: it is positive in periods of financial instability, when the insulating capacity of controls is precious, but negative when crises are absent and the direct effect an open capital account — the positive effect on resource allocation and efficiency — tends to dominate. They suggest that capital account liberalization is neither plague nor panacea, that its benefits are likely to dominate its costs when the domestic financial system is robust and the international financial system is not prone to costly and disruptive crises — in periods, in other words, when the insulating capacity of controls is least valuable."[9]

---

[5] For two recent reviews of currency crisis models and the importance of self-fulfilling behaviour, see Jeanne, O (2000). Currency crises: A perspective on recent theoretical developments, *Special Papers in International Economics No. 20*, International Economics Section, Princeton University, March and Rajan, RS (2001). (Ir)relevance of currency-crisis theory to the devaluation and collapse of the Thai baht, *Princeton Studies in International Economics No. 88*, International Economics Section, Princeton University, February.

[6] For a restatement of this dilemma about capital account openness, see Obstfeld, M. *op. cit.*

[7] Part of the problem may be due to inappropriate or inaccurate proxies of capital account liberalization.

[8] Eichengreen, B and D Leblang (2003). Capital account liberalization and growth: Was Mr. Mahathir Right? *International Journal of Finance and Economics*, 8, 205–224. In relation to this, microeconomic studies of individual country experiences (as opposed to general cross-country empirics) offer evidence that capital controls lead to economic distortion and a misallocation of resources, hence depressing productivity and growth. For instance, see Forbes, K (2003). Capital controls: Mud in the wheels of market discipline, mimeo (November). For a theoretical analysis of this issue (i.e., dichotomy between efficiency of resource allocation and heightened incidence of crisis), see Gourinchas, PO and O Jeanne (2005). The Elusive Gains from international financial integration, *Working Paper No. 9684*, NBER.

[9] Eichengreen, B and D Leblang, *ibid.*, p. 222.

For countries aspiring to enjoy some of the benefits of an open capital account while minimizing the adverse effects of such a policy, an important but belated lesson that has emerged from recent crises is the need to put in place financial self-help mechanisms against volatile capital flows. In other words, appropriate financial safeguards against liquidity crises must supplement sound macroeconomic policies.[10]

Among the more obvious ways of increasing resilience to capital account shocks are those aimed at enhancing international liquidity (via reserve holdings and contingent credit lines); adoption of "best practice" financial codes and standards and prudential regulations; and the imposition of restraints on external financial flows. Such restraints can be further subdivided into those that focus on capital account transactions, and those that pertain to foreign currency transactions *per se*. The latter in turn could involve quantitative or administrative restrictions such as limits on offshore currency trading and non-internationalization of currencies. A number of countries have, in fact, taken steps to curb currency speculation through the imposition of quantitative restrictions on foreign currency flows. Even countries with otherwise open capital accounts like Singapore and Thailand have imposed some restrictions on offshore trading of their national currencies. An IMF working paper on the issue concludes that measures to limit the offshore trading of currencies "could be effective if they were comprehensive and effectively enforced, and were accompanied by consistent macroeconomic policies and structural reforms".[11]

This leads to the following question: if such ad hoc, unilaterally imposed quantitative restrictions and administrative curbs on foreign currency and capital flows are viewed as being effective financial safeguards, would not a preferable alternative be market-based controls on financial flows that are applied uniformly across countries? This is where international currency taxation comes in.

The Tobin Tax Reconsidered[12]

Proponents of a Tobin tax have often suggested that it may have a useful role to play in reducing foreign currency outflows. This said, unlike quantitative

---

[10] For instance, see Rajan, RS (2003). *Economic globalization and Asia: Essays on Finance, Trade and Taxation*. Singapore: World Scientific Press, Chapter 3.

[11] Ishii, S, I Otker-Obe and L Cui (2001). Measures to limit the offshore use of currencies — Pros and cons, *Working Paper No. 01/43*, IMF, p. 1.

[12] This section draws on Bird, G and RS Rajan (2001). International currency taxation and currency stabilization in developing countries. *Journal of Development Studies*, 37(3), 21–38; Bird, G and RS Rajan (1999). Time to reconsider the Tobin tax proposal? *New Economy*, 6, 229–333; Also, see the papers in Weaver, J, R Dodd and J Baker (2003). *Debating the Tobin Tax: New Rules for Global Finance*. Washington, DC: New Rules for Global Finance Coalition.

restrictions on currency flows or price and administrative capital restraints, even the most ardent supporters acknowledge that the Tobin tax cannot be applied unilaterally as this will merely lead to a migration of forex transactions to untaxed countries (i.e., avoidance via migration). As long as the Tobin tax is levied on the trading site rather than the booking or settlement site, the high fixed costs involved in developing the human and physical infrastructure ought to act as a disincentive against migration. Of course, this could lead to a steady erosion of effectiveness over time insofar as new trading sites ("tax havens") gradually develop and strengthen.[13]

If the Tobin tax is limited to spot transactions (as originally suggested by James Tobin) this will lead to a tax-saving reallocation of financial transactions from traditional spot transactions to derivative instruments.[14] As such, in order to prevent tax avoidance via "asset substitution" or "changed product mix" it ought to be applied on all derivative products such as forwards, futures, options, and swaps. There is broad consensus that the tax must be levied at a rate designed to minimize the incentive to undertake synthetic transactions in order to evade the tax (i.e., geographical or asset substitution) or to alter the forex market structure from a decentralized, dealer-driven market to one that is centralized and customer-driven. Suggestions of the "most appropriate" rate of taxation have generally ranged between 0.1 and 0.25 percent.

In contrast, detractors of the Tobin tax correctly emphasize that with sizeable prospective devaluations, a marginal tax on currency transactions will be altogether ineffective. What matters is the expected returns from speculation relative to the costs (inclusive of the tax). In circumstances where expectations of currency devaluation increase, a tax will become progressively less effective. Indeed, it will be in the midst of a currency crisis, when its stabilizing properties are most required, that a currency tax will be at its least effective because of the large anticipated gains from speculation. As has been pointed out, "(a)nyone who contemplates 30 percent depreciation will happily pay 0.1 percent Tobin tax".[15] The comparison of expected exchange rate change and size of a currency tax is an important issue that has largely been ignored by the Tobin tax literature. Taking this conclusion a step further, a Tobin tax or any form of restraints on currency and capital flows imposed in the midst of a crisis could lead to a self-validating panic and crisis. Consequently they are best introduced during a period of relative calm.

---

[13] While punitive taxes exist on world stock markets without apparent problems, the only way individual countries can unilaterally impose taxes on international financial transactions is if they simultaneously impose quantitative prohibitions, as in the case of Brazil's exit tax on capital flows, for instance.

[14] Tobin, J (1978). A proposal for international monetary reform. *Eastern Economic Journal*, 4, 153–159.

[15] Dornbusch, R (1998). Capital controls: An idea whose time is gone, *Essays in International Finance No. 207*, International Economics Section, Princeton University (p. 2).

The foregoing, along with recent formal research on the Tobin, tax suggests that the international currency tax ought to be designed as a *crisis prevention* instrument rather than one for *crisis management*.[16] In other words, a Tobin tax would need to be applied counter-cyclically, i.e., stiffened during a boom and loosened during a bust. Admittedly, this policy recommendation is at odds with Tobin (and Keynes before him) and others who recommend raising of tax rates during a crisis. Nonetheless, it is consistent with other empirical studies on financial restraints in general which indicate that they are more effective at preventing "excessive" capital inflows than at stemming capital flight. The fact that a Tobin tax is relatively ineffective during a crisis period implies that a tax levied at a "moderate rate" will not be able to defend a regime that is inherently unsustainable. In other words, the discipline of the market will remain in operation despite the levy; it does not advance policy failures.

Skeptics may suggest that such a tax would still be ineffective as a preventive measure, arguing that the elasticity of foreign currency flows is low. Parallels could be drawn with the Chilean experience with, and management of, its interest-free deposit requirement which seem to indicate the restraints have not significantly affected the aggregate *level* of capital inflows and therefore, the extent of real exchange rate appreciation. (Table 1 compares the main characteristics of the oft-mentioned Chilean-type reserve requirements with the Tobin tax.) Insofar as the Chilean case of unilateral capital controls is applicable to a multilateral tax of foreign currency flows, studies suggest that the controls do appear to have been effective in altering the composition of capital flows. Specifically, they appear to have extended the *duration* or maturity structure of overall capital inflows. (Having served their purposes, the Chilean deposit requirements have come down to zero.)[17]

Conclusion

According to the World Bank, the net portfolio inflows into developing countries increased a tenfold from just over $6 billion in 2000 to over $60 billion in 2005, and is estimated at $90 billion for 2006.[18] The fact that the world

---

[16] Interested readers are referred to the following paper which develops a simple model confirming this conclusion, Bird, G and RS Rajan (2001), *op. cit.* Also see Mende, A and L Menkhoff (2003). Tobin tax effects seen from the foreign exchange market's microstructure, Discussion Paper No. 268, University of Hannover.

[17] There is a large literature on the Chilean deposit requirements. For instance, see Edwards, S (1999). How effective are controls on capital inflows? An evaluation of Chile's experience, mimeo (June).

[18] World Bank (2006). *Global Development Finance.* New York: Oxford University Press.

Table 1. Summary comparison between the Chilean deposit requirements and the Tobin tax.

	Chilean deposit requirements	Tobin tax
Motive	Prevent over-indebtedness	Reduce forex volatility (and raise revenues)
Tax applied to	Capital inflows	All forex transactions
Paid immediately by	Foreign investors	All traders (mainly interbank trade)
Paid immediately to:	Central bank (foreign currency earnings)	Global tax authority?
Relationship of tax amount to interest rate	Rises with foreign interest rate	Invariant to interest rate
Relationship to maturity	Fixed amount (falling with maturity in percent per year) when maturity is less than one year	Fixed amount in percent terms, falls continuously with maturity (if applied counter cyclically)
Where imposed?	Single country (faced with inflows)	Must be world-wide or major financial centres
Probable level of tax rate	Low-to-moderate	Low

Source: Frankel, J (1996). How well do markets work: Might a Tobin tax help? In *The Tobin Tax: Coping with Financial Viability*, ul Haq, M, I Kaul and I Grunberg (eds.). New York: Oxford University Press.

is awash with so much liquidity and such high global interconnectedness where billions can be moved at the touch of a button, it is unlikely that even a properly designed Tobin tax will be effective in reducing the intensity of capital inflows (and consequently the extent of capital outflows and crashes). In other words, international capital flows may be relatively inelastic with respect to such taxes. However, the low elasticity that limits the effectiveness of the tax in reducing capital volatility increases its capacity to raise much-needed revenues. In other words, if the international finance case for a Tobin tax proves ineffectual, this could paradoxically enhance the public finance case for the tax.

While leakages via evasion and avoidance are real concerns (as they are with any tax), the problem can, as noted, be reduced significantly if the tax rate is "punitive" and the participation is broadly multilateral. Beyond this, just as there appears to be international political will to stop money laundering, so there ought to be a similar resolve if and when leakages threaten to make a currency tax "too porous" in the event it is put in place. The issue of tax evasion via tax havens is not unique to the Tobin tax. For instance, the *Financial Stability Forum* has identified unregulated and offshore centers as a source of international financial instability.[19] Thus, to reiterate, if the elasticity turns out to be relatively low, while a currency tax may not be an effective financial safeguard, it could generate a relatively large amount of revenue if applied multilaterally that may then be used for development purposes, i.e., a financial bonanza.

How big a bonanza it will be is hard to say, as estimating the revenue from currency taxation is a complicated methodological exercise. Much depends on the rate and coverage of the tax, the level of transactions costs, the elasticity of capital movements with respect to the effective increase in transaction costs associated with the tax, as well as the extent to which it is avoided or evaded. Table 2 summarizes the estimates from various studies. Given these studies, it may not be unreasonable to assume that a transactions tax of 0.25 percent will generate annual revenues of about $150 billion. These are certainly conservative estimates, particularly because the computations are based on 1995 forex figures of $1.2 trillion as opposed to the more recent 1998 figure of $1.5 trillion. While there is clearly plenty of room to debate the numbers and assumptions used, as the numbers in Table 2 reveal, revenue from an international currency transaction tax would be large relative to other resource flows.

The revenues from a currency tax could help deal with a foreign aid "crisis" and assist in halting if not reversing the persistent downward trend in

Table 2. How much revenue can the Tobin tax generate?

Study	Tax rate assumed (percent)	Annual tax revenue derived (US$ billions)
Felix and Sau (1996)[1]	0.25	290
Felix and Sau (1996)[1]	0.10	140–180
D'Orville and Najman (1995)[2]	0.25	140
Frankel (1996)[3]	0.10	170

Source: Compiled by authors.
Notes: (1) Felix, D and R Sau (1996). On the revenue potential and phasing in of the Tobin tax. In *The Tobin Tax: Coping with Financial Viability*, ul Haq, M, I Kaul and I Grunberg (eds.). New York: Oxford University Press.
(2) D'Orville, H and D Najman (1995). *Towards a New Multilateralism: Funding Global Priorities*. New York.
(3) Frankel, J (1996). How well do markets work: Might a Tobin tax help? In *The Tobin Tax: Coping with Financial Viability*, ul Haq, M, I Kaul and I Grunberg (eds.). New York: Oxford University Press.

---

[19] See http://www.fsforum.org/publications/publication_23_45.html

aid flows. Moreover, with growing evidence that foreign aid *is* effective when combined with good domestic economic policies (i.e., "aid does work in the right circumstances"), the global political environment may become less hostile to using global taxation as a way of bringing about global income redistribution aimed at poverty reduction. To use the revenue from a currency transaction tax to augment multilateral aid flows would, in these circumstances, have the appeal of assisting countries that are largely by-passed by private international capital markets. However, all of this is probably just wishful thinking.

Chapter 8

International Capital Flows to Asia: The Never-Ending Magic Spigot?*

Introduction

While East Asia's rapid recovery from the crisis of 1997–1998 underscores the region's overall resilience, there has been a shift in the nature of the region's engagement with the rest of the world. In particular, since the financial crisis of 1997–1998 and the subsequent sharp capital outflows from economies in East Asia, the region has been running persistent current account surpluses. The region has consequently become a net exporter of capital to the rest of the world while still depending very heavily on gross financing from the rest of the world. This chapter examines balance of payments trends in the East Asian economies' and also discusses the emergence of "carry-trade" which appears to have become a force to be reckoned within global and regional financial markets.

Current Account Balances and Reserve Accumulation Since the Crisis

It is commonly noted that there has been a marked rise in developing Asia's aggregate current account surplus since the abrupt and massive capital flow reversals after the crisis of 1997–1998 (Fig. 1). However, aggregate regional data hide considerable variations across economies with respect to the timing of and reasons for the emergence of these surpluses. This diversity matters for understanding the persistence of the current situation and of the risks going forward. The economies in East Asia can be broadly divided into three groups: (i) the ASEAN-4[1] plus four newly industrializing economies (NIEs) of Hong Kong, Singapore, Taiwan, and South Korea (Korea henceforth), (ii) People's Republic of China (China henceforth), and (iii) Japan.

---

* The chapter draws on background work done by Rajan, RS and E Vostroknutova (2006). In *An East Asian Renaissance: Ideas for Competitive Growth.* Kharas, H and I Gill (eds.), Washington, DC: World Bank.
[1] Indonesia, Malaysia, Philippines, and Thailand.

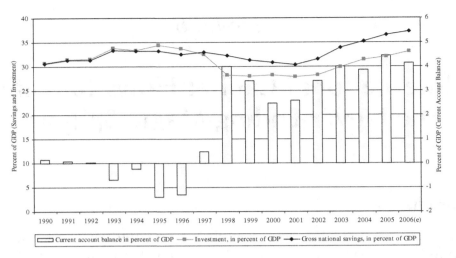

Fig. 1. Developing Asia and NIEs: Savings, investment and current account (percent of GDP) (1990–2006).

Source: IMF, WEO April 2006 database (http://www.imf.org/external/pubs/ft/weo/2006/01/data/index.htm).

Developing Asia Includes: ASEAN-9 (Brunei, Cambodia, Indonesia, Laos, Malaysia, Myanmar, Philippines, Thailand, and VietNam), NIEs (Hong Kong, Korea, Singapore, Taiwan), China and others (South Asia including India and Pacific island economies).

In the developing ASEAN and NIEs — which includes the countries most impacted by the crisis — the current account surplus only emerged immediately post-crisis. The switch from current account deficit to surplus for this group of economies as a whole was largely a result of a collapse in domestic investment rather than an increase in the national savings which has remained fairly stable. This is in part because the currency crisis turned into a full blown banking crisis (which led to a vicious cycle of illiquidity and insolvency). With the gradually improving balance sheets of companies and financial institutions; the purging of excesses and gradual dissipation of capacity overhangs; general improvement in investment climates; fading in memories of the crisis; as well as general regional asset reflation, one can expect domestic investment to continue to recover over time among this group of economies.[2] This in turn suggests that the current account surpluses for the NIEs and ASEAN economies taken in aggregate might gradually decline over the longer term if high oil prices persist.

China's current account surplus emerged in the mid-1990s and has been rising sharply in recent times accompanied by an upward trend in both

---

[2] However, to the extent that one argues that there were signs of "over investment" in the region pre-crisis (especially in construction and real estate), it is debatable whether investment ratios will ever reach pre-crisis levels.

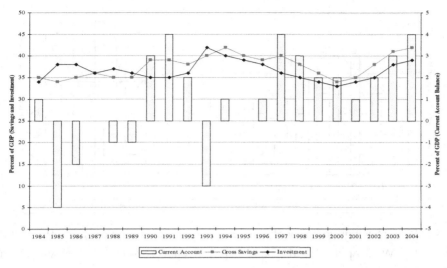

Fig. 2. China: Savings, investment and current account (percent of GDP) (1984–2004).

Source: World Bank Development Indicators.

national saving and domestic investment rate (Fig. 2). With an investment rate of 44 percent of GDP, low investment is clearly not a concern in China but there is some cause for concern regarding the overheating of the Chinese economy. It is often noted that China's high savings is deep-seated and structural in nature and is partly a consequence of a breakdown in the country's social safety structure (health, education, pension, and housing benefits having historically been provided by state-owned enterprises to their employees), along with the loss of a traditional source of social security (due to the country's one-child policy) and lack of sources or instruments for consumer finance. While these are important factors, less well recognized is that the decline in household consumption in China has been driven largely by a falling share of disposable income to GDP as opposed to a decline in consumption as a share of disposable income per se.[3] As the IMF notes:

> "During the latter half of the 1990s, much of the decline in the disposable income-to-GDP ratio was due to a fall in investment income, while in the period since, a declining share of wages in GDP was an added factor … It is striking how very little of the strong rise in corporate profits has been transferred to households. This has largely reflected the ownership structure and dividend policy in China."[4]

---

[3] See International Monetary Fund (IMF) (2006). *World Economic Outlook*, IMF, September.
[4] See International Monetary Fund (IMF) (2006). *Regional Economic Outlook: Asia and Pacific*, IMF, May.

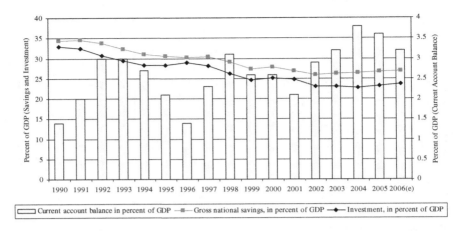

Fig. 3. Japan: Savings, investment and current account (percent of GDP) (1990–2006).

Source: IMF, WEO April 2006 database (http://www.imf.org/external/pubs/ft/weo/2006/01/data/index.htm).

In any event, the excess savings over investment in China and the consequent external surplus is a more persistent phenomenon than the case of the ASEAN economies and the NIEs.

The current account balance in Japan has been in surplus since the mid-1980s and the surplus has persisted despite the decline in both national saving and investment rates (Fig. 3). While Japan's declining national saving rate has been largely due to the deteriorating fiscal balance (as opposed to private savings), the fall in investment which started with the bursting of the asset bubble in the early 1990s has no doubt been due — and in turn contributed — to the prolonged recession in the country. With the recent pick-up in economic activity in Japan and re-emergence of consumer confidence in the country, one would expect a turnaround in consumption as well as investment. This trend can be hastened if Japan pursues much-needed structural reforms such as labor market reforms to boost investments. Counterbalancing this possible increase in private sector domestic demand is the likelihood of improvements in the fiscal balance as the Japanese government attempts to undertake fiscal consolidation on a sustained basis following years of pump priming which have resulted in a sizeable accumulation of domestic debt.[5]

Current account surpluses and limited exchange flexibility have resulted in the rapid and massive accumulation of reserves in the region (Fig. 4). The region as a whole also accounts for about one half of global reserve accumulation in the world.[6] While China and Japan have been

---

[5] See International Monetary Fund (IMF) (2005). *Regional Economic Outlook: Asia and Pacific*, IMF, September.

[6] Also see Chapter 1 of this Volume.

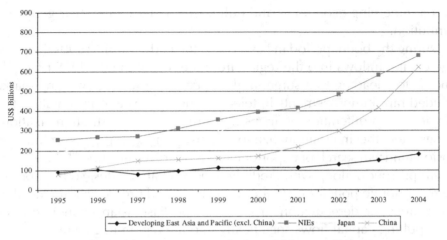

Fig. 4.   Total reserve holdings in Asia (including gold) (US$ billions) (1995–2004).

Source: World Bank Development Indicators.

Developing East Asia includes: ASEAN-9 plus Pacific island economies.

the drivers of this trend, Korea and the other NIEs have also experienced significant swelling of their reserves since the crisis.[7] There is no direct correlation between reserve stockpiling and current account surpluses in East Asia. As is well known, reserve accumulation is a consequence of an overall balance of payments surplus. Thus, even if current account surpluses in the region come down, less recognized is the fact that the region's reserve accumulation is also driven by dynamics in private capital flows. Since 2000, while the current account surplus still dominates, the private capital account surplus in East Asia has accounted for a growing share of the region's reserve accretion. In view of this, it is essential to understand the patterns and dynamics of private capital flows to East Asia.[8]

Capital Flows and International Financial Intermediation

Is capital pulled into recipient countries by their internal policies and performance, or is it pushed toward them as a consequence of external factors beyond their control, such as interest rates and economic activity in the rest of the world? Research suggests that pull and push factors may be complementary, with push factors' determining the timing and magnitude of capital

---

[7] Outside East Asia, but still in Asia, India has also seen a sharp increase in reserves from US$1 billion in 1990–1991 to US$200 billion by early 2007.

[8] A significant part of the balance of payments surplus is, of course, driven by China.

flows to emerging economies and pull factors determining their geographic distribution.[9]

During the boom period in East Asia in the early-to-mid 1990s there were large capital inflows into the region from the rest of the world. Structural or trend factors leading to a surge in global capital flows to emerging markets included rapid improvements in telecommunications and information technologies, the proliferation of financial instruments, the institutionalization of savings, and the internationalization of investment portfolios (mutual and pension funds) in search of opportunities for risk diversification.[10] The attractive growth prospects along with credibly fixed exchange rates, sound domestic macroeconomic policies (actual or perceived) and progressive financial and capital account deregulation in many of the East Asian economies, were forces pulling capital flows specifically into the region in general.

However, the subsequent loss of confidence in these economies resulted in a massive turnaround in capital flows in 1997, i.e., boom was followed by bust. What does the data tell us about this? Table 1 summarizes the balance of payments data from the IMF for developing Asia. The data reveals that emerging Asia experienced a sharp reversal in net private capital flows of over US$90 billion between 1997 and 1998. This reversal was primarily due to the "other" net private capital flows which include net short-term lending by foreign commercial banks. This component averaged about US$7 billion in inflows between 1990 and 1996 but turned into a net outflow of about US$80 billion on average in the following four years as international banks became unwilling to roll over existing short-term debts to the region. This sudden reversal in bank lending is often presented as providing strong evidence in support of a bank panic model.[11] However, a less emphasized feature of this period was the decline in portfolio flows following the initial bank panic as investors also tried to scale down their exposures in the region. In contrast, FDI flows remained remarkably stable throughout the period under consideration.[12]

---

[9] See Carlson, M and L Hernandez (2002). Determinants and repercussions of the composition of capital inflows, *Discussion Paper No. 717*, Board of Governors of the Federal Reserve System International Finance; Dasgupta, D and D Ratha (2000). What factors appear to drive private capital flows to developing countries? And how does official lending respond?, *Policy Research Working Paper No. 2392*, The World Bank.

[10] See World Bank (1997). *Private Capital Flows to Developing Countries: The Road to Financial Integration*, New York: Oxford University Press.

[11] See Chang, R and A Velasco (1998). The Asian liquidity crisis, *Working Paper No. 6796*, NBER; Radelet, S and J Sachs (1998). The East Asian financial crisis: Diagnosis, remedies, prospects. *Brookings Paper of Economic Activity*, 1, 1–90.

[12] Two caveats should be noted. One, Indonesia was the only exception since FDI collapsed due to ongoing socio-political uncertainties and two, the implicit assumption is that there is little or no relationship between the various types of capital flows.

Table 1. Net capital flows to developing East Asia (US$ billions) (1990–2006).

Developing Asia	Average							
	1990–1995	2000	2001	2002	2003	2004	2005	2006(e)
Private capital flows, net	49.0	6.5	19.6	20.8	63.5	120.3	53.8	55.2
Direct investment, net	28.9	59.0	51.6	50.7	67.9	60.0	71.8	76.5
Private portfolio flows, net	13.8	20.2	−51.2	−59.9	4.4	3.8	−31.1	−24.5
Other private capital flows, net	6.3	−72.8	19.1	30.0	−8.8	56.4	13.1	3.3
Official flows, net	4.9	−11.7	−11.7	4.6	−17.6	1.8	5.0	−0.2
Change in reserves	−34.6	−53.7	−90.2	−148.8	−226.5	−340.1	−281.9	−302.2

Source: IMF, WEO April 2006 database (http://www.imf.org/external/pubs/ft/weo/2006/01/data/index.htm).

The region remained relatively unattractive to private capital between 1997 and 2002 but has since consolidated and is again attracting foreign capital inflows. After a period of consolidation and recovery (including the IT-induced global downturn in 2001), there has been a resurgence in net capital inflows to the region since 2003. Inflows of all types of capital inflows to China were particularly high, no doubt in part due to the expectations of a renminbi revaluation, though capital flows to Korea and much of Southeast Asia also picked up, supported by rising credit ratings of emerging market issuers over the past few years. While improving fundamentals have also pulled inflows into the East Asian region, large-scale global liquidity, low industrial country interest rates and lower risk aversion have been factors pushing capital from industrial countries to emerging economies in general.

The development of bond markets, lengthening of maturities of bank loans, and stabilization of debt inflows highlight greater resilience of the region. After the outflows and de-leveraging recorded between 1998 and 2001, debt to developing countries stabilized in 2001–2002 and rose markedly in 2002–2003 as many regional economies, including Korea, China and some ASEAN economies have successfully issued bonds internationally; international creditors are once again actively participating in international syndicated loans in the region.[13] While not readily apparent from the data, it is generally reported that the average maturity of bank loans has lengthened.[14] This, along with the reserve stockpiling, has resulted in the regional economies experiencing declines in short-term debt to reserves and short-term debt to external debt ratios. Another important characteristic of debt inflows to Asia is the growing share of marketable debt instruments (i.e., bonds). This is a result of a deliberate decision by these economies to develop and upgrade their bond markets as a means of diversifying their financial systems and instruments.

Portfolio equity and FDI flows to East Asia have been on the rise, but the destination countries have changed since the crisis. Referring again to Table 1, it is apparent that after reaching the lows in 2001 and 2002, net portfolio equity flows bounced back in 2003, their highest levels since 1998. Interest in the region has been partly induced by IPO issuances by many companies, particularly from privatizations of state-owned enterprises in Korea and China. The average net FDI-to-GDP ratio in the early 1990s was about 3 percent. While this ratio remained constant during the crisis period, there are signs that it is on a gradual downward trend. What the aggregate data do not highlight though is the shift in composition in FDI. In particular, while both China and ASEAN were the primary beneficiaries of FDI inflows into East Asia prior to the crisis, China alone absorbed over three quarters of the FDI inflows to the region post-crisis, buoyed in part by the country's WTO accession.

The rise of intraregional FDI flows, especially between China and the NIEs, shows the renewed search by the regional economies. Referring to FDI flows to China, it is apparent that the sources of inflows have actually become more diversified and now not only originates from Japan and United States but also other developing countries in the region, the NIEs in particular (Fig. 5). Specifically, while the FDI inflows to China by NIEs were largely driven by Hong Kong,[15] the pattern held up for other NIEs as well. FDI outflows from East Asia have been growing and comprise about 90 percent of all investment outflows in total developing country outflows. FDI outflows from China have also increased. The outflows to the NIEs increased sharply even before the crisis — from about a quarter to more than two-thirds in 2004. There has also been a shift in the destination of these outflows over time, with a greater share of China's FDI finding its way to Asian destinations (Fig. 6).[16]

---

[13] See Capital flows to emerging market economies, International Institute of Finance (IIF), various issues. See www.iif.com.

[14] See World Bank. Global Development Finance 2003 and Global Development Finance 2004, New York: Oxford University Press.

[15] As is well known, a portion of China's FDI inflows is associated with round tripping as domestic capital from China capital leaves the country and then returns to benefit from tax incentives and other subsidies as well as to escape foreign exchange controls.

[16] Also see Chapter 15 of this Volume.

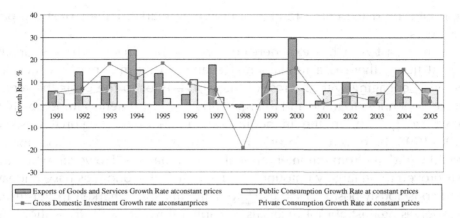

Fig. 5. East Asia: Export and domestic demand growth (percent change) (1991–2005).
Source: Asian Development Bank, Asia Regional Information Center (http://aric.adb.org/).
East Asia includes: Cambodia, Vietnam, Indonesia, Malaysia, Philippines, Korea, Singapore, and Thailand.

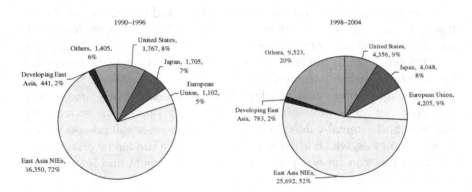

Fig. 6. Geographical distribution of intraregional FDI flows to China, 1990–1996 and 1998–2004 (Millions of US dollars and percent share).
Source: State Statistical Bureau, China Statistical Yearbook.
NIEs include: Hong Kong, Korea, Singapore, and Taiwan. Developing East Asia includes: Indonesia, Malaysia, Philippines, and Thailand.
All numbers are averages over 1990–1996 and 1998–2004.

Conclusion: The Yen-Carry Trade

International capital flows to Asia reached US$88 billion in 2006, compared to US$60 billion in 2005 and they are expected to remain high in 2007 despite the temporary market correction in May–June. Inflows of all types of capital inflows to China have been particularly high, though capital flows to Korea and much of Southeast Asia have also picked up sharply, supported by rising credit ratings of emerging market issuers over the past few years.[17]

While East Asia has experienced a resurgence in cross-border private capital flows, there is a fundamental change in the manner in which the region is engaging with the rest of the world. Prior to the crisis the region viewed openness to trade and financial flows as instruments almost solely to maximize growth. In the immediate aftermath of the regional crisis of 1997–1998 there were widespread concerns that the East Asian economies would withdraw from the international capital markets. However, while this fear proved to be largely unfounded,[18] the regional economies have endeavored consciously post-crisis to use international capital markets to self-insure themselves against abrupt reversals in capital flows as well. Indications are that the region has become somewhat less vulnerable to sudden shifts in investor sentiment than they were a few years ago. This is reflected in the dominance of FDI, lengthening of maturities of liabilities, and rapid and massive stockpiling of a war chest of reserves. The IMF has opined:[19]

> "Regional economies are now more resilient to a sudden reversal of inflows than a decade ago, because their economic fundamentals have improved, and because exchange rates in the majority of economies are more flexible. Furthermore, risks to the banking systems in the region have diminished because only a small portion of the flows, this time, have been intermediated through banks, leaving their balance-sheets largely unaffected. However, not all economies have moved at the same pace in reducing domestic and external vulnerabilities. Some economies still possess underlying weaknesses, which leave them vulnerable to a sudden reversal of capital flows that can be brought by changes in sentiment and international financial conditions."[20]

While there has been a return of capital to East Asia, there is an important dynamic in regional and global capital flows that pertains to the so-called

---

[17] See International Monetary Fund (IMF) (2006). *Regional Economic Outlook: Asia and Pacific*, IMF, September.

[18] It is "largely" because while the regional economies have generally remained open to international capital flows, there are two notable exceptions. One, Malaysia imposed capital controls in September 1998 but has since removed them. Two, some East Asian economies have tightened regulations with regard to the offshore trading of currencies. Executives' Meeting of East Asia–Pacific (EMEAP) (2002). The effectiveness of capital controls and monitoring: The case of non-internationalization of emerging market currencies, January.

[19] See International Monetary Fund (IMF) (2005). *Regional Outlook, op. cit.*

[20] In addition, while there has been a better matching in the current composition of assets and liabilities in the developing East Asia region, this is largely due to an accumulation of reserves in foreign currency terms. It is important to ensure that individual corporates and financial institutions take appropriate care to manage the risks associated with these currency mismatch risks.

"carry-trade". The IMF defines carry-trade as "a trade in which the investor borrows at a low interest rate and invests at a higher one, normally with some type of currency or basis risk".[21] *The Economist* (2006) reports:

> "The carry trade is essentially a bet on lower volatility. To take an outright gamble that markets will barely move, an investor would write (sell) options; this approach would bring in premium income, but would lose money if prices changed enough for the options to be worth exercising. In the for-eign-exchange version of the carry trade, an investor receives an income by borrowing a low interest rate currency and owning a higher-yielding one. This produces a positive return most months, but the risk is that the high-rate currency will devalue, resulting in a heavy loss."[22]

While this term is generally associated with the Japanese yen, i.e., "yen-carry trade", this is not to say that there are no carry trades associated with other currencies. The yen-carry trade has existed from the time the Japanese central bank adopted a zero interest rate policy (ZIRP) in the 1990s. The con-jecture of yen-carry trade is that there is a huge mass of money that is out there because funds and other such institutions borrowed Japanese yen at zero interest rates or near zero interest rates and used that money to invest in assets such as stocks or property in other parts of the world. The yen-carry trade has in fact been "blamed" for the rapid increase in the Asian stock mar-kets and is also believed to be the reason for the appreciation of the Australian dollar, the New Zealand dollar, as well as the Euro, as borrowers of yen have converted that money into these currencies. However, no one can give an accurate size of the yen-carry trade and no one knows where the money is. In 2007, *The Economist* reported:

> "Admittedly, the size of the market is fiendishly hard to gauge. Earlier this year Hiroshi Watanabe, Japan's deputy finance minister for international affairs, put the trade at $80 billion–160 billion. That the carry trade exists at all is gleaned only indirectly. One clue comes from financing trends among foreign banks in Japan. Whereas loans last year barely grew for Japan's banking sector as a whole, yen financing by foreign banks shot up by ¥7.4 trillion ($64 billion); foreigners are reckoned to be mainly responsi-ble for the carry trade. Another clue comes from dollar/yen positions in international money markets. As recently as last May (2006) these positions, on balance, were long yen, but that changed and in February net short posi-tions reached a record $17.8 billion. Economists at Goldman Sachs in Tokyo reckon that the total size of the yen carry trade is perhaps two to five times

---

[21] See International Monetary Fund (IMF) (2006). *Global Financial Stability Report: Market Developments and Issues,* IMF, September.
[22] Instant returns (5 October 2006). *The Economist.*

the size of money-market transactions, since much of the business is unrecorded, conducted over-the-counter. Assuming the trade's total size to be at the top of the Goldman Sachs range puts the February peak towards the bottom end of Mr. Watanabe's estimate."[23]

Many carry trade transactions are done through currency forward swaps and they are essentially off-balance sheet transactions and do not show up in official records or statistics. The important point about the yen-carry trade is that no one knows when it will end. However, it will end at some point of time and then comes the scarier part of how this "unwinding" of the carry trade will hit asset markets around the world. No one can really estimate how severe the impact will be. Doomsday proponents have predicted that when the yen-carry trade does finally unwind it will have a catastrophic effect on world financial markets. The world experienced a preview of the unwinding of the yen-carry trade in 1998 when the Japanese government decided to recapitalize its banks in the wake of the LTCM scandal and Russian financial disaster.[24] This led to the yen appreciating by around 12 percent in less than a week. Since the whole precept of the yen-carry trade rests on the belief that the yen will not appreciate significantly, this sudden rise led to a massive unwinding. However, this time around the scale of such carry trade is surely much larger. As Japan's ZIRP has come to an end in 2006 and Japanese interest rates are gradually creeping up (though still very low), many believe that the heydays of the yen-carry trade are coming to an end.

To the extent that the unwinding of such trades and subsequent sharp capital outflows could damage emerging economies in Asia, the region must consciously focus on improving the quality of domestic and regional financial institutions and financial intermediation. Deepening and diversifying domestic and regional financial markets and in particular, developing bond markets, is key to enhancing domestic demand and limiting the adverse consequences of a sudden capital account reversal as occurred in 1997–1998.

---

[23] Out with a Whimper (26 April 2007). *The Economist*.
[24] See Schinasi, G (1999). Systemic aspects of recent turbulence in mature markets, *Finance and Development*, 36(1), 30–33.

Chapter 9

Using Reserves to Finance Infrastructure in India: Will It Clear the Gridlock?*

Introduction

In addition to disciplined macroeconomic policies, a necessary condition for rapid and sustained growth is openness to international trade and investment flows. While such openness provides the right price signals and offers abundant market opportunities for firms from developed and developing countries alike, growth in many developing countries has been held back largely because of the existence of substantial supply-side constraints that have often stymied the take-off of investments and exports. Beyond regulatory and other barriers, the biggest supply-side constraint faced by developing countries is inadequate and poor quality infrastructure. Indeed, infrastructure bottlenecks (roadways, power plants, telecom networks, seaports, airports, water and sanitation, broadband connectivity, etc.) are among the main reasons that have prevented many developing countries from fully benefiting from trade and investment openness, particularly in the case of labor-intensive manufacturing.

A growing body of empirical studies points to the positive correlation between investment in quality infrastructure and a lowering of poverty rates.[1] The Monterrey Consensus has highlighted the necessity of paying adequate attention to the financing needs for development.[2] The financing of infrastructure development, which is the key to reinforcing the foundations of sustained development and poverty reduction in the Asia–Pacific region, should be viewed within the broader context of finance for development.

---

* This chapter draws on Nandy, A and RS Rajan. Improving India's Infrastructure (4 May 2005), *Business Times* (Singapore).

[1] See ADB-JBIC-World Bank (2005). *Connecting East Asia: A New Framework for Infrastructure*, ABD, IBRD, JBIC; Jones, S (2004). Contribution of infrastructure to growth and poverty reduction in East Asia and the Pacific, Oxford Policy Management, mimeo (October).

[2] Rajan, RS (2005). Financing development in the Asia–Pacific region: Trends and linkages, The Role of Trade and Investment Policies in the Implementation of the Monterrey Consensus: Regional *Perspectives, Studies in Trade and Investment No. 55*, pp. 21–65.

During a speech titled "Investing in Infrastructure: Key to Economic Growth" given in Hyderabad, India, Haruhiko Kuroda, President of the Asian Development Bank (ADB) observed:[3]

> "Infrastructure development will play a crucial role in helping India sustain high growth rates and more evenly spread the benefits of growth among its people. The critical role of infrastructure in facilitating growth is widely recognized, and well borne out by cross-country experience. For example, the miraculous transformations of Japan, Hong Kong, the Republic of Korea, Singapore, Taipei China, Thailand, Malaysia, and the People's Republic of China were preceded and reinforced by substantial investments in physical and social infrastructure. By promoting connectivity of producers and markets, lowering transactions costs, and providing people with access to important services like education and health care, a reliable infrastructure network lays the foundation for a future of sustainable economic growth. Extending roads, schools, health clinics, utilities and other services to those populations who need it most will make the process of growth more inclusive and bolster the fight against poverty."

It is estimated that the East Asian and the Pacific region needs about US$200 billion annually in infrastructure financing,[4] and it has been suggested that India alone requires some US$150–200 billion of infrastructure investment over the next five to ten years or US$30–40 billion annually.[5] This chapter explores the issue of infrastructure financing in India more specifically.

The Importance of Infrastructure in India

Investment banks, investors, and all sundry alike wax eloquently about the potential of India and how India will scale new heights in the years to come. However, their overwhelming focus tends to be on the service sector in India, which comprises the fabled software firms that, without question, deserve the praise.[6] Ask them about what they think about the manufacturing sector in India and they generally develop cold feet in a hurry. This is not to say that the manufacturing sector in India has a bleak and dismal future. It is rather that they think that the future of the manufacturing sector in India

---

[3] Available at http://www.adb.org/Documents/Speeches/2006/ms2006010.asp

[4] ADB-JBIC-World Bank, *op. cit.*

[5] Ahluwalia, MS (2005). Address of Montek S. Ahluwalia, Deputy Chairman, Planning Commission at the 42nd Convocation of the Indian Institute of Technology, Chennai (Chennai, July 29).

[6] India's services and manufacturing sectors are discussed in Chapters 13 and 14 of this volume.

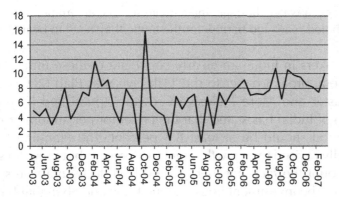

Fig. 1. Infrastructure sector growth in India (Monthly annual percentage growth) (April 2003–March 2007).

Source: Bloomberg.

is going to be handicapped by the level of infrastructure in India or, in other words, the poor infrastructure in India (However, see Chapter 14 of this volume). The performance of the infrastructure has been a mixed bag (Fig. 1), being fairly volatile in some years.

There is somewhat less concern about the effects that poor infrastructure in India might have on the software companies because, in terms of required infrastructure, all they need is a building, an electric connection (all software companies in India typically have an electric generator within the building), and a satellite connection. However, substandard infrastructure remains a significant constraint to India in its ambitions to scale up its labor intensive manufacturing activities and to boost its tourism sector which has so far failed to live up to its enormous potential.

Poor infrastructure is not a problem that is prevalent in certain sections of the country. It is prevalent in every part of India, both urban and rural. Perhaps an indication of India's shoddy infrastructure is to consider *The Economist's view in* Bangalore, the so-called "silicon-valley of India" because it is home to many big software companies[7]

> "The arriving businessman, anxious to get to grips with India's information-technology industry in its very capital, may need a little patience. He might meet his first traffic jam just outside Bangalore's airport. He can examine the skeleton of the early stages of a planned flyover on the airport road. Construction started in February 2003 and was due to be completed in April 2004. Three-quarters of the work is still to be done, but the building site is idle … Bangalore suffers the infrastructure shortcomings common to many

---

[7] The Bangalore Paradox (21 April 2005), *The Economist*.

Indian cities: a water shortage, inadequate sewers, an erratic power supply, and pot-holed roads too narrow for the traffic they need to bear."[8]

Policy-makers in India are clearly cognizant of these infrastructural bottlenecks. The approach paper to the 11th Five Year Plan (2007–2012) titled "Towards Faster and More Inclusive Growth"[9] (published by the Planning Commission of India) has stated that the target for per annum growth during the plan period should be at least 8.5 percent. The Planning Commission then upwardly revised the growth target to 9 percent but they did so after taking into account the fact that there would have to be massive spending on infrastructure. The investment house, Hong Kong and Shanghai Bank (HSBC), has estimated that for India to achieve an average of 9 percent growth during the plan period it will have to invest a minimum of US$370 billion in infrastructure which is equivalent to 48 percent of the 2005 GDP.[10] The same HSBC report says:

"The optimism concerning India's future growth prospects mainly relates to its credible regulatory and financial institutions and political situation, as well as a rapidly growing population and an associated fall in the dependency ratio. However, there also remain several well-known weak spots in India's growth path. Inadequate infrastructure is one of the most serious."

Another sign of cognizance of the problem by the government is the setting up of The Committee on Infrastructure was set up in 2004 under the chairmanship of the Prime Minister and the objectives of the committee were as follows:

- initiating policies that ensure time-bound creation of world-class infrastructure delivering services matching international standards,
- developing structures that maximize the role of public–private partnerships in the field of infrastructure; and
- monitoring progress of key infrastructure projects to ensure that established targets are realized.

The committee has estimated that the funding requirement over 2012 for national highways (roads), airports and ports is Indian Rupees (Rs.) 2,620 billion (roughly around US$60 billion). It has also estimated that Rs. 10,200 billion

---

[8] In fairness though there has some progress in Bangalore's infrastructural development since the writing of the article, though much obviously remains to be done. The aforementioned flyover started operations in August of 2006 and was finally completed in May of 2007.

[9] The approach paper is available at http://planningcommission.nic.in/plans/planrel/app11th_24.pdf

[10] HSBC "Finding USD370bn: Can India finance her infrastructure needs?" 30 October 2006.

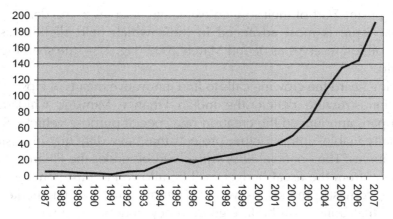

Fig. 2. Foreign exchange reserves in India (US$ billions) (1987–2007).

Source: Reserve Bank of India, Centre for Monitoring the India Economy (CMIE).

Note: The years here mean financial years. For example, 2006 would mean April 2005 to March 2006.

(around US$230 billion) will have to be spent on power and urban infrastructure during the same period. This effectively means that the total spending on infrastructure by 2012 will amount to Rs. 12,820 billion (roughly around US$290 billion).

Whatever the exact numbers, it goes without argument that the financing requirements for infrastructure are huge. Given these large financing requirements, where is the supply of funds expected to come from? Historically, infrastructure has almost solely been under the domain of the public sector and financed mainly via public money. However, the consolidated fiscal deficit of the federal and state governments was just above 7 percent of GDP in fiscal year (FY)07 (see Fig. 3) and the government has limited money to fund their own US$285 billion target. India currently spends only about 6 percent of GDP on infrastructure and is unable to raise this significantly.[11] Faced with the acute fiscal constraints, the government has to resort to innovative ways to finance the country's infrastructure needs.

Using Foreign Reserves to Finance Infrastructure

Many developing countries that have been stockpiling reserves have been exploring other innovative means of financing their infrastructure gaps,

---

[11] The aforementioned HSBC report opines that even if the private sector provides at least $148 billion or 40 percent of the required US$370 billion, the government's fiscal deficit will rise by a minimum of 3 percent a year to finance the remaining 60 percent.

including using part of their foreign exchange reserves.[12] The debate on this particular issue is most advanced in India which held slightly less than US$200 billion reserves as of end March 2007 (Fig. 2) — the sixth highest in the world.

Having heard the growing calls to find innovative means of closing India's gaping infrastructure deficit, the Indian Finance Minister, Chidambaram Palaniappan, announced the creation of a special purpose vehicle (SPV) for "financially viable" infrastructure projects that have difficulty in raising private resources. The financial SPV, which will be under the Finance Ministry but distinct from the fiscal budget, will be allowed to raise long-term funds from the domestic market as well as international capital markets. It is expected that bonds will be foreign currency denominated with sovereign-like characters, as the Indian government will provide at least a partial guarantee, thus reducing the credit risk. This in turn should help keep the cost of borrowing by the SPV fairly low. The SPV will also be partly funded from some of the country's stockpile of foreign exchange reserves, though the quantum of funding from the reserves war chest has not yet been revealed.

The SPV will in turn offer long-term loans for selected projects in key areas, namely roads, ports, airports, and the tourism sector generally to supplement other loans from banks and financial institutions. The lending limit by the SPV was set at Rs. 100 billion (roughly US$2.3 billion) for the fiscal year 2005–2006, and is to be fixed at the beginning of every financial year. An additional provision of Rs. 15 billion has been set aside from the government's budget to act as a "viability gap" fund. This long-tenure and low cost funding source are meant to fill the shortfalls in the capital funding required to make a project viable and attractive for private investments (The details, as of June 2007, have yet to be fully disclosed).

Problems with the Reserves-Funded SPV Approach

While this proposal is rather novel, there are a number of areas of concern regarding the plan to fund infrastructure using the SPV vehicle.

First, as noted, the central government will counter-guarantee the SPV's borrowings. This effectively raises the government's contingent or off-budget liabilities. This "hidden" deficit is one of the main reasons why fiscal authorities in India and elsewhere generally seem to prefer using the indirect means of capital expenditure financing (via a SPV) rather than selling bonds directly to the central bank in return for reserves. However, while the SPV scheme is a clever accounting device, the economic consequences are identical to

---

[12] See Chapter 1 in this Volume on Asian reserve build-up.

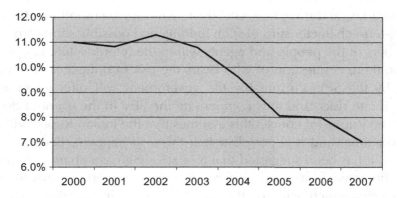

Fig. 3.   Consolidated fiscal deficit as percentage of GDP in India (2000–2007).

Source: Centre for Monitoring the India Economy (CMIE).

Note: The years here mean financial years. For example, 2006 would mean April 2005 to March 2006.

running an actual fiscal deficit. India needs to be especially concerned about the size and consequences of its overall fiscal deficit, which though falling stood at an uncomfortably high 7 percent of GDP at the end of FY07 (this excludes contingent liabilities) (see Fig. 3). Fiscal consolidation is urgently needed; failing which future growth may be derailed.

Second, there remains the nagging issue as to whether the SPV scheme will make much of a difference at all to India's infrastructure development. As noted, the government proposes to focus on "financially viable" projects. The implicit assumption here is that there are potentially solvent projects that are not moving forward because of a dearth of private investments. Is this a reasonable assumption?

Many infrastructure projects in developing countries like India may not be viewed as being financially viable to private investors because of perverse/non-economic pricing policies, ineffective delivery system, uncertain regulatory frameworks, and a slow moving bureaucracy, which hinders quick decision-making. Indeed, it may well be that these pose far greater impediments to India's infrastructure development than just the quantum of financing, and as long as they are not sorted out and reformed, it is not clear as to how effective the SPV scheme will be in filling critical gaps in infrastructure. In other words, finance may not be the major constraining factor to higher infrastructure investments.

Third, while potential projects to be financed are to be appraised by an inter-institutional group of banks and financial institutions along with the members of the Planning Commission, there are also valid concerns as to whether the funds available to the SPV will be appropriately channeled. Will appraisals of projects be based on solely economic (rather than populist) considerations, and if so, how effectively will they be monitored (in view of the long-term characteristics of such funding and possible short-term tenures of members of the people and agents within the inter-institutional group)?

Four, there is question of who bears the risk of unhedged external borrowing by the SPV. Presumably the government will offer guarantees for exchange rate risks, and thus compensate the SPV in the event of depreciations of the Rupee (of course, this assumes that the Indian Rupee will depreciate over time, and it is not clear that this will happen). Because of such concerns, it has been suggested that a relatively greater share of funding for the SPV be drawn from available foreign exchange reserves rather than external borrowing which will raise the country's overall indebtedness. As is often noted, it is like households leaving savings in low interest earning accounts while simultaneously borrowing at high interest rates to finance their expenditures. Why not just use the idle savings for the planned expenditures?

Macroeconomic Consequences of Using Reserves to Finance Infrastructure

There are also some specific concerns about channeling reserves to fund infrastructure. India's central bank, the Reserve Bank of India (RBI) has rightly been wary of the potentially inflationary consequences, as the proposal effectively implies that additional liquidity will be released into the economy. Of course, to the extent that the improvements in infrastructure raise the supply capacity of the country, the inflationary consequences due to excess liquidity may only be short-lived. However, the interim period can last for quite some time given the long gestation lag of infrastructure projects. As is often noted, inflation is like toothpaste, "easy to squeeze out but extremely difficult to push back in". In view of this, it is completely understandable why there should be concerns about the inflationary effects of such a policy.

One seemingly ingenious method of limiting of potential inflationary consequences is to require that most of the intermediate inputs needed for local infrastructure projects (steel, cement, machinery, technology, etc.) be imported. The logic is that imports do not add to domestic demand and can thus temper the immediate inflationary pressures. In addition, the rise in imports will also reduce the size of the country's balance of payments surplus, hence moderating the pace of future reserve build-up. While there is economic merit to this argument, it has two important limitations.

First, it is not clear exactly how import intensive infrastructure development really is. Most infrastructure development projects have a high local or non-tradable component (labor and transport). Thus, there is clearly a limit beyond which the inflationary impact can be offset. Therefore, these expenditures cannot possibly be entirely inflation-neutral.

Second, even if the infrastructure projects are import intensive, the fact that the country is importing intermediate goods at an undervalued exchange rate implies that it is relatively more costly for the country (compared to if the country maintained and imported at a fairly valued exchange rate).[13] In effect, therefore, the country is choosing to pay more for its capital equipment and resource needs while simultaneously subsidizing its exporters. Such a policy is hard to justify on economic terms unless one is able to argue that exports offer significant positive externalities to the rest of the society. In any event, this is just not a cost-effective means of funding infrastructure.

One way to counteract the adverse macroeconomic consequences of maintaining an undervalued currency and the additional liquidity from the release of reserves (given that the process will almost certainly not be inflation-neutral) is to concurrently reduce import tariffs. Indeed, India has continued to lower customs duties as it attempts to align its tariff structure to its East Asian neighbors and trading partners. While bringing down of protection levels should be welcomed as a means of enhancing competition and increasing economic welfare in and of itself, the immediate negative side effects of this may be to compromise the country's budgetary position. In addition, the available reserves cannot and should not be viewed as a pot of gold that can soften the budget constraint.

Conclusion

The following observation by Charan Singh, Director of the Department of Economic Analysis and Policy at the Reserve Bank of India (RBI), should be paid heed to:[14]

> "The rising levels of FER (Foreign exchange reserves) have succeeded in infusing necessary confidence, both to the markets and policy makers. However, neither the capital inflow to India nor the size of FER is disproportionately large when compared to some other countries in the region. The main sources of accretion to FER are exports of IT-related services and foreign portfolio investment-not foreign direct investment (which is more stable), as in the cases of China and Singapore. Therefore, India, which is accumulating FER for precautionary and safety motives, especially after the

---

[13] The Indian rupee did appreciate significantly in 2007.

[14] Singh, C (2005). Should India use foreign exchange reserves for financing infrastructure? *Policy Brief,* Stanford Institute for Economic Policy Research. http://siepr.stanford.edu/papers/briefs/policybrief_sep05.pdf

embarrassing experience of June 1991, should avoid utilizing reserves to finance infrastructure. Infrastructure projects in India yield low or negative returns due to difficulties — political and economic — especially in adjusting the tariff structure, introducing labor reforms, and upgrading technology. The use of FER to finance infrastructure may lead to more economic difficulties, including problems in monetary management."

While there are reasons to be skeptical about aspects of the SPV proposal and the use of foreign exchange reserves to help fund infrastructure, the good news is that Indian and other Asian policy-makers and business leaders have recognized the growth-hindering effects of India's comparatively poor quality physical infrastructure and are looking to tackle this issue with some urgency. In India, this urgency is very acute. This is because as India grows economically, there will be a move out of agriculture. It is more likely than not that these people cannot be accommodated in the service sector and will have to be accommodated in the manufacturing sector. As the approach paper to the 11th five year plan writes:[15]

"A major constraint in achieving faster growth in manufacturing that needs immediate attention is the inadequacy of our physical infrastructure. Our roads, railways, ports, airports, communication and above all electric power supply, are not comparable to the standards prevalent in our competitor countries. This gap must be filled within the next 5–10 years if our enterprises are to compete effectively. In the increasingly open trading environment that we face today, our producers must compete aggressively not just to win export markets, but also to retain domestic markets against competition from imports. Indian industry recognizes this and no longer expects to survive because of protection. But they do expect a level playing field in terms of quality infrastructure. Development of infrastructure must therefore be accorded high priority in the 11th Plan."

High project costs and large asset specificity tend to saddle infrastructure with financing risks, which then tends to place serious disincentives to private investors. According to the World Bank, between 1990 and 2005, 172 projects were undertaken by the private sector costing just above US$51 billion. The majority of the investments were in telecommunication and energy with abysmal amounts going into water and sewerage (see Table 1). Clearly more needs to be done. Since the private sector may be reluctant to enter the infrastructure sector on their own, public–private partnerships or PPPs are the new mantra as far as the infrastructure projects are concerned. PPPs are ideally suited for infrastructure projects. The premise behind PPPs in infrastructure is

---

[15] http://planningcommission.nic.in/plans/planrel/app11th_24.pdf

Table 1. Private sector participation in infrastructure projects in India (1990–2005).

Target GDP Growth Rate in 11th Plan	7.0%	8.0%	9.0%
Average investment rate	29.1	32	35.1
Average CAD as % of GDP	2.0	2.4	2.8
Domestic savings rate: of which	27.1	29.6	32.3
(a) Household	20.1	20.5	21
(b) Corporate	5	5.5	6.1
(c) Public sector companies	3.1	3.1	2.8
(d) Government	−1.1	0.5	2.4

Source: World Bank.

Table 2. Scenarios for the 11th Five-year plan.

Sector	Sub-sector	Number of projects	Total investment ($ million)
Energy	Electricity	63	17,257
	Natural gas	3	651
	Total energy	66	17,907
Telecom	Telecom	34	28,195
	Total telecom	34	28,195
Transport	Airports	4	848
	Railroads	2	198
	Seaports	14	1863
	Toll roads	50	2434
	Total transport	70	5343
Water and sewerage	Potable water and sewerage	1	0
	Sewerage	1	2
	Total water and sewerage	2	2
Total		172	51,448

Source: Planning Commission of India.

Table 3. Savings requirement as per 11th Five-year plan.

Target GDP Growth Rate in 11th Plan (%)	7.0	8.0	9.0
Public investment (as % of GDP)	8.4	9.8	11.2
Private investment (as % of GDP)	20.7	22.2	23.9
Government revenue balance (as % of GDP)	−2.9	−1.3	0.6
Government fiscal balance (as % of GDP)	−6.4	−6.2	−6.0

Source: Planning Commission of India.

that the private sector is far more efficient in getting projects completed while the government, because of its sovereign status, can guarantee the finance for the projects. The Government of India seems committed to the idea of PPPs, at least on paper.

In a document made public by the Ministry of Finance titled "Scheme for Support to Public–Private Partnerships in Infrastructure" the government lists four reasons why there needs to be PPPs:[16]

- The Government of India recognizes that there is significant deficit in the availability of physical infrastructure across different sectors and that this is hindering economic development.
- The development of infrastructure requires large investments that cannot be undertaken out of public financing alone, and that in order to attract private capital as well as the techno-managerial efficiencies associated with it, the Government is committed to promoting Public–Private Partnerships (PPPs) in infrastructure development.
- The Government of India recognizes that infrastructure projects may not always be financially viable because of long gestation periods and limited financial returns, and that financial viability of such projects can be improved through Government support.
- Therefore, the Government of India has decided to put into effect the following scheme for providing financial support to bridge the viability gap of infrastructure projects undertaken through Public–Private Partnerships.

In the final analysis, what is very clear is that rapid and massive infrastructure development is needed in India if the current rapid growth rate is to be sustained over the medium and longer terms.

---

[16] The document is available at http://finmin.nic.in/the_ministry/dept_eco_affairs/uuu/PPPGuidelines.pdf

Chapter 10

The Goldmine of Development Finance: Reassessing the Importance of Migrants' Remittances*

Introduction

A notable and much discussed trend in external finance to developing countries is the declining share of Overseas Development Assistance (ODA), as the OECD countries have consciously cut back their concessional grants since the early 1990s. Indeed, most developed countries have failed to meet the United Nation's (UN's) suggested aid target of 0.7 percent of GNP in 1970 (Tables 1(a) and 1(b)).[1] The reasons for the so-called "foreign aid crisis" are almost certainly attributable to a combination of factors. These include the global political environment, in particular the end of the Cold War which

Table 1(a). Overseas Development Assistance (ODA) by some industrial countries (US$ billions) (1990–2005).

	1990	2000	2001	2002	2003	2004	2005
Total ODA	54.5	53.7	52.3	58.3	69.1	79.5	106.4
G-7 countries	42.5	40.2	38.2	42.6	50	57.5	80
United States	11.4	10	11.4	13.3	16.3	19.7	27.4
Japan	9.1	13.5	9.8	9.3	8.9	8.9	13.1
Germany	6.3	5	5	5.3	6.8	7.5	9.9
France	7.2	4.1	4.2	5.5	7.3	8.5	10.1
Non-G-7 countries	12.0	13.5	14.1	15.7	19.1	22	26.4
EU countries	28.3	25.3	26.3	29.9	37.1	42.9	55.6

Source: OECD Development Assistance Committee.

---

* This chapter draws on Rajan, RS (2005). Growing clout of workers' remittances. *Business Times* (Singapore), 15 February and Rajan, RS (2006). The importance of workers' remittances as a source of development finance. *Georgetown Journal of International Affairs*, 8(1).
[1] Exceptions have been Denmark, Norway, Netherlands, and Sweden. While the United States has been the largest donor in absolute level, it spends just about 0.12 percent of its GDP on foreign aid (*The Economist* (3 May 2003), p. 66).

Table 1(b). Overseas Development Assistance (ODA) by some industrial countries as a percent of their Gross National Income (GNI) (1990–2005).

	1990	2000	2001	2002	2003	2004	2005
Australia	0.34	0.27	0.25	0.26	0.25	0.25	0.25
Canada	0.44	0.25	0.22	0.28	0.24	0.27	0.34
Denmark	0.94	1.06	1.03	0.96	0.84	0.85	0.81
France	0.60	0.30	0.31	0.37	0.40	0.41	0.47
Germany	0.42	0.27	0.27	0.27	0.28	0.28	0.35
Japan	0.31	0.28	0.23	0.23	0.20	0.19	0.28
The Netherlands	0.92	0.84	0.82	0.81	0.80	0.73	0.82
Norway	1.17	0.76	0.80	0.89	0.92	0.87	0.93
Sweden	0.91	0.80	0.77	0.84	0.79	0.78	0.92
Switzerland	0.32	0.34	0.34	0.32	0.39	0.41	0.44
United Kingdom	0.27	0.32	0.32	0.31	0.34	0.36	0.48
United States	0.21	0.10	0.11	0.13	0.15	0.17	0.22

Source: OECD Development Assistance Committee.

blurred ideological differences and removed much of the political motivation for aid; the desire on the part of donors to reduce their own fiscal deficits; and a general perception that aid has been ineffective at encouraging economic growth and reducing poverty (due to, for instance, the possibility that aid substitutes for, rather than supplements, domestic resources).

While there still remains a great deal of "aid pessimism", there is, however, a growing body of evidence that finds that foreign aid has been effective in many poor countries, and can be particularly effective at reducing poverty when combined with good domestic economic policy, good governance, and effective institutions.[2] Accordingly, it is important to focus on increasing both the magnitude as well as the effectiveness of ODA. The need to encourage creditor countries in the Asia-Pacific to raise their regional aid

---

[2] The debate on the links between aid and growth has given rise to a voluminous literature in the area. Notable recent papers include Burnside, C and D Dollar (2000). Aid, policies, and growth. *American Economic Review*, 90, 847–868; World Bank (1998). *Assessing Aid: What Works, What Doesn't, and Why?* New York: Oxford University Press; Radelet, S, M Clements and R Bhavani (2004). Counting chickens when they hatch: The short-term effect of aid on growth. *Working Paper No. 44*. Washington, DC: Center for Global Development; and Rajan, RG and A Subramaniam (2005). What undermines aid's impact on growth? *Working Paper No. 11657*, NBER. Without entering that debate here, it may be useful to keep in mind three caveats: (1) it might be argued that aid benefits the poor in recipient countries even if it does not contribute directly to growth, by raising expenditures on health, education, water, and sanitation; (2) aid effectiveness issues may vary by categories, and in particular, whether it is tied versus untied; (3) there may exist a macro–micro paradox. While questions remain about the general effectiveness of program aid, evidence suggests that *project*-aid has had beneficial impact when carefully targeted and administered.

commitments is particularly acute as there are concerns that aid from the United States and other donors may increasingly be influenced by strategic and political considerations (the war on terrorism, financing the reconstruction in Afghanistan and Iraq, etc.) rather than by pure development/ economic considerations. This may result (in fact, has been resulting) in a significant reallocation of aid among potential recipient countries. For instance, aid to Afghanistan and its bordering countries, Pakistan, Tajikistan, Turkmenistan, and Uzbekistan increased threefold from US$1.1 billion in 2000 to US$3.7 billion in 2002.[3]

The purpose of the United Nations Millennium Development Goal (MDG) is to reduce income poverty worldwide by about one-half between 1990 and 2015.[4] But at a time of severely curtailed ODA and other official flows, where will the *external* resources to alleviate constraints for financing development come from?[5] This is the key concern of the Monterrey Consensus of the International Conference on Financing for Development (FfD) (adopted at Monterrey Mexico, on 22 March 2002).[6] As highlighted by the Monterrey Consensus, in an era of falling aid flows, international trade (export revenues), private capital flows, particularly foreign direct investment (FDI), and worker remittances, are crucial sources of financing for development.[7] There is already an extensive literature on all aspects of FDI. In sharp contrast, workers' remittances — which are the financial counterpart of the outflow of migration flows — have generally been paid much less attention

---

[3] World Bank (2004). *Global Development Finance 2004*. New York: Oxford University Press, Chapter 4. This source also offers a succinct overview of the dynamics of foreign aid to developing countries, prospects of increasing such flows, and their development impact in the future.

[4] Income poverty reduction is not the only objective that constitutes the MDG to be realized by 2015. Other goals are: (a) attainment of universal primary education: (b) promotion of gender equality and empowerment of women; (c) reduction of the infant (under five) mortality rate by two-thirds; (d) improvement of maternal health by reducing by three-quarters the maternal mortality ratio; (e) halting the spread of HIV/Aids, malaria, and other major diseases; (f) ensuring environmental sustainability including halving the proportion of people without sustainable access to safe drinking water; and (g) development of an open, rule-based, predictable, and nondiscriminatory trading and financial system. See http://www.developmentgoals.org.

[5] We recognize, but do not discuss, the importance of internally raised resources for development (domestic resources finance most of the investment expenditures in developing countries). For a more specific discussion on budgetary resource mobilization in Asia, see Asher, MG (2004). Budgetary resource mobilisation in Asia: Growing complexity. *Economic and Political Weekly*, 38, 3639–3646.

[6] For details of the Monterrey Consensus, see United Nations (UN) Secretariat (2002). Final outcome of the international conference on financing for development. Note by the Secretariat, 15 February. Some have used the term "Monterrey development deficit" to highlight the insufficiency of financial resources to meet and surpass the MDG.

[7] Reducing the external debt burdens of many developing countries is a further element of the Monterrey Consensus. Indeed, debt relief initiative for the heavily indebted poor countries (HIPCs) (launched in 1999) remains a key component of the Monterrey Consensus. However, agreement was not reached on debt relief for middle-income countries. There are valid concerns that debt relief could lead to a reduction in the grant component of foreign aid.

to by mainstream academics and policy-makers.[8] This chapter attempts to fill that gap.

Significance of Migrants' Remittances

In many a developing country around the world, money sent by a family member working in another country, usually a more economically developed country than their birth country, is sometimes the sole lifeline of many a family. It now turns out that these remittances sent have also become lifelines for many a country. Over the years, migrants' remittances have turned out to be a huge bonanza for a number of countries. There are a number of countries where migrants' remittances amount to a significant percentage of their GDP. According to the World Bank, Tonga's inward remittances amounted to 31 percent of GDP while Haiti's remittances were just below 25 percent (see Fig. 1).

Indeed, migrants' remittances have maintained a steady and marked upward trend with remittances to developing countries reaching an amazingly high US$160 billion in 2004, compared to US$85.5 billion in 2000

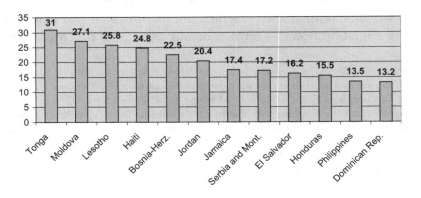

Fig. 1.   Top recipients of remittances in 2004 (as percent of GDP).

Source: World Bank (2006). *Global Economic Prospects 2006: Economic Implications of Remittances and Migration.* New York: Oxford University Press.

---

[8] Two caveats should be noted: (1) while out-migration of unskilled labor is acknowledged as offering significant economic benefits for both the sources and host countries, there is an active debate on the economic consequences of out-migration of skilled workers (i.e., "brain drain" or "brain gain"?); (2) there is some evidence that skilled migration is associated with lower remittances than migration of unskilled labor. It is, however, unclear whether these differences are robust and if they are whether they are due to different occupations of the two sets of migrants or because of differences in migration status, i.e., unskilled tend to be temporary and skilled tend more likely to be permanent migrants. Some of these issues are explored in Faini, R (2003). Is the brain drain an unmitigated blessing?, *Discussion Paper No. 2003/64*, United Nations WIDER.

Table 2.   Significance of remittance receipts to developing countries (US$ billions) (1990–2004).

	1990	1995	2000	2001	2002	2003	2004 (est)
Developing countries	31.2	57.8	85.6	96.5	113.4	142.1	160.4
Lower middle income	13.9	30	42.6	47.4	57.3	72.5	83.5
Upper middle income	9.1	14.5	20	22.3	23	27.8	33
Low income	8.1	13.3	22.8	26.8	33.1	41.8	43.9
Latin America and the Caribbean	5.8	13.4	20.1	24.4	28.1	34.8	40.7
South Asia	5.6	10	17.2	19.2	24.2	31.1	31.4
East Asia and the Pacific	3.3	9.7	16.7	20.1	27.2	35.8	40.9
Middle East and North Africa	11.4	13.4	13.2	15.1	15.6	18.6	20.3
Europe and Central Asia	3.2	8.1	13.4	13	13.3	15.1	19.4
Sub-Saharan Africa	1.9	3.2	4.9	4.7	5.2	6.8	7.7
World (developing and industrial)	68.6	101.6	131.5	147.1	166.2	200.2	225.8
Outward remittances from developing countries	6.1	12.5	12.1	14.3	18.7	20.2	24.1
Outward remittance from Saudi Arabia	11.2	16.6	15.4	15.1	15.9	14.8	13.6

Source: World Bank (2006). *Global Economic Prospects 2006: Economic Implications of Remittances and Migration.* New York: Oxford University Press.

(Table 2). Workers' remittances have in fact become the second most important type of private external finance to developing countries after FDI (Fig. 2). The data considered so far pertains only to recorded remittances and remittances through regular institutions. Thus, the magnitude of remittances noted above is clearly understated. Indeed, insofar as migrants make payments in a kind such as payments directly to schools (tuition fees) or international airlines (airfares) on behalf of relatives or friends in their home country, or channel remittances via other means (e.g., non-resident rupee deposits in India), the true magnitude of remittance transfers is probably much larger than captured by available statistics.[9] Remittances are also made through informal channels (referred to as the "hawala system" in India).

---

[9] Work is being done by the World Bank, individual countries, and international agencies and others to enhance the quality of remittance data. See http://devdata.worldbank.org/wdi2005/Section6_1.htm#fc and World Bank (2003). *Global Development Finance 2003.* New York: Oxford University Press, Chapter 7.

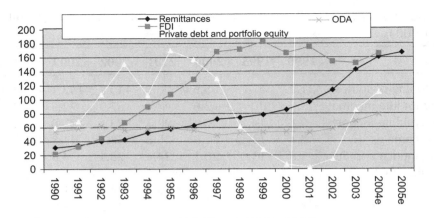

Fig. 2. The rise of remittances (US$ billions) (1990–2005).

Source: World Bank (2006). *Global Economic Prospects 2006: Economic Implications of Remittances and Migration*. New York: Oxford University Press.

Asia's share of workers' remittances to developing countries averaged almost 40 percent (Table 3).[10] The three main source countries of remittances have been the United States, Saudi Arabia, and Germany.[11] India clearly dominates as a destination for migrants' remittances (Fig. 3)[12] and these financial flows are more evenly spread out than private capital flows. For instance, in 2001, the top ten remittance recipients received 60 percent of total remittances to developing countries. This was below the share of the top ten recipient countries for FDI (almost 75 percent) though this space is dominated by China (Fig. 4).

In addition to the relative magnitudes, the relative stability (or lack thereof) of the various sources of finance is also important. The well-known story is that during the crisis of 1997–1998, FDI in Asia remained relatively stable while debt and portfolio equity flows collapsed. This is clearly borne out by the data. Specifically, FDI, workers' remittances and export revenue flows have the lowest variability, while debt flows — specifically short-term debt — are the most variable, followed by portfolio equity flows. This conclusion holds true when we limit the analysis to the crisis-hit economies in Southeast Asia (Malaysia, Thailand, Indonesia, and the Philippines) or to just China and India.[13] In addition, while FDI as well as other private capital

---

[10] As a share of GDP, remittances are particularly important to Tonga, the Philippines, and Sri Lanka in the Asian and Pacific region.

[11] World Bank (2003), *op. cit.*

[12] Remittances to India have kept its current account deficits at low levels, even registering surpluses in recent times despite large merchandise trade deficits.

[13] Rajan, RS (2005). Financing development in the Asia-Pacific region: Trends and linkages. *The Role of Trade and Investment Policies in the Implementation of the Monterrey Consensus: Regional Perspectives*, Studies in Trade and Investment, No. 55, pp. 21–65.

Table 3. Migrants' remittances received by developing countries (US$ billions) (2000–2004).

	2000	2001	2002	2003	2004
All developing countries	85.5	96.5	113.4	142.1	160.4
Asia	47.3	52.3	64.6	82.0	91.6
	55.3%	54.2%	57.0%	57.7%	57.1%
China	6.2	8.4	13.0	17.8	21.3
	7.3%	8.7%	11.5%	12.5%	13.3%
India	12.9	14.3	15.8	21.7	21.7
	15.1%	14.8%	13.9%	15.3%	13.5%
Indonesia	1.2	1.1	1.3	1.5	1.7
	1.4%	1.1%	1.1%	1.0%	1.1%
Malaysia	1.0	0.8	1.0	1.0	1.0
	1.1%	0.8%	0.8%	0.7%	0.6%
Philippines	6.2	6.2	7.4	10.8	11.6
	7.3%	6.4%	6.5%	7.6%	7.3%
Thailand	1.7	1.3	1.4	1.6	1.6
	2.0%	1.3%	1.2%	1.1%	1.0%
Pakistan	1.1	1.5	3.6	4.0	4.0
	1.3%	1.5%	3.1%	2.8%	2.5%
Sri Lanka	1.2	1.2	1.3	1.4	1. 6
	1.4%	1.2%	1.2%	1.0%	1.0%
Bangladesh	2.0	2.1	2.9	3.2	3.4
	2.3%	2.2%	2.5%	2.2%	2.1%

Source: World Bank (2006). *Global Economic Prospects 2006: Economic Implications of Remittances and Migration.* New York: Oxford University Press.
Notes: (1) Figures in percentages denote individual country's percentage share of all developing countries' flows; (2) Asia constitutes of South Asia and East Asia and Pacific as defined by the World Bank.

flows tend to be pro-cyclical (rising as the host country is doing well and there is general bullishness about the country's prospects), the same may not be true remittances. This is so as remittances could be viewed as a self-insurance mechanism for developing countries, or there may be an element of philanthropy (i.e., altruistic motive) in the sense that the overseas diaspora increases remittances at times when it is most needed (e.g., during periods of economic crises or natural disasters).[14] This relatively low positive correlation

---

[14] Admittedly, however, we cannot say whether remittances are actually *counter cyclical* as market considerations and signals clearly also play some role in remittance inflows. Buch, C and A Kuckulenz (2004). Worker remittances and capital flows to developing countries. *Discussion Paper No. 04-31*, ZEW Centre for European Economic Research; and Solimano, A (2003). Remittances by emigrants: Issues and evidence. mimeo (August).

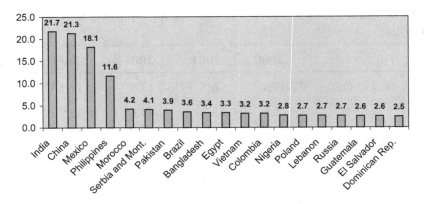

Fig. 3.   Top 20 developing country recipients of workers' remittances in 2004 (US$ billions).

Source: World Bank (2006). *Global Economic Prospects 2006: Economic Implications of Remittances and Migration*. New York: Oxford University Press.

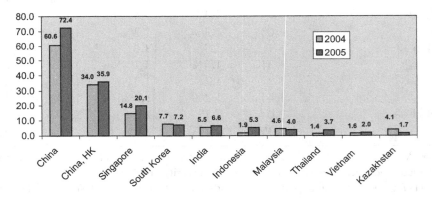

Fig. 4.   Top 10 recipients of FDI inflows in the Asian and Pacific regions (US$ billions) (2004–2005).

Source: UNCTAD Foreign Direct Investment database.
Note: (1) Ranked on the basis of the magnitude of 2005 FDI inflows.

between remittances and other private capital flows and its well-targeted nature (i.e., person-to-person flows), makes it a particularly important source of finance to developing countries. Such a stabilizing role was historically played by ODA.

Economic Effects of Remittances

Remittances have been growing in absolute terms as well as in comparison to other sources of external finance and they are a relatively stable form of finance. Admittedly, there needs to be much more empirical work on the links between remittances and private capital flows (substitutes or complements?), and remittances and growth. With regard to the latter, while most of the literature generally holds a benign view on the growth and development impact of remittance inflows, it has been suggested that remittances may actually hinder growth for two reasons.[15] At a microlevel, there is a moral hazard problem in that remittance inflows might provide less incentive for the remitter to enter the labor force. At a macrolevel, large-scale remittances could lead to a "Dutch Disease" phenomenon of overvalued real exchange rates, loss of export competitiveness, over-consumption, under-investment, and delay much-needed policy reforms.[16] However, more recent work suggests that, at least at a macrolevel, remittances are less likely than foreign aid to have perverse macroeconomic effects (i.e., loss of competitiveness, etc.).

Since inward remittances by migrants have become a more stable source of income and, in the past few years, a large source of income, they have had a profound impact on the macroeconomics of many a country. The World Bank in its annual publication *Global Economic Prospects* (GEP) chose "Economic Implications of Remittances and Migration" as the topic for its 2006 edition. The GEP outlines various macroeconomic effects of remittances. First, remittances are stable and may be countercyclical because migrants tend to send more money when there is a downturn in the economy or when there is a natural calamity. These remittances tend to smooth out consumption. Second, remittances can improve country creditworthiness because of their sheer size when compared to the respective countries' GDPs.[17] Third, remittance securitization can help countries raise external financing. As noted by the World Bank, several banks in developing countries (such as Brazil) have been able to access international capital markets to raise relatively cheap and long-term financing via securitization of future remittance flows. The GEP also observes:

"High levels (or large increases) in remittance flows can be expected to have direct repercussions on foreign exchange rates, domestic interest rates, and

---

[15] Chami, R, C Fullenkamp and S Jahjah (2004). Are immigrant remittance flows a source of capital for development? *IMF Staff Papers*, 52, 55–81.

[16] This suggests the need for the government to work in concert with financial institutions not only to promote more efficient financial intermediation, but also to offer remittance recipients new and innovative financial services that would be useful to them, as well as proactively encourage a "savings culture".

[17] The World Bank lists some examples of countries that benefit enormously from this. For Serbia and Montenegro, remittances in 2004 were equal to 7 percent of GDP and their S&P rating increased to BB– from B+ when remittances were included. This also meant that their savings in terms of spreads was equal to 150 basis points. The creditworthiness of Haiti, whose remittances equaled 28 percent of GDP in 2004, rose from CCC to B+ and the spread savings they had was a significant 334 basis points. Nicaragua went from a CCC+ to a B– and had a spread savings of 209 points while Lebanon went from B– to B+ and had a spread savings of 130 basis points.

the balance of payments, and indirect repercussions on macro-variables. Because of their relative stability and targeting (directly to households), they may bring some additional benefits. However, as the experience with and analysis of natural resource booms have shown, large inflows can also have some undesirable side effects."[18]

Conclusion

Workers' remittances have been and will continue to be an important and stable source of external finance for developing countries, and it is incumbent on policy-makers to facilitate such flows. It is generally recognized that the remittances business is extremely segmented and inefficient; transactions costs are high as a few players dominate the market and charge "excessive fees". Specifically, remittances have hitherto largely been channeled via Money Transfer Operators (MTOs), post offices, ethnic stores, couriers, and such (some of these go unrecorded). Reduction of the intermediation costs by encouraging more players to enter the remittance business (particularly by establishing partnerships between retail banks with extensive branches and government post office network) can provide a significant fillip to this source of financing for development. The World Bank notes:

> "Despite the clear welfare benefits of remittances, weaknesses in the financial sector and in government administration impose substantial transaction costs on migrant workers who send them. Easing these constraints could increase remittance receipts, while bringing a larger share of remittance payments into the formal financial system. Anecdotal evidence suggests that inefficiencies in the banking system — long delays in check clearance, exchange losses, or improper disclosure of transaction costs — deter inward remittances."[19]

World Bank economist Dilip Ratha goes on to suggest four ways of cutting transaction costs:

> "First, the remittance fee should be a low fixed amount, not a percent of the principal, since the cost of remittance services does not really depend on the amount of principal. Indeed, the real cost of a remittance transaction — including labor, technology, networks, and rent — is estimated to be significantly below the current level of fees.

---

[18] World Bank (2003). Workers' remittances: An important and stable source of external development finance. New York: Oxford University Press. p. 9.
[19] World Bank (2003), *op. cit.*

Second, greater competition will bring prices down. Entry of new market players can be facilitated by harmonizing and lowering bond and capital requirements, and avoiding overregulation (such as requiring full banking licenses for money transfer operators). The intense scrutiny of money service businesses for money laundering or terrorist financing since the 9/11 attacks has made it difficult for them to operate accounts with their correspondent banks, forcing many in the United States to close. While regulations are necessary for curbing money laundering and terrorist financing, they should not make it difficult for legitimate money service businesses to operate accounts with correspondent banks.

Third, establishing partnerships between remittance service providers and existing postal and other retail networks would help expand remittance services without requiring large fixed investments to develop payment networks. However, partnerships should be nonexclusive. Exclusive partnerships between post office networks and money transfer operators have often resulted in higher remittance fees.

Fourth, poor migrants need greater access to banking. Banks tend to provide cheaper remittance services than money transfer operators. Both sending and receiving countries can increase banking access for migrants by allowing origin country banks to operate overseas; by providing identification cards (such as the Mexican matricula consular), which are accepted by banks to open accounts; and by facilitating participation of microfinance institutions and credit unions in the remittance market."[20]

Economic migration is a reality, and steps must be taken to ensure that there are as few hurdles as possible for inward remittances since the beneficiaries are usually people who need it the most.

---

[20] Ratha, D (2005). Remittances: A lifeline for development. *Finance and Development,* December, 42(4), http://www.imf.org/external/pubs/ft/fandd/2005/12/basics.htm.

Section 3

Trade, Investment and the Rise of China and India

Chapter 11

The "Do's and Don'ts" of Attracting Foreign Direct Investment*

Introduction

There is something about the word "Foreign Direct Investment" (FDI) that makes practically every government in the world sit up and take notice. In economics, there is an often-used term called "signaling". The *Penguin Dictionary of Economics* defines signaling as "the use of a mechanism by which someone indicates to someone else that they have certain characteristics, even though these characteristics are not directly observable". FDI is viewed as an excellent signaling device that suggests to other investors that it is worth investing in a particular country.

Indeed, the working assumption nowadays is that in a *relatively nondistorted* domestic policy environment, FDI brings in much-needed financial capital, technical know-how, organizational, managerial and marketing practices, and global production networks, thus facilitating the process of economic growth and development in host countries.[1] For instance, according to the UNCTAD,[2] FDI can complement local development efforts in a number of ways, including boosting export competitiveness; generating employment and strengthening the skills base; enhancing technological capabilities (transfer, diffusion, and generation of technology); and increasing financial resources for development.[3] In fact, FDI has become one of the

---

* This chapter draws on Rajan, RS (2004). *Economic and Political Weekly*, 39, 3 January, 12–16 and Rajan, RS (2005). FDI, Trade and the internationalization of production in the Asia-Pacific region: Issues and policy conundrums. *Asia-Pacific Trade and Investment Review*, 1(1), 3–26.

[1] Lall, S (2000). FDI and development: Policy and research issues in the emerging context, *Working Paper No. 43*. Queen Elizabeth House: University of Oxford; and Organisation of Economic Cooperation and Development (OECD) (2002). *Foreign Direct Investment for Development: Maximising Benefits, Minimising Costs*, Paris: OECD, Chapters 1 and 3.

[2] UNCTAD (1999). *World Investment Report 1999*. New York and Geneva: Oxford University Press.

[3] Technology transfer from FDI in turn operates via four related channels: (i) vertical (backward and forward) linkages with suppliers or purchasers in the host countries; (ii) horizontal linkages with competing or complementary companies in the same industry; (iii) migration of skilled labor; and (iv) the internationalization of R&D. OECD, *op. cit.*, p. 69. For a critical overview of some of the often suggested positive spillovers from FDI to the host country, see Hanson, GH (2001). Should countries promote foreign direct investment. *G-24 Discussion Paper Series No. 9*. United Nations Conference on Trade and Development.

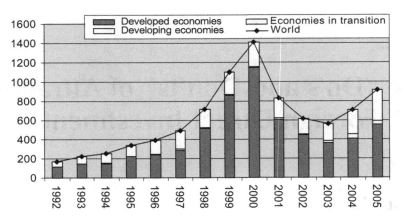

Fig. 1. FDI inflows, global and by groups of economies (US$ billions) (1980–2005).
Source: UNCTAD FDI Statistics Online.

largest and most stable sources of external financing for most developing countries.

Figure 1 shows the FDI inflows for the world, developing economies, developed economies, and economies in transition. If one looks at the component for developing countries, barring a dip during 2000 and 2001, FDI has been increasing every year since 1992. In view of this largely benign view of FDI, there has been an intense "global race" for such forms of capital inflows. Indeed, FDI is attracted into countries for a variety of reasons — resource seeking (natural or human resources), market seeking, efficiency seeking, or strategic-asset seeking.[4] However, at a general level, in order for a country to be more attractive to investors (both local and foreign), there is a need to put in place measures to ensure an enabling environment by reducing the so-called "hassle costs".

But what are these costs? Apart from costs arising from an unstable macroeconomic and regulatory environment, administrative barriers and red tape (Table 1) can significantly raise the costs of establishing and doing business. A prominent study involving 32 developing economies indicates that there exists a statistically and economically significant negative nexus between administrative costs and FDI to GDP ratio after controlling other factors.[5] This chapter discusses selected steps commonly used by governments to enhance their attractiveness as a destination for FDI.

---

[4] For an elaboration of these and other locational determinants as well as other issues relating to FDI (including definitions and financing), see Working Group of the Capital Markets Consultative Group (CMCG) (2003). Foreign direct investment in emerging market countries. mimeo, IMF (September). Also see general overview by Goldin, I and K Reinert (2005). Global capital flows and development: A survey. *Journal of International Trade and Economic Development*, 15, 453–481.

[5] Morisset, J and OL Neso (2002). Administrative barriers to foreign investment in developing countries. *Transnational Corporations*, 11, 99–121.

Table 1. Summary of administrative procedures faced by an investor.

Category	Items
Entry Approvals	Company registration
	Investment code registration
	Initial bank deposit
	Residence and work permits
	Tax office registration
	Foreign investment licensing
	Business and trading permits
	Statistical office registration
	Existence, conformity, opening reporting
	Health care and pension plans
	Social security registration
Land, Site, Development, Utilities	Access to land
	Town planning certificate
	Site inspections and general approvals
	Building permits
	Electricity and power connection
	Telephone and telex
	Water and sewerage
	Post box and private bag
Operation requirements	Import–export intention and permits
	Import–export clearance process
	Foreign exchange control
	Fiscal situation certificate
	Health and safety inspections
	Labor inspections
	Social welfare plan payments

Source: Morisset, J and OL Neso (2002). Administrative barriers to foreign investment in developing countries. *Transnational Corporations*, 11, 99–121.

Investment Promotion and Government Intervention Policies

Over and above the creation of a business-friendly environment, it may be important for a potential host country to actively undertake investment promotion
policies to fill in information gaps or correct the perception gaps that may hinder FDI inflows. A commonly used definition of investment promotion is "activities that disseminate information about, or attempt to create an image of the
investment site and provide investment services for the prospective investors".[6]

---

[6] Wells Jr, L and A Wint (1990). *Marketing a Country: Promotion as a Tool for Attracting Foreign Investment*. Washington, DC: IFC and MIGA.

Table 2. Annual FDI promotion budget of selected countries, 1999.

Country	Annual FDI promotion budget (US$ millions)	Population (millions)	Per capita budget (US$)
Asian countries			
Indonesia (BKPM)	2.8	207	0.01
Malaysia (MIDA)	15	22.7	0.66
Philippines (BOI)	3	76.8	0.04
Singapore (EDB)	45	3.2	14.06
Memo: Non-Asian countries			
Dominican Republic (IPC)	8.8	8.4	1.05
Mauritius Export Development and Investment Authority (1996)	3.1	1.2	2.58
Ireland (IDA, 1999, including grants)[1]	213 (41)	3.7	57.57 (11.16)
Costa Rica (CINDE)	11	3.5	3.14

Source: Te Velde, DW (2001). *Policies Towards Foreign Direct Investment in Developing Countries: Emerging Issues and Outstanding Issues*. London: Overseas Development Institute. *Note*: [1]Figures in parenthesis exclude grants.

Any investment promotion strategy must be geared toward the following: (a) image-building activities promoting the country and its regions and states as favorable locations for investment; (b) investment-generating activities through direct targeting of firms by promotion of specific sectors and industries, and personal selling and establishing direct contacts with prospective investors; (c) investment-service activities tailored to prospective and current investors' needs; and (d) raising the realization ratio (i.e., percentage of the FDI approvals translated into actual flows). Table 2 summarizes the annual budgets on investment promotion by selected countries in Asia and elsewhere. As is apparent, Singapore — a major success story as far as FDI-led development is considered[7] — massively outspent the other countries on a per capita basis.

A case might be made for the establishment of a one-stop investment promotion agency (IPA) to assist in the entry and operation of FDI. The need and logic for an IPA appears to have been embraced by a number of countries and by 2001 there were about 160 national IPAs and over 250 sub-national ones.[8]

---

[7] Rajan, RS (2003). Sustaining competitiveness in the new global economy: Introduction and overview. In *Sustaining Competitiveness in the New Global Economy: A Case Study of Singapore*, Rajan, RS (ed.), Chapter 1, Cheltenham: Edward Elgar.

[8] UNCTAD (2001). The world of investment promotion at a glance: a survey of investment promotion practices. *United Nations Advisory Studies No. 17*, UNCTAD/ITE/IPC/3, New York and Geneva.

While a one-stop investment promotion agency could facilitate FDI by lowering administrative delays and associated cost overruns, Sanjaya Lall correctly notes:

> "Unless the agencies have the authority needed to negotiate the regulatory system, and unless the rules themselves are simplified, this may not help. On the contrary, there is a very real risk that a 'one-stop shop' becomes 'one more stop'."[9]

The foregoing finds justification from a recent empirical analysis of IPAs in 58 countries between February and May 2002.[10] In particular, while there is some evidence that IPAs have a positive impact on FDI, this is more likely to be the case in circumstances where IPAs (a) have a high degree of political visibility (for instance, by being linked to the highest government official such as the Prime Minister's office); (b) have active private sector involvement via, for instance, participation in the IPAs board; and (c) operate in a country with a good overall investment environment. The study further finds that the types of functions that IPAs undertake have bearing on their effectiveness (see Table 3 for definitions). "Policy advocacy", which is defined as steps to

Table 3. Functions of an Investment Promotion Agency (IPA).

Image Building: Refers to the function of creating the perception of a country as an attractive site for international investment. Activities commonly associated with image building include focused advertising, public relations events, and the generation of favorable news stories by cultivating journalists.

Investor Facilitation and Investors Servicing: Refers to the range of services provided in a host country that can assist an investor in analyzing investment decisions, establishing a business, and maintaining it in good stand. Activities include information provision, "one-stop shop" service aimed at expediting approval process, utilities, and various types of assistance in obtaining sites.

Investment Generation: This entails targeting specific sectors and companies with the aim of creating investment leads. Activities include identification of potential sectors and investors, direct mailing, telephone campaigns, investor forums, and seminars and individual presentations to targeted investors.

Policy Advocacy: This consists of the activities via which the agency supports initiatives to improve the investment climate and identifies the views of the private sector on that matter. Activities include surveys of the private sector, participation in task forces, policy and legal proposals, and lobbying.

Source: Reproduced with minor changes from Morisset, J (2003). Does a country need a promotion agency to attract foreign direct investment?: A small analytical model applied to 58 countries. *Policy Research Working Paper No. 3028*, The World Bank.

---

[9] Lall, S, *op. cit.*, p. 10.
[10] Morisset, J (2003). Does a country need a promotion agency to attract foreign direct investment?: A small analytical model applied to 58 countries. *Policy Research Working Paper No. 3028*. The World Bank.

improve the overall investment climate and identify views of private sector, appears to be the most effective function. This is followed by investment facilitation or servicing (the roles conventionally attributed to a one-stop shop), and image building. IPAs seem least effective in actually generating sector-specific investments.

This suggests that growth-enhancing policy intervention probably ought *not* to be biased by sector. Instead, industrial policy should be focused on enhancing a country's general capability to benefit from FDI by: (a) improving the general quality of the country's labor force and infrastructure; (b) developing local skills and technology and local learning; and (c) ensuring a stable and conducive overall macroeconomic and regulatory environment.

This said, UNCTAD continues to advocate a policy of targeted promotion, suggesting it has potentially high payoffs, though also acknowledging that it can be a risky proposition.[11] The UNCTAD position finds support from the successes of countries like Singapore whose investment promotion authority, the Economic Development Board (EDB), has quite successfully targeted specific global corporations or broad sectors to invest in the city state.[12] Interestingly, however, even policy-makers in Singapore are somewhat circumspect about the use of selective industrial promotion and targeting. Consider the following observation by one senior Singapore Minister:

> "Within manufacturing and services, we will have to leave it to the market to spot future winners. Some broad clusters of growth activity are clear enough in global markets — within manufacturing, these include electronics — notwithstanding its cyclical gyrations — chemicals and the biomedical sciences. But we cannot tell what proportions of Singapore manufacturing each of these clusters will occupy in future, or which firms and which specific industries within these clusters will remain winners. Nor can we tell if other new clusters will emerge as major growth potentials for Singapore. We should therefore leave room for more 'white space' in our economic structure. The Government can support market players where they decide it is worth basing their operations in Singapore. But we should aim to make our tax system and other incentives less targeted and more broad-based, in order to accommodate a greater degree of market experimentation, whether in manufacturing or services."[13]

---

[11] UNCTAD (2002). *World Investment Report 2002.* New York and Geneva: Oxford University Press, Chapter 3.

[12] For instance, see Oman, C (2000). *Policy Competition for Foreign Direct Investment: A Study of Competition Among Governments to Attract FDI.* Paris: OECD Development Centre, Chapter 2. However, to date there has not been a careful cost-benefit analysis of the EDB's promotion activities given unavailability of data.

[13] Shanmugaratnam, T (2002). Succeeding in an unpredictable world — Moving from a managed to an entrepreneurial economy. Speech by the Senior Minister of State, Ministry of Trade & Industry and Ministry of Education at the Singapore 1000/SME 500 Awards Ceremony (Singapore, 18 January). Also see Rajan RS, *op. cit.* for a further discussion on Singapore's growth strategy.

More generally, the choice of the exact type and extent of such investment promotion activities and agencies must be based on a careful and systematic evaluation of potential costs and benefits. One size cannot fit all countries at all times. Particularly in cases where administrative capacity is weak, government failure is pervasive, and resources are scarce, it may be advisable for countries to eschew selective policy intervention.

An insufficiently recognized point is that for FDI to have a significantly positive impact on the host country it must have attained a minimum threshold of development itself.[14] Indeed, a careful examination of the empirical studies linking FDI and technological development suggests that FDI is more likely to be a significant catalyst to overall industrial development, and the higher the income of the host country. This in turn is often interpreted as signifying that the host country must be capable of absorbing the new technologies manifested in FDI.[15] Another common finding is that greatest technological spillovers from FDI occur when the technological gap between local and foreign enterprises is "not very large", and crowding in of domestic investments and technology transfer from FDI is more likely the higher the level of human capital.[16]

In view of the above, and at the risk of generalizing, the most effective type of policy intervention appears to involve broad measures to enhance overall human capital and technical capabilities of the domestic economy on a nondiscriminatory basis rather than selective intervention to maximize linkages between local firms and local subsidiaries of multinationals or technology transfer domestically from FDI. In any event, policies such as domestic content or performance requirements, joint venture requirements, caps on foreign ownership, technology licensing, location or local employment requirements have generally had mixed results at best.[17] There may, in fact, be a tradeoff in the sense that "artificial" attempts to indigenize FDI activities may make the affiliate operations of multinationals less integrated with the production network of the parent to the detriment of the host country (i.e., "screwdriver operations").[18] To maximize spillover benefits from FDI on a sustained basis, host country characteristics (in terms of human capital, technological

---

[14] OECD, *op. cit.*, Chapter 3.

[15] For instance, see Blomström, M, R Lipsey and M Zejan (1994). Host country competition and technology transfer by multinationals. *Weltwirtschaftliches Archiv*, 130, 521–533. For a review of the literature on the subject of FDI and technological transfer, see Fan, EX (2002). Technological spillovers from foreign direct investment — A survey. *Working Paper No. 33*. Economics and Research Department, Asian Development Bank.

[16] See OECD, *op. cit.*, Chapters 5 and 6; and Borensztein, E, J De Gregorio and J Lee (1995). How does foreign direct investment affect growth. *Journal of International Economics*, 45, 115–135.

[17] For instance, see OECD, *op. cit.*, Chapter 10.

[18] In addition, there are acute risks in restricting FDI inflows or activities so as to promote the development of local enterprises (conventional "infant industry" argument). For instance, it is often quite difficult in reality to distinguish between crowding out and legitimate competition.

capacity, etc.) must be improved. Any other policy is likely to be ineffective or short-lived at best, distortionary and detrimental at worst.

Fiscal and Financial Incentives

Countries have and will increasingly compete with each other to attract FDI by offering a number of incentives and other concessionary measures. Apart from *fiscal or tax incentives*, broadly defined as a set of policies designed primarily with a view to lower the tax burden of a firm (including loss write-offs and accelerated depreciation), countries could offer *financial incentives*, defined as direct transfers from the government to the form (including direct capital subsidies, subsidized loans, or dedicated infrastructure).[19]

Many East Asian economies have been particularly aggressive in using preferential tax treatments and other implicit and explicit subsidies to attract FDI, i.e., "bidding wars" or "fiscal wars". To be sure, while systematic evidence of such phenomenon is limited to specific industries (like automobiles and regional headquarter services), "the prisoner's dilemma nature of the competition creates a permanent danger of such wars".[20] This is particularly problematic in the case of larger federal countries like Brazil, India, and the United States where there is the danger of fiscal wars among various states with the rents being transferred from the states to the foreign investors to the detriment of national welfare.[21] From the viewpoint of the country as a whole, broad national codes of conduct may be useful for effective and economically rational use of such incentives.[22]

Table 4 highlights some common tax incentives: (a) reduced corporate income taxes; (b) tax holidays; (c) investment allowances and tax credits; (d) accelerated depreciation; (e) exemptions from selected indirect taxes; and (f) export processing zones (EPZs) — and their relative merits. Tax holidays and accelerated depreciation appear to be the least desirable, while accelerated depreciation seems to be the most efficient.[23]

---

[19] The World Bank (2003). *Global Economic Prospects and the Developing Countries 2003*. New York: Oxford University Press, Chapter 3.

[20] Oman, C, *op. cit.*, p. ii.

[21] For instance, for a discussion of competition for FDI among Brazilian states, see Nelson, R (2002). State competition for foreign direct investment in Brazil: The case of dell computer. *Brown Journal of World Affairs*, 8, 139–153.

[22] Of course, if one argues that in the absence of competition states might impose taxes that are higher than what is nationally optimal, because, for instance, they do not take into account interstate spillovers from FDI, then tax competition may not reduce national welfare. For a formalization of this point, see Davies, R (2002). *Working Paper No. 228*, Department of Economics, University of Oregon.

[23] For an elaboration of the various tax incentives, see Fletcher, K (2002). Tax incentives in Cambodia, Lao PDR, and Vietnam. Paper prepared for the *IMF Conference on Foreign Direct Investment for Cambodia, Lao PDR and Vietnam* (Hanoi, Vietnam: August 16–17).

Table 4. Relative pros and cons of selected types of fiscal and financial incentives.

Pros	Cons
Lower corporate income tax rate on a selective basis	
• Simple to administer. • Revenue costs more transparent.	• Largest benefits go to high-return firms that are likely to have invested even without incentive. • Could lead to tax avoidance via transfer pricing (intracountry and international). • Acts as windfall to existing investments. • May not be tax spared by home country tax authorities.
Tax holidays	
• Simple to administer. • Allows taxpayers to avoid contact with tax administration (minimizing corruption).	• Similar to lower Corporate Income Tax rates, except that it might be tax-spared. • Attracts projects of short-term maturity. • Could lead to tax avoidance through the indefinite extension of holidays via "redesignation" of existing investments as new investments. • Creates competitive distortions between existing and new firms. • Costs are not transparent unless tax filing is required, in which case administrative benefits are foregone.
Investment allowances and tax credits	
• Costs are relatively transparent. • Can be targeted to certain types of investment.	• Distorts the choice of capital assets toward projects of short-term maturity since an additional allowance is available each time an asset is replaced. • Qualified enterprises might attempt to abuse the system by selling and purchasing the same assets to claim multiple allowances. • Greater administrative burden.

(Continued)

Table 4.   (*Continued*)

Pros	Cons
	• Discriminates against investments with delayed returns if loss carry-forward provisions are inadequate.

Accelerated depreciation

Pros	Cons
• Similar benefits to investment allowances and credits. • Generally does not discriminate against long-lived assets. • Moves the corporate tax closer to a consumption-based tax, reducing the distortion against investment, typically produced by the former.	• Some administrative burden. • Discriminates against investments with delayed returns if loss carry-forward provisions are inadequate.

Exemptions from indirect taxes (VAT, import tariffs, etc.)

Pros	Cons
• Allows taxpayers to avoid contact with tax administration (minimizing corruption).	• VAT exemptions may be of little benefit (under regular VAT, tax on inputs is already creditable; outputs may still get taxed at later stage). • Prone to abuse (easy to divert exempt purchases to unintended recipients).

Export processing zones

Pros	Cons
• Allows taxpayers to avoid contact with tax administration (minimizing corruption).	• Distorts locational decisions. • Typically results in substantial leakage of untaxed goods into domestic market, eroding the tax base.

Source: Fletcher, K (2002). Tax incentives in Cambodia, Lao PDR, and Vietnam. Paper prepared for the IMF *Conference on Foreign Direct Investment for Cambodia, Lao PDR and Vietnam* (Hanoi, Vietnam: 16–17 August) with slight modifications.

As noted, tax incentives form only a part of the overall picture. Even though formal tax incentives may not be available, businesses may still benefit significantly from financial incentives.[24] For instance, Singapore provides subsidies to investors that go well beyond traditional tax measures involving

---

[24] See Asher, MG and RS Rajan (2001). Globalization and tax systems: Implications for developing countries with particular reference to Southeast Asia. *ASEAN Economic Bulletin*, 18, 119–139; and Asher, MG and RS Rajan (2003). Economic globalization and taxation: With particular reference to Southeast Asia. In *Economic Globalization and Asia: Essays on Finance, Trade and Taxation*, RS Rajan (ed.). Singapore: World Scientific, Chapter 9.

training, expenditure, pricing of land and utilities, and even taking rather large equity stakes in selected ventures.[25] As with the formal tax incentives, financial incentives are likely to benefit large companies (both domestic and foreign) disproportionately. In turn, states like Singapore with strong fiscal positions can use a combination of low tax rates and aggressive fiscal incentives as competitive strategies to attract FDI vis-à-vis fiscally weak states in neighboring Southeast Asia (given that such competition tends to be largely intraregional), but elsewhere as well.

While the theoretical literature on FDI incentives is burgeoning,[26] the empirical literature in this area is rather lagging. However, the available empirical evidence to date suggests that such fiscal incentives may be important *at the margin* in influencing investment decisions. Incentives are particularly useful when used essentially as signaling devices about the government's country's general (welcoming) attitude toward foreign investment and the overall business environment.[27] Indeed, an OECD study suggests the existence of a two-stage investment decision process.[28]

Investors will typically first shortlist countries where they can invest their money on the basis of some parameters. These parameters are usually economic and political. Investment incentives do not play much of a role at this stage. It is only after the shortlist is made that investors consider and in fact seek out investment incentives before deciding where to invest (by playing off one potential host country against another). From the potential host country's perspective, apart from being costly (given the tax revenues foregone as well as costs of implementation and oversight), such incentives will be least effective when used as substitutes for necessary investment-conducive policies like disciplined macroeconomic policies, adequate infrastructural and supporting facilities, a stable and transparent regulatory environment and relatively noncorrupt environment.

In the final analysis, countries will no doubt continue to employ FDI incentives, not least because unilateral withdrawal of incentives as policy instruments by any single country might be potentially costly to it. However, three points bear emphasis. First, the complexity and uncertainty

---

[25] Take the Local Industrial Upgrading Program (LIUP) of Singapore's EDB as an example. The aim of this scheme is for the multinationals to help raise the efficiency of local suppliers in stages. A large part of the success of this scheme has been due to the financial incentives offered by the EDB in the form of subsidizing of training programs by the EDB itself (OECD, *op. cit.*, Chapter 10).

[26] See the review by Deveruex, M (1990). Tax competition and impact on capital flows. In *Reforming Capital Income Taxation*, H Siebert (ed.). Germany: J.C.B. Mohr (Paul Siebeck).

[27] This conclusion with regard to fiscal incentives in East Asia is drawn by Tanzi, V and P Shome (1992). The role of taxation in the development of East Asian countries. In *The Political Economy of Tax Reform*, T Ito and A Krueger (eds.). Chicago: University of Chicago Press.

[28] Oman, C (2000). *Policy Competition for Foreign Direct Investment: A Study of Competition Among Governments to Attract FDI*. Paris: OECD Development Centre.

(i.e., frequent changes) in FDI-related policies (be they incentives, taxes or laws) can have a significant deterring effect on inflows. Second, beyond a signaling role, FDI incentives do not make up for deficiencies in the overall investment climate. Third, the fiscal costs of such incentives along with those of investment promotion activities noted above can be burdensome and must always be kept in mind when deciding if and the extent to which such measures are to be utilized. The use of such incentives ought to be guided by certain commonsensical principles. Ad hoc, discretionary regimes which could give rise to rent-seeking activities should be eschewed. Focus should instead be on deploying a simple and predictable tax system with low rates for all investors, with there being no preference between domestic and foreign investors (i.e., uniformity).[29] Corporate tax rates ought to be comparable to those prevailing in capital exporting countries.[30]

Conclusion

A 2003 UNCTAD research note refers to "the most dramatic downturn of FDI inflows in history" to describe the current global investment climate.[31] While global FDI inflows did rise modestly in 2004 following large declines in 2001 (41 percent), 2002 (13 percent), and 2003 (12 percent),[32] this increased global "supply" of FDI is not expected to satiate the ever-growing "demand" for FDI. In other words, the global competition for FDI will remain intense. It is therefore incumbent on the developing countries to take steps to ensure an enabling business environment. These steps might include enhancing intersectoral factor mobility (and especially reducing labor market rigidities), dismantling barriers to the free entry and exit of firms, relieving some infrastructural bottlenecks (roads, ports, and storage), reducing other transaction costs of doing business (investment approvals, custom clearance, etc), including regulatory and legal impediments, and strengthening overall governance and intellectual property rights (IPRs).

---

[29] Blomström, M and A Kokko (2003). The economics of foreign direct investment. *Working Paper No. 9489*, NBER.

[30] Moran, T (1998). *Foreign Direct Investment and Development: The New Policy Agenda for Developing Countries and Economies in Transition.* Washington, DC: Institute for International Economics. Indeed, the close nexus between host and source country tax policies is a rather under-appreciated but significant factor in determining the effectiveness of tax incentives (for instance, see Asher and Rajan, 2001 and 2003, *op. cit.*).

[31] UNCTAD (2003). Prospects for global and regional FDI flows. *Research Note* (14 May). General reasons behind this decline include continued weakness and uncertainty in global economic prospects, weakening of equity markets worldwide, and drop in the value of cross-border mergers and acquisition (M&A) activities.

[32] UNCTAD (2005). *World Investment Report 2005.* New York and Geneva: Oxford University Press.

Returning to the issue of investment promotion and industrial targeting, the following observation by Sanjaya Lall hits the nail on the head and is a good way to conclude:

> "FDI strategy is an art not a science … If administrative capabilities are not appropriate to the skill, information, negotiation and implementation abilities needed, it may be best to minimize interventions with the market: to simply reduce obstacles in the way of FDI, minimize business costs and leave resource allocation to the market … (T)here is no ideal universal strategy on FDI. Strategy has to suit the particular conditions of the country at the particular times, and evolve as its needs change and its competitive position in the world alters."[33]

---

[33] Lall, S, *op. cit.*, pp. 20–21.

Chapter 12

Chips from East Asia, Hardware from Southeast Asia, and Assembled in China: Production Sharing and Trade in Asia*

Introduction

When the aircraft manufacturer Boeing announced the process of production of its new plane, the 787 "Dreamliner", it startled many a person. What was startling was not the fact that Boeing was building a new plane, but the fact that Boeing was going to make only 30 percent of the airframe in-house and outsource almost 70 percent of the airframe to different vendors around the world. Some of the airframe parts outsourced were the nose section to Spirit Systems in the United States, the rudder to the Chengdu Aircraft Industrial Group of China, and the mid-fuselage section to Kawasaki Heavy Industries of Japan.[1] Even the part of production process to be undertaken by the Boeing company itself was to be undertaken by Boeing-owned factories around the world. The plane itself would be assembled in Boeing's facilities in Everett, which is in the state of Washington in the United States.[2]

The process of Boeing outsourcing different parts of the airframe to destinations all over the world and then assembling the whole plane at a central location is known as "production sharing", defined as the decoupling of previously integrated goods into their constituent parts, components, and accessories (PCAs) which in turn are distributed across

---

* This chapter draws on Rajan, RS (2003). Production sharing in East Asia. *Economic and Political Weekly*, 38, 6 September, 3770–3772.
[1] A fuller list is available at http://transport.seekingalpha.com/article/17727.
[2] See *Business Week* (2006). Boeing's global strategy takes off. 30 January. Available at: http://www.business week.com/magazine/content/06_05/b3969417.htm.

countries on the basis of comparative advantage.[3] Other terms sometimes used in the international economics literature to describe this phenomenon include "intra-product specialization", "international product fragmentation", "delocalization", "disintegration of production", "Heckscher–Ohlin (HO) plus production fragmentation", "slicing the value chain", "intra–mediate trade", "delocalization", "co-production", or "super-specialization".[4] The international business literature has used terms such as "global commodity or value chains" or "fragmentation of value chains" to describe this phenomenon. This sort of cross-border multi-staged production process has in turn been facilitated immensely by major improvements in transportation, coordination, and information communication technologies (ICTs).

To be sure, production sharing could involve either intra-firm transactions (i.e., Boeing owns the production facilities overseas which undertake part of the production), or inter-firm or arms-length in nature (i.e., Boeing subcontracts to third parties to produce a certain part of the airframe). Of course, a transaction that is arms-length (i.e., "outsourced") could be done, but within the same country. This is sometimes referred to as "onshore outsourcing" as opposed to "offshore outsourcing" or "offshoring" which is the focus of this chapter. In other words, we are concerned here about cross-border transactions in parts and components, independent of who owns the production facility.

Trade, both intraregional and otherwise, in Asia and around the world, is increasingly characterized by production sharing. The Asian Development Bank says that "International production sharing ... has been associated with a high and rising degree of intraregional trade in parts and components that are produced and assembled into final goods within Asia, particularly in East and Southeast Asia".[5] While production sharing has been used extensively in commodity trade (consumer goods like garments, footwear, toys, handicrafts) for decades in Asia and elsewhere, it is now being applied more intensively to trade in airliners, computers, electronics, semiconductors, automobiles,

---

[3] The term "production sharing" was coined by Ng, F and A Yeats (1999). Production sharing in East Asia: Who does what for whom, and why? *Policy Research Working Paper No. 2197*, The World Bank. For recent trends in this sort of components trade, see Kimura, F, Y Takahashi and K Hayakawa (2005). Fragmentation and parts and components trade: Comparison between East Asia and Europe. mimeo (July); Athukorala, PC (2005). Product fragmentation and trade patterns in East Asia. *Asian Economic Papers*, 4, 1–27; and Athukorala, PC and N Yamashita (2006). Production fragmentation and trade integration: East Asia in a global context. *North American Journal of Economics and Finance*, 17, 233–256.

[4] For references, see Rajan, RS (2003). Economic globalization and Asia: Trade, finance and taxation. *ASEAN Economic Bulletin*, 18, 2001, 1–11 and RS Rajan (2003). *Economic Globalization and Asia: Essays on Finance and Trade*. Singapore: World Scientific Press.

[5] Asian Development Bank (2006). *Asian Development Outlook 2006*, p. 272.

Table 1. Main characteristics of producer-driven versus buyer-driven production sharing.

	Producer-driven production sharing	Buyer-driven production sharing
Drivers	Industrial capital	Commercial capital
Core competencies	R&D, production	Design, marketing
Barriers to entry	Economies of scale	Economies of scope
Economic sectors	Consumer durables, intermediate goods, capital goods	Consumer non-durables
Typical industries	Automobiles, computers, aircraft, semiconductors	Apparel, footwear, toys
Ownership of Manufacturing firms	TNCs	Local firms, predominantly in developing economies
Main network lines	Investments-based	Trade-based
Predominant structure	Vertical	Horizontal

Source: Based on Gereffi, G (2001). Shifting governance structures in global commodity chains, with special reference to the Internet. *American Behavioral Scientist*, 44, 1616–1637.

aerospace, and many other products.[6] This said, as highlighted in Table 1, there are some important distinctions between "old" or "buyer-driven" pro-duction sharing and "new" or "producer-driven" production sharing. The dif-ferences in the two can be broadly summarized as follows:

> "Producer-driven and buyer-driven chains are rooted in distinct industrial sectors, they are led by different types of transnational capital (industrial and commercial, respectively), and they vary in their core competencies (at the firm level) and their entry barriers (at the sectoral level). The finished goods in producer-driven chains tend to be supplied by transnational corporations in core countries, whereas the goods in buyer-driven chains are generally made by locally owned firms in developing countries. Whereas transna-tional corporations establish investment-based vertical networks, the retail-ers, designers, and trading companies in buyer-driven chains set up and coordinate trade-based horizontal networks."[7]

Production sharing is not limited to trade in goods as transnational cor-porations (TNCs) have fragmented and dispersed various services functions

---

[6] In line with the increasing significance of production sharing, there is a growing body of analytical lit-erature on the subject. See the collection of papers in Arndt, SA and H Kierzkowski (eds.) (2003). *Fragmentation: New Production Patterns in the World Economy*. New York: Oxford University Press.

[7] Gereffi, G (1999). *op. cit.*, p. 1621.

worldwide to take advantage of marginal differences in costs, resources, logistics, and markets. In the Asia-Pacific region, Singapore and India have benefited significantly as many TNCs have used the former as a regional headquarter (RHQ) given the city state's excellent infrastructural quality, political stability, low tax regime, and strategic location, while they are increasingly using the latter for their backroom and related operations in view of the ready availability of excellent, low cost, high-quality skilled labor.[8] The specific issue of servicing outsourcing is the focus of Chapter 13. This Chapter focuses primarily on manufactured goods.

The Importance and Implications of Production Sharing

Table 2 reveals that growth of PCA trade involving developing economies has outpaced growth in manufactured trade in general and aggregate trade as well. Thus, PCA exports involving developing economies rose from 13.2 percent of total exports in 1981–1990 to 18.5 percent in 1990–2000. The share of developing economies in global PCA exports increased from a mere 4 percent in 1981 to 21 percent in 2000. As noted by the World Bank, the involvement of developing countries in the global production networks has offered them the opportunity to raise their share of the world's fastest growing export products (transistors and semiconductors, computers, and computer and office machine parts) from 2.4 percent in 1980 (about the same as the share of those products in global exports) to

Table 2.   Growth of exports of parts, components and accessories (PCAs) involving developing economies, 1981–2000 (average annual percentage change in US dollars).

Type of export	1981–1990	1990–2000
Manufactured exports	10.6	7.2
PCA exports	12.1	9.6
Memo:		
Share of PCA in total exports	13.2	18.5

Source: World Bank (2003). *Global Economic Prospects and the Developing Countries 2003.* New York: Oxford University Press, Chapter 2.

---

[8] For a discussion of India's emerging strength in information and communication technologies (ICT) services, see Chapter 17 of this Volume. For a discussion of Singapore's services sector, see Findlay, CF and A Sidorenko (2003). Opportunities and challenges in Singapore's services trade. In *Sustaining Competitiveness in the New Global Economy: A Case Study of Singapore*, Rajan, RS (ed.), Cheltenham: Edward Elgar, Chapter 5.

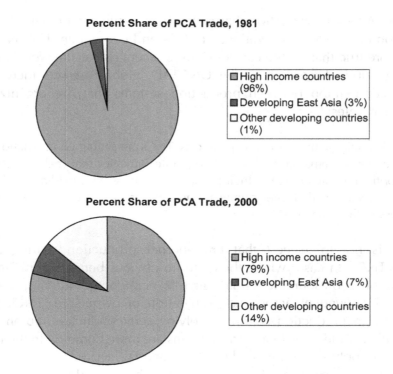

Percent Share of PCA Trade, 1981

☐ High income countries
   (96%)
■ Developing East Asia (3%)
☐ Other developing countries
   (1%)

Percent Share of PCA Trade, 2000

☐ High income countries
   (79%)
■ Developing East Asia (7%)

☐ Other developing countries
   (14%)

Fig. 1.   Developing countries' share of global parts, components and accessories (PCAs), 1981 and 2000 (as a percentage of total trade).

Source: World Bank (2003). *Global Economic Prospects and the Developing Countries 2003.* New York: Oxford University Press, Chapter 2.

16.3 percent by 1998 (almost 7 percentage points higher than the share of such products in global exports).[9]

Nonetheless, trade of PCAs involving developing economies is highly concentrated, far more than total trade or manufactured goods trade in general (Fig. 1). According to the same World Bank source, nine of the top ten developing economies are from East Asia (except Brazil). South Asia, Sub-Saharan Africa, and the Middle East and North Africa together account for only 2 percent of developing economies' PCA exports (and two-thirds of that involves just two countries, India and South Africa), compared with 11 percent of developing economies' total manufactured exports.[10]

To a large extent this concentration of PCA trade in a handful of countries in East Asia is not altogether surprising, being a reflection of the concentration of export-oriented foreign direct investment (FDI) in core

---

[9] World Bank (2003). *Global Economic Prospects and the Developing Countries 2003.* Washington, DC: The World Bank, Chapter 2.
[10] *Ibid.*

countries. After all, production sharing has been facilitated immensely by the expansion of the global operations of TNCs and consequent FDI. Nowhere is this more true than in the case of China's recent rise as the world's manufacturing hub.[11] According to the UNCTAD, global markets increasingly involve competition between production systems that are organized by TNCs. As it notes:

> "While retaining their core competencies, TNCs are setting up international production systems on the basis of corporate strategies that seek to obtain the optimal configuration of their production process by spreading production to locations that offer significant advantages in production costs and access to third markets."[12]

This is not to suggest that cross-border production sharing always requires TNCs. In cases where there are no obvious benefits from "internationalization", outsourcing could also be conducted at "arm's-length" between independent actors, i.e., separation of ownership. TNCs play a major role in production sharing involving semiconductors, automobiles, and the like, while arms-length transactions are more common in the case of textiles and footwear and related products (see Table 1).

The importance of production sharing is that by reducing the costs of production of a product it makes the entire set of countries that participates in the integrated production system more attractive as export markets and investment destinations — a win–win arrangement for all participants. Lower income developing economies are not only able to gain a comparative advantage in lower-end light industries, but also in the lower-end production stage of higher-tier industries. Middle and higher income developing countries are able to graduate to higher ends of the value-added chain, i.e., more advanced stages of the Original Equipment Manufacturing (OEM) and eventually into Original Design Manufacturing (ODM). Countries could also move horizontally, e.g., improve product quality and serve higher value-added market segments. This so-called Original Brand Manufacturing (OBM) essentially involves moving from selling under a foreign label to developing and selling under their own label, hence allowing them to capture brand name rents. Hong Kong has done this effectively in the case of apparels, Korea has done so effectively in automobiles, electronic products and household appliances, Taiwan is known for computers, bicycles and sporting equipment, and other economies in the

---

[11] For an in-depth analysis of China's role as a processing center, see Gaulier, G, F Lemoine and D Ünal-Kesenci (2005). China's integration in East Asia: Production sharing, FDI & high-tech Trade, *Working Paper No. 2005–09*, Centre d'Etudes Prospectives et d'Informations Internationales (CEPII), France.

[12] UNCTAD (2002). *World Investment Report 2002*. New York and Geneva: Oxford University Press, p. 141.

Asia-Pacific region such as Singapore are developing their own "brand names" in other areas.[13]

On the plus side, the splitting of goods into finer sub-parts which are then outsourced is a means of including more countries in the production network (i.e., multiplication of supplier networks). On the minus side, in view of the footloose nature of such production, there are well-founded concerns that small variations in costs could lead to large swings in comparative advantage thus necessitating large and sudden domestic adjustments.[14] Jagdish Bhagwati refers to this phenomenon as "kaleidoscope" or "knife-edge" comparative advantage.[15] As he notes:

"Gone are Adam Smith's days ... (when) ... (c)omparative advantage was 'thick', shielded by big buffers. This is no longer so: not predictably from India and China, but almost certainly from somewhere. Hence I use the metaphor: 'kaleidoscopic comparative advantage'. Today, you have it; but in our state of knife-edge equilibrium, you may lose it tomorrow and regain it the day after ... It is as if the design of trade patterns that you see now gives way to another, as if a kaleidoscope had turned. In this situation of flux and change, we see the Friedman metaphor turned on its head. Faced with fierce competition, firms and unions often seek to iron out whatever differences they can so that the cost conditions for foreign rivals are brought closer to what they are for oneself. Producer interests, including labor, lobby to narrow (if not equalize) as far as politically possible the cost advantages that accrue to rivals from differences in all sorts of domestic policies and institutions. They try, through political agitation, to shield themselves."[16]

Countries therefore need to be ever aware of their relative cost competitiveness in the short run as well as ensure constant industrial upgrading over time so as to remain important cogs in the larger regional or global production system. As UNCTAD notes:

"In locational decision-making ... production costs are always evaluated relative to the efficiency and productivity of a location. This point is often overlooked in discussions of comparative costs, but it is particularly crucial in that a major focus of TNCs geographic allocation of value-chain activities is to achieve systemic efficiencies across their entire international production systems. A given location, therefore, is judged by how cost-efficiently it performs a given function in coordination with functions located elsewhere, and not merely in isolation."[17]

---

[13] Gereffi, G (2001). *op. cit.*, pp. 38 and 56.

[14] After all, the whole basis of production sharing has been to exploit factor price differentials.

[15] Bhagwati, JN (1997). The global age: From a sceptical South to a fearful North. *The World Economy*, 20, 259–283.

[16] Bhagwati, JN (2005). A new vocabulary for trade. *The Wall Street Journal*, 4 August.

[17] UNCTAD, *op. cit.*, pp. 124–125.

Conclusion: Production Fragmentation and Regional Trade Arrangements (RTAs)

The growing significance of production sharing emphasizes the need for governments seeking export-oriented FDI "to go beyond trade and FDI policies and assess their locational advantages in the international production system context".[18] It is in this sense that regional integration efforts that lower the costs of cross-border transactions can be an especially attractive tool to promote trade, FDI, and technological progress.[19] Indeed, it is not surprising that Japanese and other businesses have been among the most enthusiastic proponents of the ASEAN Free Trade Area (AFTA) and ASEAN Investment Area (AIA).

To be sure, such RTAs are clearly the second-best solutions, multilateral trade liberalization being the first best.[20] Given the second best nature of RTAs, neither theory nor empirics is able to offer definitive insight into whether there are any net benefits from a country being a member of such trade alliances. Nonetheless, it is almost certain that a country that is *not* a participant in any of the new RTAs will be adversely impacted due to trade and investment diversion and possible adverse movements in their terms of trade. Thus, there is a strong case for joining RTAs for "defensive reasons".[21] In other words, "RTAs are like street gangs: you may not like them, but if they are in your neighbourhood, it is safer to be in one".[22] It is therefore imperative that developing economies that are hitherto not part of the new regionalism look to consciously establish such linkages with other high-income countries. For such liberalizing economies, "open" RTAs with higher income liberal trade partners may strengthen the hand of exporters and other pro-trade forces, and thus the political support for further liberalization.

At the very least, such RTAs should be geared toward trade facilitating measures such as streamlining and standardizing customs procedures and providing timely and relevant information on cross-border trade and investment opportunities. Trade facilitation has been among the more significant areas of economic cooperation pursued by the Asia-Pacific Economic

---

[18] Quoted in UNCTAD, *op. cit.*

[19] This issue is explored analytically by Arndt, SA (2001). Regional enterprise in preference areas. In *Wirtschaftsstandort Oesterreich: Von der Theorie zur Praxis,* W Fuchs and O Horvath (eds.). Vienna: Ministry for Economic Affairs and Labor; and Arndt, SA (2001). Production networks in an economically integrated region. *ASEAN Economic Bulletin*, 18, 24–34.

[20] Also see Chapter 17 of this Volume.

[21] This issue is elaborated upon in Whalley, J (1996). Why do countries seek regional trade agreements? In *The Regionalization of the World Economy,* J Frankel (ed.). Chicago: Chicago University Press.

[22] Quoted in Crawford, J and S Laird (2001). Regional trade agreements and the WTO. *North American Journal of Economic and Finance*, 12, 193–211.

Cooperation (APEC) Forum.[23] From the perspective of promoting trade, FDI, and overall development, APEC should be encouraged to open membership to other countries like India which have shown a willingness to enhance their degree of integration with the global economy in a market-consistent manner. Unfortunately, this appears unlikely in the near term in view of the self-imposed moratorium on new members by APEC.[24] Whether APEC extends membership to new deserving members such as India remains to be seen. As a keen observer of APEC has noted,

> "APEC members will have to again take up the issue of whether to expand the organization and, especially, if it can afford to not have India in the fold. This issue is of at least as much importance to APEC's continued relevance as a trans-Pacific institution as it is to India."[25]

Independent of this, other regional trade alliances in East and South Asia should place trade facilitation on the top of their respective economic agendas since production sharing is something that is extremely sensitive to the costs of trade,[26] while still remaining open to third countries. As the Asian Development Bank fittingly concludes:

> "Ultimately, Asia's growth and prosperity will be a function of the health of the global trading system, of which the region is an important part. Asia has a significant interest in a strong, healthy, ambitious multilateral agenda. After all, Asia's trade interests overwhelmingly lie in having unfettered access to the largest markets of the US and EU. Intraregional trade integration through production sharing actually reinforces Asia's interests in keeping open access to industrial-country markets. This is because these markets are the ultimate destination of most exports of final goods assembled from parts and components traded in Asia."[27]

---

[23] For instance, see Wilson, J, C Mann, YP Woo, N Assanie and I Choi (2002). Trade facilitation: A development perspective in the Asia-Pacific region. mimeo. Available at www.asiapacific.ca/analysis/pubs/apec/apec_tf_report.pdf.

[24] Of course, this runs counter to APEC's much-touted goal of "open regionalism". For a discussion of APEC's open regionalism concept, see Woo, YP (1999). APEC after 10 years: What's left of open regionalism? mimeo. Available at www2.auckland.ac.nz/apec/papers/woo.html.

[25] See Woo, YP (2005). A review of the APEC membership debate and prospects for India's admission after 2007. mimeo. Available at www.asiapacificresearch.ca/caprn/cisp_project/2005/papers/woo_back.pdf. Also see Rao, VVB (2007). Does APEC membership really matter for India? *Business Line*, 23 January. The issue of India and the East Asia is discussed in Chapter 16 of this Volume.

[26] De, P (2007). Impact of trade costs on trade: Empirical evidence from Asian countries. *Asia-Pacific Research and Training Network on Trade*, Working Paper Series, No. 27, January 2007. Available at http://www.unescap.org/tid/artnet/pub/wp2707.pdf.

[27] Asian Development Bank (2006). *op. cit.*, p. 298.

Chapter 13

All Paths Lead to India: Do Other Asian Countries Pose a Challenge to Its Dominance in Services Outsourcing?*

(With Sadhana Srivastava)

Introduction

The consulting firm A.T. Kearney defines "outsourcing" as taking place "when a company assigns its activities, and sometimes its people, to a third party".[1] Outsourcing can be done both offshore as well as onshore. They define "offshoring" as "the search for a lower cost location for business processing. It includes migrating existing processes or augmenting a current global footprint". Offshoring in turn can be done through an unrelated third party outsourcing arrangement or through a unit that is set up to exclusively service its needs (i.e., a captive unit).

Contemporary international trade flows are increasingly characterized by "production sharing" which essentially refers to the cross-border multi-staged production, and trade in parts, components, and accessories (PCAs). This sort of trade has been facilitated immensely by major improvements in transportation and information communication technologies.[2] Production sharing is not limited to trade in goods as companies have also fragmented and dispersed various service functions worldwide to take advantage of marginal differences in costs, resources, logistics, and markets. This has led to a rapid rise in the offshore outsourcing of and trade in many service activities that may have been considered nontradable in the recent past. The often repeated mantra nowadays is "anything that one can send over the wire is up for grabs"!

---

* This chapter draws on Rajan, RS and S Srivastava (2005). The growing importance of business process outsourcing. *ARTNET Policy Brief No. 3*, UNESCAP, 23 September, 2005 and Rajan, RS (2004). Economic reasons behind outsourcing. *Business Times* (Singapore), 27 July.

[1] Kearney, AT (2004). The real offshoring question. *Executive Agenda*, 7(3), Third Quarter.

[2] See Chapter 12.

Table 1. Hourly wages for selected occupations in the United States and India, 2002/2003 (in US dollars).

Occupation hourly wage	Hourly wage rate, US	Hourly wage rate, India
Telephone operator	$12–$13	Under $1
Health record technologists/ medical transcriptionists	$13–$14	$1.50–$2
Payroll/Data entry clerk	$15–$20	$1.50–$2
Legal assistant/paralegal	$17–$18	$6–$8
Accountant	$23–$24	$6–$15
Financial researcher/analyst	$33–$35	$6–$15
Software developer	$60	$6

Sources: Bardhan, AD and CA Kroll (2003). *The New Wave of Outsourcing*. Research Report. Berkeley: Fisher Center for Real Estate and Urban Economics, University of California; and McKinsey Global Institute (2003). *Offshoring: Is it a Win-Win Game?*. San Francisco, August.

Many US, British, and other multinationals as well as smaller enterprises routinely outsource a number of their service activities. They have come to appreciate that if they do not outsource to reduce costs, while their competitors continue to do so aggressively, they stand to lose global and local market shares to their foreign rivals. The resultant stagnant corporate profit growth will limit the creation of new capital and re-investment in domestic technology.

India has become the leading destination for service outsourcing for a number of reasons, including the widespread use of English, relatively low wages (see Table 1), large pool of science and engineering graduates, and the presence of strong indigenous service sector enterprises. However, other countries like China, Hungary, Israel, South Africa, Philippines, Poland, and Russia are also emerging as important players (see Table 2). Outsourcing to India, in particular, has not only involved low- to mid-skill areas like call centers and routine data-crunching tasks, but also more sophisticated and skills-based services including software development, research and development (R&D), financial portfolio analysis, patent writing, and product design and development.

Extent and Types of Outsourcing

The World Trade Organisation (WTO) describes four types of outsourcing using location and organization control as distinguishing criteria. With regard to international trade flows, what is important is not so much organizational

Table 2. Leading destinations of offshore outsourcing.

Today's Leader (1st Tier)		Up and Comers (3rd Tier)	
India		Belarus	Lithuania
		Brazil	New Zealand
		Caribbean	Singapore
		Egypt	Ukraine
		Estonia	Venezuela
		Latvia	

Challengers (2nd Tier)		Beginners (4th Tier)	
Canada	Mexico	Bangladesh	Nepal
China	Northern Ireland	Cuba	Senegal
Czech Republic	Philippines	Ghana	Sri Lanka
Hungary	Poland	South Korea	Taiwan
Ireland	Russia	Malaysia	Thailand
Israel	South Africa	Mauritius	Vietnam

Source: Gartner Research Inc. (2003). *The Changing Shape of Outsourcing*, June.

control — i.e., intra-firm versus arms-length — but rather, location of economic activity. What we are concerned with here is all forms of international outsourcing as opposed to any type of domestic offshoring. International outsourcing involving arms-length transaction with no direct interface requirement between consumer and producer comes under the rubric of Mode 1 services trade. This category needs to be distinguished from captive offshoring that involves establishing a commercial presence by foreign providers in another country, as represented under Mode 3 of General Agreement on Trade in Services (GATS).

Measuring the extent of outsourcing activity is an extremely difficult task in view of the acute lack of comprehensive and internationally harmonized data. Although data on computer and information services and other business services reported in the *IMF Balance of Payments* provides some broad indication of the magnitude of international cross-border trade in some services, not all such service transactions can necessarily be characterized as being of the outsourcing variety.

As an indication of the severe measurement difficulties noted above, the OECD has estimated the global volume of the offshoring market (excluding domestic outsourcing) in 2003 to have been anywhere between US$10 billion on the low end to US$50 billion on the high end.[3] Many of the countries that

---

[3] Organization for Economic Co-operation and Development (OECD) (2004). *Economic Outlook of the OECD*. Paris: OECD, Chapter 2.

are witnessing an offshoring wave viz. India and China in the Asia-Pacific region as well as Ireland, Brazil, and many smaller Eastern European countries (such as Estonia, Latvia), have inevitably experienced rapid growth in the exports of Business services and Computer and information services.[4]

The offshored/outsourced service activities to India first started with companies sub-contracting software coding work to Indian companies (so-called IT "Business Processing Outsourcing" or BPO). Then came the labor-intensive jobs but they were less-skilled activities, usually referred to as IT-enabled services (ITES-BPO). The IT-BPO activities in India predominantly deal with the writing of software. On the other hand, activities under the ITES-BPO category have included call center support and other back-end business process operations such as data entry and handling, coding, medical and legal transcriptions, and testing.[5]

The growth of the IT and ITES sectors is fairly evident by looking at Table 3 which shows the revenues of both sectors. According to the National Association of Software and Service Companies (NASSCOM), the trade body of software and service companies in India, the total revenues of IT and ITES companies, grew from US$ 16.7 billion in FY 2004 to US$ 29.5 billion in FY 2006. Of this, US$ 12.9 billion was exported in 2004 while US$ 23.4 billion

Table 3.   Performance of the IT and ITES Industries (US$billions) (2004–2006).

	FY 2004	FY 2005	FY 2006
IT Services	10.4	13.5	17.5
Exports	7.3	10	13.2
Domestic	3.1	3.5	4.3
ITES-BPO	3.4	5.2	7.2
Exports	3.1	4.6	6.3
Domestic	0.3	0.6	0.9
Engineering services and R&D, software products	2.9	3.9	4.8
Exports	2.5	3.1	3.9
Domestic	0.4	0.7	0.9
Total software and service revenues	16.7	22.6	29.5
Of which, exports are	12.9	17.7	23.4

Source: National Association of Software and Service Companies, India.

---

[4] Amiti, M and SJ Wei (2004). Fear of service outsourcing: Is it justified? *IMF Working Paper, WP/04/186,* October.

[5] For a discussion of outsourcing to India, see Dossani, R and M Kenney (2007). The next wave of globalization: Relocating service provision to India. World Department, 35(5), 772–791.

was exported in FY06. Table 4 shows the regional breakdown of where the exports were headed to and the Americas clearly dominate — accounting for 68 percent of all software and service exports in 2005. Europe comes in second at 23 percent, while Australasia accounts for 8 percent.

This tremendous increase in revenues has also been marked by a sharp increase in the number of people employed in these two sectors. According to NASSCOM, the number of people employed in the IT and ITES sectors rose from 284,000 in 2000–2001 to 1.2 million in 2005–2006. Table 5 shows the employment levels in these industries and it confirms that there has been a very high growth in employment in the ITES sector. Using data in Tables 3 and 5, it is apparent that in 2004, the per-employee export level in the IT industry was $24,662 and this increased to $25,730 in 2006. However, for ITES, the per-employee export level was $14,351 in 2004 and this increased to $15,403 in 2006. This confirms — albeit in a crude manner — the greater labor intensity (and presumably lower skill levels) of the ITES sector compared to the IT sector.

Table 4.　Geographical breakdown of exports (2004–2005).

Location	FY 2004 (%)	FY 2005 (%)
Americas	69.4	68.4
Australasia	7.4	8.0
Europe	22.6	23.1
Others	0.6	0.5

Source: National Association of Software and Service Companies, India.

Table 5.　Employment in the IT and ITES sectors (2000–2006).

	FY 2000	FY 2001	FY 2002	FY 2003	FY 2004	FY 2005E	FY2006E
IT, Engineering and R&D, software products exports	110,000	162,000	170,000	205,000	296,000	390,000	513,000
IT-enabled service exports	42,000	70,000	106,000	180,000	216,000	316,000	409,000
Domestic sector	132,000	198,114	246,250	285,000	318,000	352,000	365,000
Total	284,000	430,114	522,250	670,000	830,000	1,058,000	1,287,000

Source: National Association of Software and Service Companies, India.

Outsourcing is also increasingly taking place in higher end activities or the so-called "Knowledge Process Outsourcing" (KPOs) that include valuation and investment analysis, market research, consulting, legal and insurance claims processing, software design, architecture, drafting and filing of patent applications, drug discovery and other types of R&D activities, chip design and embedded systems, analytics and inventory management, and so on and so forth. The potential of the KPO business is huge. According to one report, the global KPO market is expected to grow to US$17 billion in 2010 of which US$12 billion will be outsourced to India.[6] The same report also claims that the number of KPO jobs will rise to 300,000 in 2010 from 25,000 jobs that existed at the end of 2005. The profiles of these jobs are very different from the regular BPO jobs. While BPO jobs require an employee to have a basic undergraduate degree, a KPO employee will typically have a graduate degree with some amount of work experience. The same report says this of jobs in the KPO sector. "KPO is a new sector that promises to provide long-term jobs for intellectual, analytical and knowledgeable people with a pay scale much higher than the BPO sector".

An example of how KPO works can be exemplified by the example of equity research. A KPO firm in India will approach an equity research firm in say the United States and offer to do their research on their equity research reports for a particular price. Once both have agreed on a price, the operation starts. The equity research firm in the United States will send a template on which all reports would need to be done. They will then send what research reports would need to be done via a secure server. These research reports will typically contain the name of the company to be researched as well as some financials and most importantly the rating such as buy, sell, or hold that the research house puts on the company. However, the written component will be largely blank. It is the job of the KPO firm to fill in this written section and this "fundamental" section will be written based on the rating that the research firm has given that particular company. If the rating is a "buy", then the report will sound very positive and if it is a "sell", it will sound negative and so on. The researcher in India will use resources available to them such as Bloomberg and the Internet to find out more about the company as well as get the latest news about the company. After the report is written, it will be uploaded back onto the research house's server. It will be downloaded in the United States, where someone will edit the document for grammar as well as to ensure that all reports are consistent. The report is then distributed to the clients of the research house. At no point, however, will the research document ever say that it was actually written in India.

---

[6] Evalueserve (2005). Global sourcing now. Report was cited by Rediff (2005). 300,000 KPO jobs coming to India, 26 December, http://www.rediff.com/money/2005/dec/26bpo1.htm.

The interesting development in the KPO industry is that unlike the IT and BPO industry, the payment model is shifting from the model where the company in the United States or Europe pays the Indian KPO on per-employee basis to one where the payment is made on a per-transaction basis. In other words, for equity research, the research house will pay the KPO firm based on the number of quality research reports done, quality being based on the number of errors that the research house has to correct.

An example of a company that has outsourced high-end work to India is General Electric (GE). GE started sending high-end work to India much before the concept of KPO was even coined. GE's outsourcing of its high-end work, unlike many other companies, has been primarily for its own captive use. GE opened the John F. Welch Technology Center (JFWTC) in Bangalore, India on 17 September 2000. It started with 275 employees and by November 2003, the number of employees increased to 2200. The employees that are hired by GE for JFWTC are typically highly educated people who engage in very high-end work. The GE web site describes the JFWTC as follows[7]:

> "The John F. Welch Technology Center (JFWTC), Bangalore, is General Electric's (GE) first and largest integrated, multidisciplinary Research and Development Center outside the US. JFWTC, the US$80 million state-of-the-art facility is GE's hub for technology, research and innovation. Scientists, researchers and engineers work in virtual teams with their counterparts worldwide, in areas like Electromagnetic Analytics, Composite Material Design, Color Technology, Additive Technology, Non-Destructive Evaluation, Corrosion Technology, MEMS, Molecular Modeling, Power Electronics, Analysis Technologies, Computational Fluid Dynamics and Engineering Analysis. Over 2200 scientists, researchers and engineers work on GE's global technology initiatives at JFWTC, and help create game-changing technologies and innovations to ensure GE's growth and leadership."

Economic Benefits of Outsourcing

In 2003, *The Economist* penned an article titled "America's Pain, India's Gain"[8] which essentially talked about how cost-cutting in American technology companies led them to outsource services to Indian IT and ITES companies. The article summarized why Americans have come to fear outsourcing and how this issue has become a political hot potato. The economics of

---

[7] More information on John F. Welch Technology Center is available at http://www.ge.com/research/grc_3_3.html.
[8] *The Economist* (2003). America's pain, India's gain, 9 January.

outsourcing is easy to understand for a country like India, but it is counter-intuitive for someone in the United States but no less important.

From an economy-wide perspective, offshore outsourcing of service activities from developed to developing countries will inevitably lead to some white-collar job losses in the former, just as production sharing has been leading to the displacement of certain blue-collar workers. Such domestic adjustments are an inescapable outcome of resource reallocation to their more productive uses following international trade (which is the reason motivating such trade in the first instance). However, this in no way justifies embracing protectionist attitudes or policies that prevent the optimal allocation of resources globally. Rather, the focus of well-meaning labor unions and policy-makers should be to empower people to take advantage of, rather than hinder and lament, the process of economic globalization and interrelated forces. Why?

International trade lowers the costs of final goods and services available to the consumers. This so-called consumer "surplus" will far outweigh the job losses faced by a select group of workers in developed countries. Indeed, outsourcing is responsible for only a small portion of recent job losses in the United States, with the general business cycle and rapid automation being the main reasons behind sluggish job creation and concomitant job insecurities that have gripped the country. Thus, even in a simple *static* sense, outsourcing and production sharing will be beneficial on a net basis to society as a whole, though there will inevitably be some transitional costs.

An August 2003 report by McKinsey Global Institute estimates that for every US$1 offshored by the United States to India, the former gains US$1.12 to US$1.14, while the latter gains US$0.33. While such estimates should be taken with a pinch of salt, they are indicative of the static gains to be reaped from offshoring.[9] In a more *dynamic* sense, the trade-induced growth in income levels in developing countries will have further positive feedback effects for the rest of the world in terms of rising exports and increased tourism inflows. This is the age-old global-wealth-creation story, which is a win-win game. There are already signs of this happening with rapid growth in China and India leading to a sharp increase in imports by these countries as well as increases in outbound tourism from them.

Outsourcing wisely to take advantage of the new international division of labor in both the trade of physical goods as well as services, should be an integral part of every company's corporate and economic restructuring. Many Asian companies have been rather slow off the mark in embracing the benefits of offshore outsourcing compared to their American and European

---

[9] McKinsey Global Institute (2003). Offshoring: Is it a win-win game? San Francisco: McKinsey Global Institute. http://www.mckinsey.com/knowledge/mgi/offshore.

counterparts. It is time that they started tapping countries in their neighbor-hood like India and China, not solely for their large domestic markets (i.e., as new revenue sources), but also because of their potential to enhance the global cost competitiveness of Asian companies.

Conclusion: Can Asian Countries Challenge India's Dominance?

The consulting firm, A.T. Kearney publishes an annual list called the "A.T. Kearney Global Services Location Index".[10] India topped this list in 2005 (as it did in 2004), followed by China, Malaysia, Philippines, Singapore, and Thailand. The list is compiled by scoring 40 different metrics under three broad categories. The three categories are financial attractiveness, people skills and availability, and business environment. The study says that India will be dominant as a service outsourcing destination because of its first mover advantage and having had almost 20 years to develop this sector. By contrast, countries like China and the Philippines have only been in the game for less than five years. The study also states that the other Asian coun-tries, other than Singapore, are lower down on the totem pole when the kinds of services offered are compared.

Nasscom and McKinsey undertook a study in 2005 and the conclusion of that report was that the Indian IT and ITES industry would export at least US$60 billion by fiscal year 2009–2010. The report also concludes that this will lead to an increased demand for professionals with the demand for IT professionals expected to rise by 850,000 and the demand for ITES profes-sionals anticipated to rise by 1.4 million.[11] However, one factor that could derail this forecast as well as the success and well-being of Indian IT and ITES companies is the rising costs of labor and lack of talent. The fact that India is facing a talent squeeze surprises almost everyone because of the large population and favorable demographics. However, only a small percent of the population actually obtains a degree in college and an even smaller per-cent get technical degrees. It addition, it has been estimated that of the people getting technical degrees, only around 25 percent are "employable". Software companies are trying to get around this hurdle by hiring people with social and physical science degrees and training them on to code soft-ware. As costs escalate in India, the sustainability of doing low-end services will be called into question.

---

[10] Kearney, AT (2006) Building the optimal global footprint: AT Kearney's Global Services Location Index. A.T. Kearney.
[11] See NASSCOM web site at http://www.nasscom.in.

Countries in Asia are enhancing their capabilities to offer services, but none have achieved the maturity of India. However, countries such as China and the Philippines may challenge India in the lower-end areas such as call centers. *The Economist,* in an article on Chinese outsourcing industry and the potential challenge it offers India, wrote[12] "for the moment, China is likely to capture an increasing share of low-level BPO tasks, such as data entry, form processing and software testing, while India continues to dominate higher-value functions, such as research and design, which require greater creativity and language skills". However, they go on to write that "it isn't just pure competition between the two countries: last year, (India's) TCS signed a deal with the Chinese government and Microsoft to build China's first big software company, which aims to provide IT services for the Olympics".

This said, for India's IT and ITES sectors to survive and to maintain its pre-eminent position in the global outsourcing market, Indian businesses have to necessarily move to higher end service offerings. For that to happen, India must improve the quality of students coming out of educational institutions and create a sustainable mass of people to service this industry.[13]

[12] *The Economist* (2006). Watch out India, 4 May.
[13] "See Agarwal, P (2007), "Higher education and the labor market in India", for a discussion of India's higher education and implications of the labor market. Available at http://siteresources.worldbank.org/INTABCDE2007BEI/Resources/PAgarwal.PDF.

Chapter 14

The Rise of the Indian Manufacturing Sector: A True Underdog Story*

Introduction

There is a word that has been attracting a great deal of attention in recent times, particularly in the United States and that word is "Bangalored". If the word is "googled", the search result that one most commonly gets is "people who have been laid off from a multinational because their job has been moved to India". This is obviously in reference to the fact that some Information Technology (IT) and IT-enabled jobs have been relocated from the West to Bangalore, the so-called "silicon valley of India". However, there are two perspectives on that word. In the United States, it is considered a rather derogatory word, while in India it refers to a coming-of-age term and a badge of pride. Anywhere around the world, India is now associated with IT outsourcing and is seen sometimes as the lynchpin of Indian economic growth.

"The service sector is to India what the manufacturing sector is to China" is the oft-repeated mantra. Indeed, in the story of India's rapid economic growth since the 1990s, the share of manufacturing in India has been stagnant for over a decade at about 15 percent of GDP, while the share of services has increased from 49 percent in fiscal year (FY)00 to 54 percent in FY06 (see Figs. 1 and 2). This is clearly atypical among developing economies in East Asia and elsewhere which have historically experienced a surge in the manufacturing sector in the early stages of liberalization and structural transformation.[1]

The Economist wrote that India missed out on developing a manufacturing sector on a global scale fueled by foreign direct investment (FDI) (akin to China and other East Asian nations) because of "poor quality, outdated products, bad management, indolent self-serving businessmen and appalling infrastructure". But it goes on to add that India's big companies have undergone

---

* This chapter draws on Rajan, RS and S Rongala (2006). Made in India: The next big story in the making. *East Asian Brief* (Korea), pp. 117–125.

[1] For an overview of growth of India's services sector, see IMF (2005). India: Selected Issues. *IMF Country Reports No. 05/87*, IMF, Chapter 2.

159

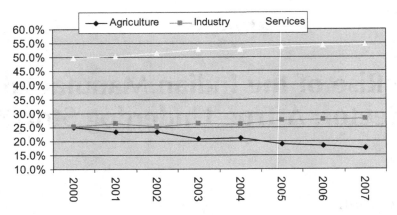

Fig. 1.   Sectoral contribution to GDP in India (2000–2007).

Source: Centre for Monitoring the India Economy (CMIE)
Note: The years here mean financial years. For example, 2006 would mean April 2005 to March 2006.

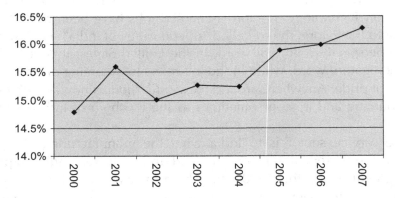

Fig. 2.   Contribution of manufacturing to GDP in India (2000–2007).

Source: Centre for Monitoring the India Economy (CMIE)
Note: The years here mean financial years. For example, 2006 would mean April 2005 to March 2006;
Manufacturing is a component of the Industry Sector.

major restructuring over the years to become internationally competitive by "shedding labor, designing new products and improving management".[2] *The New York Times* wrote "India's annual growth in manufacturing output, at 9 percent and accelerating, is close to catching growth in services, at 10 percent. Exports of manufactured goods to the United States are now rising faster in percentage terms than China's, although from a much smaller base. More than two-thirds of foreign investment in the last year has gone into

---

[2] *The Economist* (2004). Manufacturing in India: Old India awakes, 12 February.

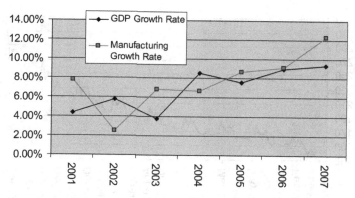

Fig. 3.   GDP and manufacturing growth rate in India (2001–2007).

Source: Centre for Monitoring the India Economy (CMIE)

Note: The years here mean financial years. For example, 2006 would mean April 2005 to March 2006.

manufacturing in India, not services".[3] Other numbers bear out the resurgence in Indian manufacturing. Industrial activity in India has seen a sharp uptick since 2002. The manufacturing sector grew at over 8 percent in FY05 and 9 percent in FY06 and an unprecedented growth rate of over 12 percent in FY07. This resurgence in manufacturing activity (due to both strong domestic and export demand) has helped propel India's GDP annual growth rate to an average of 8.6 percent between FY04 and FY07. Both manufacturing activity and overall economic growth appear to be set to grow on a steep trajectory in the future (Fig. 3).

Further evidence of the recent resurgence of the Indian manufacturing sector can also be seen in the Manufacturing Index (Fig. 4). The Manufacturing Index with a base of 100 in 1993 took 10 years to reach 200 in 2003 and only 3 years since 2003 to reach 250 in 2006. The growth in the manufacturing sector from 2004–2006 has been spectacular, where the monthly average growth has exceeded 9 percent. The manufacturing sector appears to have shaken off its previously erratic performance. Manufactured goods exports rose roughly by 23 percent in FY06 over the previous year (Fig. 5). A study by the Confederation of Indian Industry (CII) and McKinsey & Co has estimated that Indian manufacturing exports have the potential to reach $300 billion by 2015 of which nearly $70–90 billion will be captured by apparel, auto components, specialty chemicals, and electronic products.[4]

---

[3] *The New York Times* (2006). A younger India is flexing its industrial brawn, 2 September. http://www.ysr.in/userArticle.aspx?id=107.

[4] See http://www.ibef.org/download/CompetitiveIndustry.pdf.

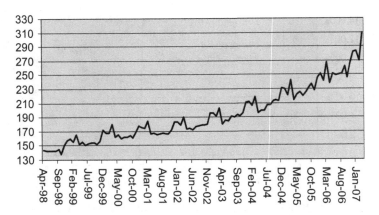

Fig. 4. Monthly manufacturing sector growth index in India (1993–1994 = 100) (April 1998–March 2007).

Source: Bloomberg.

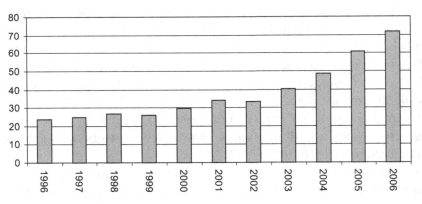

Fig. 5. Manufacturing sector exports (US$ billions) (1996–2007).

Source: Directorate General of Commercial Intelligence and Statistics, India.
Note: The years here mean financial years. For example, 2006 would mean April 2005 to March 2006.

Indian Companies Going Global

Another facet of Indian manufacturing is that a number of manufacturing companies are going the multinational route. No longer content with just operating in India, many companies have spread their operations well outside India. In fact, a number of large Indian manufacturing conglomerates now have a significant percentage of their revenues coming from operations outside India. The Indian company becoming a multinational company route has been through acquisitions.

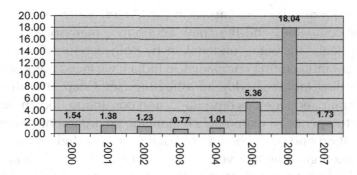

Fig. 6. Overseas deals by Indian companies (US$ billions) (2000–2007).

Source: Bloomberg.

Note: The years here refer to calendar years. 2007 deals are from January to April (both inclusive); The numbers do not include deals where the amount was not disclosed. The numbers would be substantially higher if they are included too;

The deals include deals done by all types of companies and not necessarily manufacturing companies.

During the days of British rule in India, a famous slogan was "Be Indian, Buy Indian". The slogan basically meant that Indians should only buy products made by Indian companies thus ensuring that "Indian money" did not get into the hands of foreign companies, especially British ones. How times have changed since then. Indian companies are spreading their wings externally and have been actively involved in major overseas acquisitions. The market value of the acquisitions has increased tremendously from $5.36 billion in 2005 to $18.04 billion in 2006 (see Fig. 6). To date most of the acquisitions have been in Europe, but attention is increasingly being focused on the United States and Asia.

Certainly, many Chinese companies too have been on a hectic buying spree over the last few years, spurred by the government's desire to build "national champions" and as a means of ensuring energy security. However, India Inc's internationalization thrust has been more decentralized and calibrated, a reflection of the differing political systems in the overall development strategies of the two countries. Many Indian companies have been involved in outward ventures for longer than their Chinese counterparts and have developed knowledge and acumen to deal with the complex issues relating to the management of cross-border alliances.[5]

---

[5] For instance, see Giridharadas, A and S Rai (2006). Out of India: A "Third Wave of Globalization" Emerges. *International Herald Tribune*, 17 October; Boston Consulting Group (BCG) (2006). *The New Global Challengers: How 100 Companies from Rapidly Developing Economies are Changing the World*, The Boston Consulting Group, May. Accenture (2005). *China Spreads its Wings — Chinese Companies go Global*, Accenture; Aguiar, M, A Bhattacharya, T Bradtke, P Cotte, S Dertnig, M Meyer, DC Michael and H Sirkin (2006). *The New Global Challengers: How 100 Top Companies from Rapidly Developing Economies Are Changing the World*. The Boston Consulting Group, 25 May.

While India may be best known in the United States and elsewhere for its software companies and the "new economy", many of India's overseas acquisition deals are being undertaken by "old economy" manufacturing companies. Manufacturing companies in India have faced innumerable challenges including India's shoddy infrastructure (see Chap. 9 of this volume), the bureaucratic red tape ("license Raj"), and corruption. Indian industry has learnt how to operate in extremely challenging environments. After a period of consolidation and strengthening of balance sheets, Indian manufacturing sector has been growing at a very healthy pace in the last half decade. This has given rise to a new confidence among Indian corporates which is manifesting itself in the form of an increasing number of overseas acquisitions.

Most of the overseas acquisitions undertaken by Indian companies recently have been aimed at buying brand names, acquire technology, processes, management know-how and marketing and distribution networks, and to solidify existing markets or seek new ones. Such market-seeking investments can be expected to grow in importance as Indian companies are beginning to face intense foreign competition at home and are looking to expand overseas market shares. Indian government has, in recent times, taken a positive attitude toward this trend and has been taking steps to liberalize foreign exchange policies and related rules to promote outward investments by the country's corporates.

The Tatas, the second largest corporate house in India, is the perfect example of an Indian corporate playing the acquisition game. It is a household name in India, being involved in everything from trucks to cars to watches to steel to tea to hotels among many others. The Tata Group comprises of over 90 companies and their revenues during the past year were about US$22 billion. While the revenues and profits of the Tatas have been growing at a steady pace, they have also been very actively focused on acquiring companies throughout the world. In the past 6–7 years, they have bought some 20 companies in countries ranging from the United Kingdom to Chile to Australia to the United States. Their first big acquisition was in February 2000 when they acquired the UK based tea company Tetley for $407 million. However, of all their foreign acquisitions, the coup de grace was their acquisition of UK-based Corus Steel in 2006 for a whopping $12.8 billion. This deal, as of June 2007, was the largest ever acquisition done by an Indian company.

Perhaps what spurred the Indian CEO psyche toward bigger and more deals was the $38 billion acquisition of Arcelor Steel by smaller rival, Mittal Steel earlier this year. While Mittal Steel is technically not an Indian company (it is European-based), it started in India and the Chairman and CEO of Arcelor-Mittal, Lakshmi Mittal is an Indian national. Coverage around the world referred to Mittal Steel as an Indian steel company and the

Government of India exerted considerable pressure when obstacles were placed in front of the acquisition plan. When the deal was done, there was extensive coverage in India about how an Indian could pull off such a big deal.

The Tata conglomerate and other cash-rich Indian corporates in manufacturing and heavy engineering, IT-related services, pharmaceuticals, healthcare, and other areas, are intent on making their brand names truly global via possible overseas acquisitions. Like their Chinese counterparts, Indian multinational corporations have come of age; they are ambitious and hungry and are slowly but surely shaping the process of globalization.

Selected Manufacturing Industries in India

The manufacturing sector in India produces items ranging from machine tools to boilers to air conditioners. Some examples of the more important industries are automobiles and auto parts, mobile telephones, textiles, and pharmaceuticals, among other areas.[6] We discuss recent trends in some of these sectors below.

Automobiles and Auto Components

India became the fastest growing car market in the world in 2004 with a growth rate of 20 percent. The automobile industry in India includes the production of passenger cars, multi-utility vehicles, commercial vehicles, two-wheelers and three-wheelers. It also includes the production of auto components. The growth of the automobile sector has been explosive. The number of automobiles manufactured has grown from 5.3 million in FY02 to 9.73 million in 2005–2006. The revenues of automobile manufactures nearly doubled from INR 422 billion ($9.75 billion) in 1999–2000 to INR 835 billion ($19 billion) in FY05. It has been estimated that the automobile industry in India will receive an investment of $6.7 billion by 2007 and that the market for passenger cars will grow at a rate of 10 percent till 2014. However, more than the impressive numbers, the remarkable story of the automobile sector in India is the fact that the market has changed from one where consumers were at the mercy of manufacturers to the other way around. In around 15 years, the number of variants available has increased to over 150 from just a handful. The other impressive turnaround is that while previously, Indian auto production was mainly for domestic consumption,

---

[6] Much of the information on the four industries is from the India Brand Equity Foundation web site (www.ibef.org) which is run by the Ministry of Commerce. The fiscal year in India is April–March.

companies like Hyundai and other major car manufacturers are increasingly seeking to make India their global production base for small cars (Hyundai Motors has made India its global hub for the Santro hatchback). The number of automobiles that have been exported from India has increased exponentially. A total of 0.18 million was exported in FY00 and that increased to 0.80 million in FY06.

The auto components industry has had blistering growth too on the back of the booming automobile sector. In 1999–2000, total auto component manufacturing amounted to $3.8 billion and this increased to $10 billion in FY06 and is expected to increase to $13 billion in FY07. Auto components exports increased from $456 million in FY00 to $1.8 billion in FY06. Among the companies that are outsourcing from India are General Motors, Ford, Daimler Chrysler, Hyundai, Fiat, Toyota, Delphi, Navistar, Visteon, Cummins, and Caterpillar. General Motors now plans to source components worth at least $1 billion a year from India by 2010. According to a joint Auto Component Manufacturers Association and McKinsey study, given India's strengths, especially its competitiveness in manufacturing labor-intensive, skill-intensive parts, India can achieve a 3–4 percent share of the potential sourcing market (estimated by them at US$700 billion) by 2015.[7]

Mobile Telephony

India is the world's fastest growing large mobile telecoms market, with 79 million subscribers as of June 2006 and is expected to cross 100 million in 2007. This is in comparison to 11.1 million subscribers in January of 2003. The retail market for handsets is currently at around $17 billion and is growing at a phenomenal 20 percent a year. LG Electronics was the first foreign multinational to establish a factory in India (Pune) to create a Made-in-India handset. By 2010, LG aims to produce 20 million mobile phone units of which 50 percent will cater to the export market. The facility will involve an investment of US$60 million by the year 2010. Nokia is setting up a plant in Chennai (India) and its investment in India is estimated at $100 million to $150 million.

Textile Industry

The Indian textile industry is one of the largest and most important sectors in the economy. It accounts for 20 percent of industrial production, 9 percent

---

[7] See http://www.automonitor.co.in/show_article.asp?code=568.

of excise collections, 18 percent of employment in industrial sector, and nearly 20 percent of the country's total export earnings. The Indian textile industry currently contributes to around 4 percent of GDP and is the second largest employer after agriculture, directly employing around 30 million people. In terms of exports, the textile industry exported $10.7 billion worth in 2001–2002, which increased to $13.04 in FY05. Though the increase has not been stellar, neither has it been anemic. A possible reason for this less than stellar growth is likely the result of the Multifiber Arrangement (MFA) and its successor the Agreement on Textiles and Clothing (ATC). However, with the dismantling of the ATC, there have been predictions in many quarters that the textile industry is set to boom. CRISIL, an India rating agency, says that the Indian textile and apparel industry can potentially reach a size of $85 billion by 2010 with a domestic market size of $45 billion and exports accounting for the rest. This potential, they say, can result in the creation of 12 million new jobs both directly and indirectly.[8]

Pharmaceuticals

According to the Foreign Ministry, there are 15,000 pharmaceutical manufacturing units in the country of which 5,000 are large-scale units, while 45 have an international presence. The Indian pharmaceutical industry is among the top 15 in the world. The Indian pharmaceutical industry has the highest number of plants approved by the US Food and Drug Administration outside the United States. It also has the largest number of Drug Master Files filed which gives it access to the high growth generic bulk drugs market. However, the Indian pharmaceutical industry is comparatively very small when compared to the industry in the United States. The industry, in FY05, amassed $4.5 billion in domestic sales and $3.8 billion in exports. It has been estimated that the Indian pharmaceutical market will be $11.6 billion in 2009–2010. However, the Indian pharmaceutical industry faces a major hurdle. In 1970, as a result of high drug prices, the government allowed domestic companies to manufacture patented medicines in India without paying a royalty. Though they were not given a "product patent", they were given a "process patent", which enabled companies to manufacture these drugs albeit through a slightly altered process. On 1 January 2005, the government amended the act to conform to the Trade-Related Intellectual Property Rights (TRIPS) Agreement. The amendment has now closed the "process patent" loophole which means that companies will now have to pay full royalties to

---

[8] The report was done by CRISIL for The Indian Cotton Mills Federation as part of their "Vision Statement 2004". A press release of the report is available at http://www.crisil.com/Ratings/Brochureware/Media/PressRelease/ICMF.pdf. The full report can be purchased from the ICMF at http://www.citiindia.com/.

companies which own the original patent. While this will have no impact on the manufacture of drugs whose patent has expired, it will likely have an impact, especially in terms of price, on drugs whose patents are yet to expire. However, to compensate for this, the government is offering incentives to companies that set up Research and Development facilities. According to the Economic Survey of 2004–2005, "the pharmaceutical industry, with its rich scientific talent and research capabilities, supported by Intellectual Property Protection regime, is well set to take a great leap forward".[9]

Impediments for Manufacturing in India

In 2004, the World Bank published a report on the investment climate in India.[10] The report, based on a questionnaire sent to and answered by various private sector participants, listed some top bottlenecks to the manufacturing sector in India. These bottlenecks have been responsible for hindering the manufacturing sector from achieving its full potential as well as hindering FDI in manufacturing when compared to China. These bottlenecks are:

Regulation and Corruption — This bottleneck refers to India's excessive regulations in the manufacturing sector and such regulations inevitably breed corruption. Because of these regulations, it typically takes 89 days to start a business in India while it takes 41 days in China. It takes 10 years for a company in India to complete bankruptcy procedures while it takes 2.5 years in China. The other regulatory concern is the rigid labor market where employers have difficulty firing people. On a scale of 0 to 100, 100 being most rigid, the report ranked India at 90 in terms of difficulty of firing while China was at 40 and Malaysia at 10. Because of this Indian firms reported overstaffing of around 11 percent in factories.

Tax Administration and Customs Clearance — The government through customs officials, tax officials, and others regulates businesses through a number of acts and standards that apply to all establishments that employ 10 or more people. These acts give officials considerable discretion in enforcing rules and these are typically done through arbitrary visits and inspections. The report says that much of these visits are a veiled demand for bribes. The World Bank uses these visits as proxy for "cost-of-tax administration". In India,

---

[9] See http://indiabudget.nic.in/es2004-05/chapt2005/chap73.pdf.

[10] See "*India: Investment Climate and Manufacturing Industry*" published by the World Bank in November 2004. The study is based on two previous studies conducted by CII. The study is available on the World Bank's web site. Much of the information on the various hindrances are from the study unless specifically stated.

the number of inspections was 6.7 per year while China had 26.7 per year. However, Indian management of small firms spent 11.9 percent of their time dealing with regulations compared to 7.8 percent in China. However, in the area of custom clearance, India's average is 7.3 days when compared to 9.9 days in China.

Infrastructure — The report chose three indicators to measure the quality of infrastructure. They are power, telephones, and quality of transport services for freight movement. In India, it takes 47.8 days to get connected to the power grid while it takes 25 days in China. Firms in India can expect power outages every day while a power outage occurs once in two weeks in China. These outages cause the average manufacturer in India to lose 8.4 percent a year in sales while Chinese firms lose less than 2 percent. India's cost of power is higher at $0.08 per kilowatt hour compared to $0.06 in Southeast Asia.

Elaborating on the issue of power losses, the Economic Survey of 2004–2005 notes:

> "End-consumers of electricity continue to experience shortages in terms of 'reliable access to electricity'. The problem in India is the massive transmission and distribution (T&D) losses incurred. While officially, the T&D losses are at 23 percent, which is extremely high by any measure, there have been studies that show T&D losses to be as high as 50 percent. These high loss rates are a direct result of severe under-investment, which in turn is the result of under-pricing electricity to homes as well as free and subsidized power given to farmers as electoral ploys have left the state power sector with massive accumulated losses. The *Economist* (2005) says that this electrical shortage 'may thwart India's rush to modernity'."[11]

Regarding telephones, it takes 29.8 days for a company in India to get a new phone connection while it takes 9.3 days in China. However, this number in India will reduce as more firms enter the telephony business. On the issue of quality of transport of freight, a proxy is the average inventory kept by businesses. In India it is 32.5 days while it is 24.2 days in China. There are some serious deficiencies in road and rail transport in India. India has only 3,000 km of four-lane highways while China has over 25,000 km of four- to six-lane highways.[12] The quality of roads is not good either and an indicator is the average speed of trucks which is 30–40 km per hour. Though India's rail network is the second largest in the world, transporting freight is

---

[11] *The Economist* (2005). India's electricity reforms: Underpowering, 22 September.

[12] The government is promoting a highway system called the quadrilateral because it aims to connect the four corners of India and work is progressing steadily on it. Though India has only 3,000 km of four-lane highways, there is around 65,000 km of two-lane highways called national highways.

expensive because it cross-subsidizes passenger costs. In a world of zero cross-subsidization, the ratio of passenger earning per passenger km to freight earning per metric ton of freight km should be 1. In India, it is 0.3 while in China it is 1.1.

Access to Land — According to the report, urban land policies and regulations are creating an artificial scarcity of land and driving up prices. These distortions included unclear land ownership, widespread institutional ownership, inflexible land use and property rights, and high transaction costs in the form of stamp duties.

Access to Finance — 54 percent of small businesses in India have access to bank credit and this is higher than in China but lower than 50 percent when compared to Brazil. The report suggests that "A greater proportion of small business might thus have been rationed out of formal credit markets in India than could otherwise be the case even by emerging market standards". The problem seems to be that Indian small- and medium-size enterprises (SMEs) have relied on debt from banks and NBFIs. However, with increased regulation, the number of NBFIs has shrunk and SMEs now have to rely on debt that is of a short duration, typically less than a year, and is more expensive. Another problem faced by Indian manufacturing is the inadequacy of finance. This can be traced to the high fiscal deficits of the federal and state governments that have tended to "crowd-out" money, which could have otherwise been used for investment in industry.

Availability of Skills — The report states that it is easier to get skilled people in India than in China or Brazil. However, the caveat is that it does not mean that India has more skilled workers but an indicator that there is a shortage of skilled workers in China and Brazil given the large number of industries requiring skilled workers. This high number is directly proportional to the FDI these countries received.

Going Forward: Overcoming Obstacles

The question that arises naturally is why has India undergone a manufacturing revival in recent years despite these significant disadvantages, which has prevented India from becoming a major source of labor-intensive manufactured exports? First, there has been a bias in manufacturing activities away from traditional low-cost, labor-intensive manufacturing (toys, kettles, etc.) to those that are able to harness India's brainpower and technical skills and complement the country's experiences in product design and development,

IT services, and back-office work. Second, existing large-scale, home-made Indian manufacturers with experience in producing in the Indian conditions have become more prevalent. Third, the availability of domestic enterprises has allowed many foreign multinationals to use domestic companies to source the whole product or one or more critical components. Fourth, the large size of the Indian market and the higher share of consumption to GDP compared to many East Asian economies has made India a very attractive market for domestic goods as opposed to just an export platform. Finally, India has a very favorable demographics; by 2020, 47 percent of Indians will be between 15 and 59, compared with 35 percent now. This suggests that companies will have available a youthful and a potentially dynamic labor force.

While India has clearly increased competency in manufacturing, the government has set a priority of sustaining manufacturing growth at about 10–12 percent over the coming years. Particular attention has been given to attracting FDI into labor-intensive manufacturing as a means of tackling the country's unemployment. In relation to this, in the Economic Survey of 2004–2005, the government fixed a target of increasing merchandise exports from the current level of $80 billion a year to $150 billion a year by 2008–2009 which means, by their own calculations, exports need to grow at around 20 percent annually. The government is not alone in targeting or predicting ambitious numbers. As mentioned previously, a joint CII and McKinsey & Company report came to the conclusion that India has the potential to reach $300 billion in merchandise exports by 2015. The prediction is based on the current trend to manufacture products in low-cost countries and that India is ideally placed because of vast and cheap manpower.[13] The study states that this in turn will create 25–30 million new jobs and lead to a rise in India's share of world trade to 3.5 percent from the current 0.5 percent.

The key point here is the need for manufacturing to not only grow rapidly, but also to be able to generate employment on a large scale as has happened in the cases of China and the rest of East Asia. Indeed, while India's manufacturing prowess is growing, there is a key difference between India's manufacturing competency and much of East Asia. Much of India's manufacturing is relatively of smaller scale and high value-added. The industry was also initially largely driven by domestic corporates, however more recently selected multinationals have become more important. In contrast, the East Asian model of investment and export-led manufacturing growth has

---

[13] The source of this information is from a news release from the CII web site and is available at http://www.ciionline.org/news/newsMain.asp?news_id=1025200440617PM. The title of the report is "Made in India" and is a study of the manufacturing sector in India.

been largely fueled by multinationals creating production networks across countries, with each country producing and exporting parts and components. Such fragmented trade has involved very high volume but rather low value-added. While India has become part of such networks in the area of design and services (finance, customer services, etc.), the Indian manufacturing sector has not been part of the regional division of labor. These production networks are invariably driven by FDI, which — though growing in India — has remained somewhat disappointing.

In order to attract more large-scale FDI manufacturing operations, the Indian government is belatedly taking actions on a number of fronts to overcome the various bottlenecks — building a network of highways, deregulating of the power sector, upgrading ports and airports, further streamlining of customs duties, improving basic literacy, reducing transactions costs of doing business, etc. However, the pace of change in a democratic, large and decentralized country with a coalition-based government has inevitably been less rapid than many East Asian economies and rather uneven.[14]

In view of this, one key instrument that the government has begun to use to overcome some of the hindrances to large-scale investments in the manufacturing sector is by enacting a Special Economic Zones (SEZ) law in February 2006, which covers issues pertaining to establishment, operation, and fiscal oversight. The main advantages of the SEZs are related to tax incentives offered to businesses established within such zones. Thus far the government has given in-principle approval to 267 applications for setting up new SEZs across the country, with 80 percent concentrated mainly in the northern and western regions (states of Haryana, Gujarat, and Maharashtra).[15] It is hoped that the SEZs can act as an interim means of boosting investments in manufacturing and other industries until the government is able to improve the business environment on a country-wide basis. It is often noted that such a strategy was successfully undertaken by China and used effectively by the government in policy experimentation before being replicated on a larger scale. Nonetheless, there are some concerns that the policy may not be nearly as successful in India given the relatively small size of the proposed SEZs (most are about 1 sq. km compared to the mega-sized SEZs of 100 sq. km in China). The high concentration in India makes such large and seamless SEZs less viable. Apart from the scale-related issues, there are also valid concerns regarding the fiscal implications of the SEZs given the large tax breaks offered to businesses in the Indian SEZs. In other words, SEZs may merely lead to uneven regional development (via a diversion of investments

---

[14] For a discussion of factors that have hindered FDI into India, see IMF (2005). India: Selected issues. *IMF Country Reports No. 05/87*, IMF, Chapter 3.

[15] For detailed description and critical analysis of India's SEZs, see Ahya, C and M Sheth (2006). India economics — SEZ rush: 267 and counting ... Morgan Stanley Research Asia-Pacific, 22 September.

from the other areas of the country to the SEZs) and worsen the country's fiscal position.

SEZs are not the panacea that Indian policy-makers are looking for and it is clearly not a substitute for needed infrastructural, regulatory, and institutional reforms on a macro-basis. However, these and other institutional innovations in India emphasize that the country's policy-makers are consciously attempting to improve India's attractiveness as an investment destination and a global manufacturing hub. The investment climate in India has undoubtedly become friendlier and investing in India is a much more attractive proposition today than in yesteryears. India is definitely in the early stages of an industrial renaissance.

Chapter 15

Will the Big Tiger Leave Any Crumbs for the Little Dragons? China vs. Southeast Asia*

Introduction

In the 1992 US presidential election, Ross Perot made a statement about a "giant sucking sound". He was of course referring to Mexico sucking away American jobs because of NAFTA. Ten years later, an American newspaper, *The Nation*, had this to say about China in 2001:

> "The 'giant sucking sound' Ross Perot used to talk about is back, only this time it is not Mexico sucking away American jobs. It is China sucking away Mexico's jobs. And jobs from Taiwan and South Korea, Singapore and Thailand, Central and South America, and even from Japan. Globalization is entering a fateful new stage, in which the competitive perils intensify for the low-wage developing countries much like the continuing pressures on high-wage manufacturing workers in the United States and other advanced economies. In the race to the bottom, China is defining the new bottom."[1]

China has had phenomenal industrial growth over the last two decades and it has emerged as a major Asian and global economic power. In 2006, China was the biggest economy in Asia after Japan in constant dollars and the largest in purchasing power parity (PPP) terms (second largest in the world behind the United States). China's GDP grew at an average rate of 10 percent between 1990 and 2006. China's accession to the World Trade Organisation (WTO) in December 2001 gave further impetus to the country's export, FDI, and overall growth prospects. By 2006, China had become the third biggest merchandise trading nation in the world and the largest

---

* This chapter draws on Rajan, RS (2003). Emergence of China as an economic power: What does it imply for Southeast Asia? *Economic and Political Weekly*, 38(26), 28 June, 2639–2644. It also draws on Srivastava, S and RS Rajan (2004). What does the economic rise of China imply for ASEAN and India: Focus on trade and investment flows. In *Foreign Investment in Developing Countries*, H Kehal (ed.), pp. 171–204. Palgrave: McMillan.
[1] See http://www.thenation.com/doc/20011231/greider.

recipient of foreign direct investment (FDI) among developing countries for a number of years. In 2006, China also had the largest current account surplus, amounting to close to US$180 billion, while foreign exchange reserves crossed US$1,000 billion in 2006. The World Bank estimated that China contributed to one-third of global economic growth in 2004.

While some troubling questions about the accuracy and reliability of official Chinese statistics on growth and investment persist,[2] there can be no doubt that the economic ascendancy of China is a very real phenomenon. While terms used to describe China's industrial strength such as "global factory", "the world's manufacturing center", or "export processing zone of the world" are surely colorful exaggerations, they do underscore how far the country has come in the last two decades.

Nowhere has the rapid economic ascendancy of China been more closely watched than in Southeast Asia whose policy-makers are anxious to know the answer to the six-million dollar question — *"Is the emergence of China as an economic power a boon or bane?"* No doubt Indian policy-makers and those in other parts of Asia are asking themselves the same question.

China's Impact on Southeast Asia's Exports

Bilateral merchandise trade between the 10 members of the Association of Southeast Asian Nations (ASEAN) and China totaled US$133 billion in 2005 compared to US$7–8 billion in 1990, a compounded annual growth rate of 21 percent year-on-year (Table 1). While both ASEAN's exports to and imports from China have increased in tandem, the latter has consistently exceeded the former, ensuring that China has enjoyed a persistent trade surplus with Southeast Asia but this pattern changed in 2005 when ASEAN became a net exporter vis-à-vis China (Fig. 1). In 1990, China accounted for 1.8 percent of Southeast Asia's total global exports and this increased to 10.2 percent in 2005. Most ASEAN economies are all fairly dependent on China and in the case of the Philippines 19.5 percent of their exports went to China in 2005 (Tables 2 and 3).

A simulation exercise suggests that China will be Southeast and East Asia's largest exporter by about 2010.[3] This anticipated growth of China's internal market and domestic demand suggests that there exist innumerable opportunities for ASEAN to significantly accelerate their export growth, while

---

[2] For instance, see Economist Intelligence Unit (EIU) (2002). Does anyone believe China's numbers? *EIU Viewswire*, 28 March and Berthelsen, J (2003). China's GDP figures: Are they bogus? *Asia Times*, 6 February.

[3] Roland-Holst, D (2002). An overview of PRC's emergence and East Asian trade patterns to 2020. *Research Paper No. 44*, Asian Development Bank Institute (October).

Table 1.   ASEAN exports to and imports from China and total bilateral trade (US$ billions) (1990–2005).

	ASEAN exports to China	ASEAN imports from China	Total bilateral trade
1990	2.63	4.79	7.42
1991	3.27	5.64	8.91
1992	4.01	5.79	9.80
1993	5.27	6.04	11.31
1994	6.88	7.98	14.86
1995	8.75	11.18	19.93
1996	10.00	11.61	21.61
1997	10.71	13.82	24.53
1998	10.55	11.85	22.40
1999	11.55	13.86	25.41
2000	16.38	18.65	35.03
2001	16.70	19.85	36.55
2002	21.82	26.95	48.77
2003	30.96	33.83	64.79
2004	40.96	47.72	88.68
2005	67.85	65.21	133.06

Source: Compiled by authors, using data from Asian Development Bank.
Note: All data is for calendar year and in some cases may not correspond to financial year.

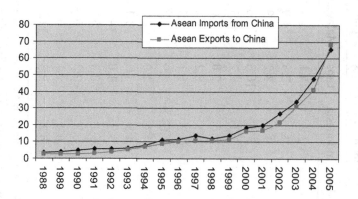

Fig. 1.   ASEAN exports to and imports from China (US$ billions) (1988–2005).
Source: Asian Development Bank.

also offering a number of lucrative opportunities in China for regional investors. The study finds that an "East Asian trade triangle" is gradually developing, with China running a sustained trade surplus with Western economies (the United States and the European Union) and a deficit of about

Table 2. Exports to China as a percentage of total exports (1990–2005).

	Brunei	Cambodia	Indonesia	Laos	Malaysia	Myanmar	Philippines	Singapore	Thailand	Vietnam	ASEAN
1990	0.1	0.4	3.2	9.1	2.1	8.1	0.8	1.5	1.2	0.3	1.8
1991	0.1	0.8	4.1	2.5	1.9	18.3	1.4	1.4	1.2	0.9	2.0
1992	0.2	0.1	4.1	3.2	1.9	17.5	1.2	1.8	1.2	3.3	2.1
1993	0.0	0.4	3.4	10.6	2.6	17.3	1.5	2.6	1.2	4.5	2.5
1994	0.0	0.4	3.3	2.7	3.3	13.8	1.2	2.2	2.0	7.3	2.6
1995	0.0	1.5	3.8	2.8	2.6	11.3	1.2	2.3	2.8	6.4	2.7
1996	0.0	2.1	4.1	0.2	2.4	10.6	1.6	2.7	3.3	4.6	2.9
1997	0.0	7.3	4.2	0.1	2.3	5.9	1.0	3.2	3.0	5.0	3.0
1998	0.0	4.5	3.8	1.9	2.7	4.9	1.2	3.7	3.2	4.7	3.2
1999	0.4	0.9	4.1	1.9	2.7	6.6	1.6	3.4	3.2	6.5	3.2
2000	1.8	2.1	4.5	1.5	3.1	5.7	1.7	3.9	4.1	10.6	3.8
2001	4.0	1.3	3.9	1.8	4.3	4.6	2.5	4.4	4.4	9.4	4.3
2002	6.4	1.3	5.1	2.3	5.6	4.5	3.9	5.5	5.2	9.1	5.4
2003	6.7	1.1	6.2	2.3	6.5	5.6	5.9	7.0	7.1	9.3	6.8
2004	4.5	1.1	6.4	2.1	6.7	5.9	6.7	8.6	7.4	9.0	7.4
2005	3.8	0.9	8.2	3.3	11.3	6.8	19.5	9.5	8.3	7.5	10.2

Source: Compiled by authors, using data from Asian Development Bank.
Note: All data is for calendar year and in some cases may not correspond to financial year.

Table 3. Trade surplus/deficit with China (US$ millions) (1990–2005).

	Brunei	Cambodia	Indonesia	Laos	Malaysia	Myanmar	Philippines	Singapore	Thailand	Vietnam	ASEAN
1990	−24	−3	182	−10	58	−104	−120	−1,296	−838	3	−2,152
1991	−28	−2	356	−10	−164	−219	−115	−1,369	−814	1	−2,365
1992	−43	−14	645	−27	−203	−166	−70	−1,140	−834	64	−1,787
1993	−38	−21	314	7	108	−207	−15	−499	−475	50	−777
1994	−49	−38	−47	−12	570	−276	−156	−787	−458	151	−1,104
1995	−88	−52	247	−13	180	−544	−451	−1,283	−453	32	−2,426
1996	−92	−63	460	−22	6	−448	−325	−1,044	−85	11	−1,603
1997	−78	−11	711	−5	−380	−560	−728	−1,616	−516	70	−3,112
1998	−10	−53	926	−12	145	−530	−855	−787	−52	−75	−1,304
1999	−8	−77	767	−16	179	−355	−465	−1,777	−633	73	−2,312
2000	39	−89	746	−32	−209	−433	−123	−1,739	−571	135	−2,275
2001	116	−70	358	−53	17	−425	−182	−1,866	−848	−189	−3,143
2002	197	−254	476	−51	−903	−673	104	−2,006	−1,375	−641	−5,127
2003	230	−300	845	−98	−490	−845	347	−938	−360	−1,255	−2,864
2004	152	−453	503	−97	−1,879	−841	−6	−819	−1,083	−2,235	−6,759
2005	130	−564	−1,543	−92	6,600	−778	5,579	−774	−2,034	−3,885	2,636

Source: Compiled by authors, using data from Asian Development Bank.
Note: All data is for calendar year and in some cases may not correspond to financial year.

the same magnitude with the rest of East Asia. This in turn suggests the growing importance of China as an import market for the rest of East Asia. Thus, if current growth trajectories persist, China may eventually act as an independent engine of growth for ASEAN in the long run on its own, or at least could provide a much needed cushion to smaller ASEAN economies against gyrations in the industrial country economic environment. More generally, with China's WTO accession there will be greater scope and demand for services by China, particularly with regard to distribution, professional, and infrastructural services (telecommunications and financial).

China will certainly continue to alter the division of labor in Southeast and East Asia. This is turn will involve some degree of economic dislocation as other countries adjust to these changing dynamics. This said, there is little basis for the high degree of export pessimism that has been voiced by a number of regional observers and some policy-makers. Such pessimism — "fallacy of composition" — has often been expressed in the past by some but has always proven to be largely unfounded. International trade is not a zero sum game and neither is it one that is static. By definition, one country — no matter how big — cannot have a comparative advantage in the production of all goods and services.

To be sure, with the major improvements in transportation, coordination, and communication technologies, globalization provides vastly increased opportunities for the fragmentation of previously integrated goods and activities into their constituent parts, components, and accessories (PCAs) which in turn may be spread across countries on the basis of comparative advantage. The importance of such "production sharing" is that it suggests that openness, by expanding opportunities for international specialization and trade, will be beneficial to all parties involved.[4] Thus, over time, free trade ought to be an unambiguously positive-sum game (i.e., all round wealth-creating outcome). This is of particular relevance to East Asia where machinery and electrical equipments constitute a high and growing proportion of intraregional trade.[5] Seen through the lens of production sharing, the cost effectiveness of China ought to benefit all countries that are part of the production network (this leads on to the issue of the Southeast Asia–China Free Trade Agreement which we will discuss later on). In particular, countries that are at the more advanced production stage than China — i.e., those that import intermediate inputs from China — will specifically benefit given the availability of lower cost intermediate products from China. This should help maintain profit margins of businesses that are being faced with an increasingly harsh economic environment.

---

[4] The issue of production sharing is explored in Chapter 12 in this Volume.
[5] Lemoine, F and D Ünal-Kesenci (2002). China in the international segmentation of production process. *Working Paper No. 2002-02*, CEPII.

There are well-founded concerns that small variations in costs could lead to large shifts in comparative advantage, thus necessitating large and sudden domestic adjustments. The eminent trade economist, Jagdish Bhagwati, refers to this phenomenon as "kaleidoscope" or "knife-edge" comparative advantage.[6] Countries need to be ever aware of these potential cost shifts and ensure constant industrial upgrading so as to remain important players in the larger regional production network. In other words, the continued opening of China may well contribute to a far more uncertain and competitive environment for ASEAN economies (especially as China's western regional developing and labour-intensive industries migrate to the inland regions). In relation to this, opportunities for lower income ASEAN members to upgrade to higher value-added stages of production may be harder to come by compared to the transition made by their higher income neighbors in earlier periods. However, offsetting these concerns is the significant potential upside gains noted previously.

In addition to production sharing which usually involves *vertical* specialization; openness to international trade allows countries to also specialize *horizontally* based on price/quality. Thus, even if a country's comparative advantage happens to coincide with China, it can still develop its own export market niche by specializing in differentiated products. However, a concern often voiced about China's ascendancy and price competitiveness is that "cheap Chinese imports" will keep the price pressures on imperfect substitutes down, i.e., other countries will import price deflation from China with consequent depressing effects on profit margins and factor returns, including wages. It is in this sense that ASEAN economies may have complementarities with China in production and export structures (i.e., vertical specialization) while other parts are simultaneously competitive (horizontal specialization).

These global competitive pressures emanating from China and the potential deflationary effects are of particular concern in the areas of textiles and clothing where China's WTO accession is expected to be a significant boon to Chinese exporters who are no longer limited by the quantitative restrictions under the Multifiber Arrangement (MFA). Quantitative analyses suggest that the eventual removal of these quotas will lead to a significant increase in China's exports in these areas at the expense of many ASEAN economies as well as other Asian countries more generally.[7] While the possibility of

---

[6] See discussion in Chapter 12.

[7] See Martin, W and E Ianchovichina (2001). Implications of China's accession to the World Trade Organisation for China and the WTO. *The World Economy*, 24, 1205–1219 and Francois, J and D Spinanger (2001). With rags to riches but then when? Paper presented at the *Fourth Annual Conference on Global Economic Analysis* (Purdue University, Indiana: 27–29 June). There are, however, some safeguard measures in place to phase in the transition and to minimize disruption.

horizontal specialization (i.e., trade in differentiated goods) suggests that the above costs are probably over-estimates, there are bound to be non-negligible price pressures and adjustment cost effects on other textile- and clothing-exporting countries.

That said, it is clear that China is not inhibiting ASEAN's exports. Table 4 actually shows that export growth of most ASEAN countries appear to be healthy. Notwithstanding the fact that none of them can or have ever matched China's explosive growth, their exports do not seem to have been hurt tremendously by the increased competition. ASEAN's exports did see a dip in 1998, but that was the result of the Asian crisis and not that of China.[8]

China's Impact on Southeast Asia's Investment Prospects

There have been growing fears that Southeast Asia is "losing out" in the intense competition for FDI inflows to China. To the extent that China's industrialization strategy, like that of Southeast Asia, is fueled largely by inflows of FDI, there will invariably be a degree of competition involved in terms of attracting FDI inflows.

But has the rise and opening up of China actually altered the flow of FDI to Asia? The commonly noted statistic is that in the early 1990s, three-fifths of FDI to Asia were channeled into the Southeast Asian countries and less than one-fifth to China. By 1999–2000, over two-fifths went to China (more than two-thirds went to Mainland China plus Hong Kong) while only about one-fifth found its way to Southeast Asia. The share of Southeast Asia to global FDI, which averaged about 6.7 percent during 1993–1996, registered a substantial decline since 1997, hovering at around 1.6 percent during 1999.

However, even at a superficial level one must doubt the importance of direct competition from China as it too suffered a marginal decline in the net FDI inflows in recent years, albeit less than Southeast Asia (the FDI decline to China reversed itself in 2001).[9] Indeed, the relatively sharp decline in Southeast Asia's FDI flows and its share of total FDI to East Asia was primarily due to Indonesia which was the only Southeast Asian country to experience an outright erosion in the cumulative stock of FDI in the

---

[8] According to one study, "countries specializing in the production and export of components, capital goods and raw materials feel positive effects from China's growth, while countries specializing in the production of consumer goods feel negative effects". See Eichengreen, B and H Tong (2006). How China is reorganizing the world economy. *Asian Economic Policy Review*, 1, 73–97.

[9] Wu, F, TS Pao, HS Yeo and KK Phua (2002). Foreign direct investments to China and Southeast Asia: Has ASEAN been losing out? *Economic Survey of Singapore*, Third Quarter, Singapore: Ministry of Trade and Industry.

Table 4. Total merchandise exports from ASEAN (US$ billions) (1990–2005).

	Brunei	Cambodia	Laos	Indonesia	Malaysia	Myanmar	Philippines	Singapore	Thailand	Vietnam	ASEAN	China
1990	2.2	0.0	0.1	25.7	29.4	0.4	8.2	52.8	23.1	2.5	144.4	62.8
1991	2.5	0.1	0.1	29.2	34.4	0.5	8.8	59.2	28.9	2.2	165.9	72.0
1992	3.9	0.2	0.1	34.0	40.7	0.7	9.8	63.5	32.5	2.9	188.3	85.6
1993	3.6	0.3	0.2	36.8	47.1	0.9	11.3	74.1	37.3	3.0	214.7	91.7
1994	3.3	0.2	0.3	40.1	58.8	0.9	13.4	96.9	46.1	4.1	264.1	120.9
1995	3.4	0.4	0.3	45.5	73.7	1.2	17.4	118.2	58.7	5.6	324.4	149.0
1996	3.7	0.3	0.3	49.9	78.2	1.2	20.6	125.2	56.5	7.5	343.3	151.2
1997	4.0	0.6	0.2	53.4	78.9	1.1	25.2	125.4	58.4	9.5	356.8	182.9
1998	2.0	0.9	0.4	48.9	73.5	1.1	29.5	109.9	55.4	9.3	330.9	183.7
1999	2.6	1.0	0.5	48.7	84.6	1.4	35.5	114.8	58.5	11.5	358.9	194.9
2000	3.2	1.1	0.4	62.1	98.2	2.0	38.2	138.0	69.0	14.5	426.6	249.2
2001	3.3	1.3	0.4	56.3	88.2	2.6	32.2	121.8	65.1	15.0	386.3	266.7
2002	3.4	1.8	0.4	57.2	93.4	2.8	35.2	125.2	68.9	16.7	404.9	325.7
2003	4.4	2.1	0.4	61.0	105.0	2.8	36.2	144.3	80.3	20.1	456.7	438.4
2004	4.5	2.6	0.5	71.6	126.5	3.2	39.7	179.7	96.2	25.8	550.3	593.4
2005	5.0	2.9	0.7	92.9	161.5	3.6	52.4	207.3	110.1	30.8	667.2	762.3

Source: Asian Development Bank.

Note: All data is for calendar year and in some cases may not correspond to financial year.

country since 1997, as there has been a sharp outflow of FDI between 1998 and 2000. Indonesia in turn has been hurt by domestic socio-political convulsions and investor uncertainty as opposed to competition from China *per se*.

More detailed analysis of the sources of FDI into Southeast Asia and China is also suggestive of limited direct "competition" between the two. For instance, the bulk of FDI to the former has been from Japan and the United States in particular. Japan has hitherto been a rather reluctant investor to China. The declines in FDI flows to Southeast Asia have in large part been due to lower investment levels from Japan. The extent of decline in Japanese FDI can be seen from the fact that while it has consistently been the single largest investor in Southeast Asia since the late 1980s, it did not even figure in the top ten investors in 2000. In contrast, the bulk of investments to China has been from overseas Chinese in Hong Kong and Taiwan.

Insofar as the accession of China to the rules-based WTO system as well as the removal of uncertainty regarding China's Most Favored Nation (MFN) treatment and granting of permanent normal trade relations (PNTR) has made it an even more attractive host for FDI, there may well be (further) diversion of FDI from ASEAN. As trade barriers in China continue to decline and infrastructural and communications facilities improve further, FDI may move from some Southeast Asian countries to China, and the Southeast Asian markets will be served from China in the presence of competitive pressures and squeezing of profit margins.

Probably of most concern to the lower- and middle-income Southeast Asian countries (such as Indonesia, Thailand, Philippines, and Indonesia) is the fact that Japanese investors, who hitherto have been reluctant investors in China, have begun to make plans to invest in China. Whether Japanese investments into China involve relocation from Japan or from other Southeast Asian countries remain to be seen. A survey of Japanese companies by the Japanese External Trade Organisation (JETRO) in October 2001 suggests that much of that of those planning to relocate operation to China, the distribution will be from Japan (67.5 percent) and only about 7–8 percent from Southeast Asia.[10]

All of this said, it is likely that the competition dimension can and has been rather overblown. There are a number of reasons to remain positive about ASEAN's FDI potential.

First, some multinational enterprises (MNEs), concerned about what might be "excessive" exposure to China, are considering setting up factories in

---

[10] McKibbin, W and WT Woo (2002). The consequences of China's WTO accession on its neighbours. mimeo (October).

some other Southeast Asian countries as a form of "risk hedging". The need for such risk diversification to ensure minimal disruption to global supply chains has been made especially apparent in recent times with the outbreak of the SARS crisis which has impacted China and Greater China far more than Southeast Asia. In fact an article in *The Economist* titled "The Problem with Made in China" states that "China is choking on its success at attracting the world's factories. That has handed its Asian neighbors a big opportunity".[11] It goes on to say that three companies, which have huge manufacturing facilities in China, have decided to invest in various ASEAN economies as "they chose to avoid China's thundering economy in order to put their factories elsewhere in Asia. These companies are not alone. In the calculus of costs, risks, customers and logistics that goes into building global operations, an increasing number of firms are coming to the conclusion that China is not necessarily the best place to make things".

Second, China's opening and growth China businesses may lead to Chinese investments in Southeast Asia and other countries. There is growing anecdotal evidence of this. For instance, CNOOC, which is China's state-owned offshore oil company, has acquired assets in a major Indonesian oil company. There is also significant interest by Chinese firms in infrastructural projects in Indonesia and other less-developed ASEAN members.

Third, the lowering of import barriers (both actual trade barriers as well as "behind the border" ones) in China may reduce the incentive to establish tariff-jumping FDI in China as the Chinese market may, in some instances, be well served via exports. This appears to be the case in some areas such as automobiles and petrochemicals which have hitherto been heavily protected in China.

Academic studies seem to suggest that China is not crowding out FDI investment to Southeast Asian countries. Using data between 1986 and 2001, Zhou and Lall find that there is no competition whatsoever between China and Southeast Asia for FDI.[12] As they note:

"While fears of a Chinese 'threat' to FDI inflows are understandable, it is not clear that they are justified. The supply of FDI to the region is not strictly limited. Whether or not countries compete for FDI depends on the nature of the investment: a large portion of FDI flows into activities that do not actually compete with each other. There may still be FDI substitution by China, but it should be considered in an analytical framework that takes the other determinants of FDI location into account."

---

[11] *The Economist* (2007). The problem with made in China, 11 January.
[12] Zhou, Y and S Lall (2005). The impact of China's FDI surge on FDI in South-East Asia: Panel data analysis for 1986–2001. *Transnational Corporations*, 14, 46–67.

In fact, Fung *et al.*[13] find that "in terms of the levels of foreign direct investment flows, the China Effect is on balance positive for the East and Southeast Asian economies". Table 5 does not show any clear indication that China has been sucking away FDI from ASEAN countries.

While there is little doubt that in the long run ASEAN will benefit from a prosperous and economically strong and stable large neighbor, the issues tend to be more complex in the short and medium terms. Inevitably, like all other neighbors, China can be expected to be both a formidable economic competitor as well as a reliable partner. China's WTO accession has not been a sudden, one-off event. Rather, it is part of an ongoing process that was initiated over two decades back. Southeast Asian countries have hitherto been able to adjust to China's initial opening up between 1990 and 1997 fairly successfully. However, the crisis of confidence following the regional crisis of 1997–1998, the loss of forward momentum with regard to regional integration among ASEAN members, and the feeling of vulnerability to an increasingly volatile global economy are some of the reasons for heightened concerns about the economic ascendancy of China.

Conclusion: The ASEAN–China Free Trade Agreement (ACFTA)

It is a fact that in an increasingly globalized world decisions about production, investment and trade are closely interlinked and often cannot be made independently of one another. From Southeast Asia's perspective, this implies the need for more aggressive and urgent steps to deepen regional economic integration and reduce the extent of fragmentation that currently exists among Southeast Asian markets.

In relation to this, special mention should be made of the proposed ASEAN–China Free Trade Area (ACFTA) first mooted by Chinese Premier Zhu Rongji during the ASEAN–China Summit in November 2001. After a series of negotiations, the so-called ASEAN–China Closer Economic Partnership Framework Agreement was given concrete shape during the ASEAN Summit in Cambodia in November 2002 and was formally agreed to by 2004.[14] A key feature of the ACFTA agreement is the "early harvest" clause which commits ASEAN and China to reduce their tariffs for certain products within 3 years,

---

[13] See Chantasasawat, B, KC Fung and H Iizaka (2005). The giant sucking sound: Is China diverting foreign direct investments from other Asian economies? UCSC: Department of Economics, *Working Paper 594*, 30 November. http://repositories.cdlib.org/ucscecon/594.

[14] For background of the origins and motivations for the ACFTA, see Lijun, S (2003). China–ASEAN Free Trade Area: Origins, developments and strategic motivations. *Working Paper*, Institute of Southeast Asian Studies (ISEAS).

Table 5. Net FDI inflows (US$ billions) (1994–2005).

	Brunei	Cambodia	Indonesia	Laos	Malaysia	Myanmar	Philippines	Singapore	Thailand	Vietnam	ASEAN	China
1994	0.67	0.07	2.11	0.06	4.34	0.13	1.59	3.97	1.37	0.00	14.31	33.79
1995	-0.63	0.15	4.35	0.10	4.18	0.28	1.48	4.75	2.07	0.00	16.71	35.85
1996	0.12	0.29	6.19	0.16	5.08	0.31	1.52	1.73	2.34	2.40	20.14	40.18
1997	0.13	0.20	4.68	0.00	5.14	0.39	1.22	2.85	3.90	2.22	20.72	44.24
1998	N.A.	0.24	-0.24	0.00	2.16	0.32	2.29	5.15	7.32	1.67	18.91	43.75
1999	N.A.	0.23	-1.87	0.00	3.90	0.26	1.73	8.58	6.10	1.41	20.33	38.75
2000	N.A.	0.15	-4.55	0.03	3.79	0.26	1.35	10.57	3.37	1.30	16.26	38.40
2001	0.06	0.15	-2.98	0.02	0.55	0.21	0.99	-4.52	3.89	1.30	-0.32	44.24
2002	0.23	0.15	0.15	0.03	3.20	0.15	1.79	5.05	0.95	1.40	13.09	49.31
2003	0.12	0.08	-0.60	0.02	2.47	0.25	0.35	7.23	1.95	1.45	13.33	53.51
2004	0.07	0.13	1.02	0.02	4.62	0.21	0.47	6.31	1.41	1.61	15.88	54.94
2005	0.29	0.38	6.11	0.03	3.96	0.07	1.13	20.08	4.01	2.02	38.08	53.00

Source: Asian Development Bank and World Bank.

as a reflection of their commitment to tariff reduction. These early harvest products are mainly agricultural products that represent about 10 percent of all tariff lines in the Harmonized System (HS) of tariff classification.[15]

The timetable for the formation of the ACFTA in goods for the older ASEAN members (Indonesia, Malaysia, Singapore, Thailand, and Brunei) is 2010, and that for the others (i.e., Cambodia, Myanmar, Laos, and Vietnam — so-called CMLV countries) is 2015. In other words, newer members have been offered more time to adjust to the requirements of the ACFTA. The framework agreement identified five priority areas for economic cooperation apart from trade liberalization and facilitation measures. These are agriculture, human resource development (HRD), information and communication technology (ICT), investment, and the Mekong River basin development. It has agreed to implement capacity building programs and provide technical assistance for the CMLV members to help catch up with the more advanced ASEAN members and increase their trade and investment cooperation with China.

While the ACFTA ought to speed up the growing mutual interdependence between Southeast Asia and China, its impact on individual Southeast Asian economies is likely to be felt differentially, depending upon the extent to which its economic structure and composition of trade complements or competes with that of China. Differential potential effects of the ACFTA may well act as a roadblock preventing its full implementation.[16]

Nonetheless, an immediate positive side effect of the ACFTA proposal is that it appears to have provided an impetus for Southeast Asian countries to hasten the process of intra-ASEAN integration. It has had further domino effects, with the other major economic powers in Asia, viz. Japan, India, and Korea also seeking out trade pacts with ASEAN. All of these in turn have offered Southeast Asia the potential to act as a hub with the consequent benefits of being one. ASEAN needs to encourage and act on such courtships in parallel with the implementation of the ACFTA for their own sake, and also to act as buffers against China's dominance in the Southeast Asian region.

At the same time, it is imperative that Southeast Asia maintain its cohesion and reinvigorate efforts to foster more intensive intra-ASEAN economic integration. Failure to do so could lead to a loss of hub status as the larger economic powers may come to view ASEAN as a body that is disjointed and uncoordinated. A related concern for ASEAN is how to manage the tensions within the heterogeneous alliance given the existence of a two-tier ASEAN

---

[15] The early harvest products belong to the following categories: Live animals, meat and edible meat offal, fish, dairy produce, other animal products, live trees, edible vegetables, and edible fruits and nuts.

[16] For a fuller discussion of the implications of the ACFTA, see Tongzon, JL (2005). ASEAN–China Free Trade Area: A bane or boon for ASEAN countries? *The World Economy*, 28, 191–210.

(older six ASEAN members versus the CMLV economies).[17] There are no easy answers to this hard question, but it is one that the alliance needs to give more serious thought to if it is to remain cohesive and effective and continue to be seen as such by the rest of the world.[18]

In the final analysis, the greatest challenge faced by Southeast Asia is not the economic ascendancy of China or anything external. As the famous cartoonist Walt Kelly once said, *"We have met the enemy and it is within us"*. Adjustment and flexibility are crucial. Countries that remain alert to the changing dynamics of comparative advantage and are able to position themselves to respond effectively to them, will benefit. On the other hand, countries that are bogged down by domestic socio-political problems and poor leadership could find the varying landscape in Asia especially painful to adjust to in the short- and medium-terms. This lesson rings equally true for ASEAN's neighbor, India as it continues along the path of economic reforms.

---

[17] In fact, one could probably further subdivide the six ASEAN members into two subtiers — for instance, Singapore, Malaysia, and Thailand in the first tier and Indonesia, the Philippines, and possibly Brunei in the next tier. The same concerns with regard to large and growing income gaps between various regions plague China as well.

[18] Conversely, in view of the heterogeneity of ASEAN in terms of development and economic structures, it makes sound sense for non-ASEAN countries like China, India, and Korea to engage strategically with ASEAN as a whole while simultaneously doing so with individual interested ASEAN members on a bilateral basis (assuming that these countries have sufficient negotiating capacities to do so).

Section 4

Economic Regionalism in Asia

Chapter 16

Embracing One's Neighbor: Redefining the Importance of India to ASEAN*

Introduction

"India has the potential to show the fastest growth over the next 30 and 50 years. Growth could be higher than 5 percent over the next 30 years and close to 5 percent as late as 2050 if development proceeds successfully". The above is an excerpt from the famous "BRICs" report from the investment bank Goldman Sachs in 2003, where BRICs refers to Brazil, Russia, India, and China.[1] The report then went on to say "Overall, growth for the BRICs is likely to slow significantly over this time frame. By 2050, only India on our projections would be recording growth rates significantly above 3 percent". This report has been a watershed as far as the world's perception of India is concerned.

To say India has had an image problem in the past is a bit of an understatement. While India has been among the top 10 biggest economies in the world, it was never perceived to be an energetic economy; an economy that just preferred to trudge along especially when compared to the "Tiger" economies in East Asia. India had a rate of growth that was sub-par and it was disparagingly referred to as the "Hindu rate of growth", a play of words comed by economist Raj Krishna on "Secular rate of growth" which means an increasing growth rate. The term also disparagingly refers to the majority Hindu population who are supposedly context with their "lot in life."

It does not help that the first thing that anybody flying into Mumbai, the financial capital of India, sees is "Dharavi", the largest slum in Asia. Then the drive into the city is marked by potholed roads, beggars and the poverty that exists side by side with gleaming buildings. Compare this to Shanghai where the roads are wide and superb, the buildings gleaming and virtually no poverty visible. That is not to say that poverty does not exist in China; it certainly does,

* This chapter draws on Rajan, RS and S Rongala. Warmly welcome India into the east Asian summit (11 May 2005), *Business Times* (Singapore) and Rajan, RS. Will Asia come together? (1 February 2005) *Business Times*.
[1] Wilson, P and R Purushothaman (2003). Dreaming with BRICs: The path to 2050. *Global Economics Paper No. 99*, Goldman Sachs (October).

but is better concealed than in India. India is said to suffer from what is called the "skyscraper effect" where visitors to China see the huge and very fancy sky-scrapers compared to almost none in Mumbai and based on that decide that China is a much better place to do business compared to "backward" India.

On the back of solid economic performance, the image that the outside world has of India has been changing quite dramatically for the better since the early 2000s. The solid performance in turn has only been possible because of the economic reforms instituted in 1991; a set of reforms that have crossed the point of no return.[2] This economic performance has also generated a buzz among investors and investment banks alike about the potential that India offers. Suddenly words like "favorable demographics" and "trillion dollar economy" have sprung into many a lexicon. The former is an obvious reference to the huge percentage of the Indian population that is below 25 years and offers a sort of ready-made market for many a product of the potential investors, while the latter is because India became a trillion dollar economy in FY07.

India has rapidly emerged as a leading provider of offshore services. India is slowly, but most definitely, becoming a key component of the regional value-added chain.[3] With India's favorable demographics (a rising proportion of the population will be in the working age group over the next few decades), and latent potential, if India continues on its path of economic reforms, tack-les governance issues, and alleviates some of the supply-side constraints and microeconomic distortions, it promises to continue to be the best — or at least second best — performing major economy over the medium and longer-terms. Stephen Roach from Morgan Stanley has observed:

> "I am returning from India with great enthusiasm. Many serious problems remain — especially the ravages of poverty. But in the past couple of years, India has faced many of its macro imperatives head-on — especially low saving, inadequate infrastructure, and lagging foreign direct investment. It is now making solid progress on two of those counts — saving and FDI — and infrastructure seems set to follow. These are the breakthroughs that can unshackle India's greatest strengths — a high-quality stock of human capi-tal and the magic of its entrepreneurial spirit. As a result, there is now good reason to believe that the macro and micro are coming together in the world's second most populous nation. India is now on the move and could well be one of the world's most exceptional economic development stories over the next 3–5 years."[4]

---

[2] For instance, see Panagariya, A (2005). The triumph of India's market reforms: The record of the 1980s and 1990s. *Policy Analysis*, November 7, CATO.

[3] See Chapter 13 in this Volume.

[4] See Roach, S (2007). India on the Move, *Global Economic Forum*, 05 February 2007. http://www.morganstanley.com/views/gef/archive/2007/20070205-Mon.html

India–ASEAN Relationship

India's economic awakening has also had a dramatic effect on India's links with its Southeast Asian neighbors. India and ASEAN have had a rather tortuous relationship. It has been a very complex relationship fraught with misunderstandings and ill-will. Jawaharlal Nehru, the first prime minister of India, distrusted many of the Southeast Asian countries because during his lifetime, most of them were still ruled by colonial powers.

However, the deeper fissure occurred during the 1960s. Indonesia, Malaysia, Philippines, Singapore, and Thailand, the founding members of ASEAN invited India to be a founding member of ASEAN and India declined. There were many reasons for rejecting this offer, but one of the most important was that India was looking more to becoming an autarkic economy rather than being dependent on others, much less having a formal economic relationship with other countries. The other important reason was that India was considering creating a socialistic type of economy, while the Southeast Asian countries were obviously leaning towards more free-market oriented policies. Obviously, the ASEAN countries viewed this as a snub and India and ASEAN became estranged in the 1970s and 1980s. Ideological differences and the divisions brought about by the cold war as well as differing growth strategies (India's import substitution and ASEAN's export orientation) kept these two regions apart despite their geographically proximity and cultural affinity. There were many instances when ASEAN leaders took jabs at India making remarks about its lethargy, red tape and all but declaring it a failure.

The relationship started changing in 1991 and is no coincidence that it was the same time that India started liberalizing her economy. After decades of neglect, India has shown a strong desire to integrate and interact more intensively with ASEAN and the larger East Asia since the early 1990s. To this end, former Prime Minister, P.V. Narasimha Rao, initiated the so-called "Look East" policy in 1991, an initiative that was pursued energetically by subsequent governments regardless of their political affiliations.

However, India's overtures were initially spurned by some ASEAN members who tended to view India with some hostility and even a degree of scorn and were reluctant to engage India. However, ASEAN has started to adjust its views in light of India's economic emergence on the world stage. India, on the strength of its economic growth as well as its economic potential, is now being accepted as a partner with whom business can be conducted with. ASEAN has only recently started to adjust its views in light of India's economic emergence on the world stage.

Sub-regional cooperation between India and some of the ASEAN members such as Vietnam, Thailand, Myanmar, and Laos has also accelerated.

Singapore's former Prime Minister, Goh Chok Tong, has been an important proponent of an Asian Economic Community linking South Asia, North and Southeast Asia. As he noted:

> "(T)he vision that we have..(is)..to bring India closer to Southeast Asia and to East Asia so that, together, we can realise, over the longer term, the Asian economic community — small 'e' small 'c'. Not with rules and regulations like the European Union, but a more integrated Asia. I see China becoming a very powerful economy. Of course, Japan will remain developed. Korea, Singapore, Thailand will also become developed economies, together with Malaysia. East Asia will therefore comprise developed countries and middle-income countries. It's my hope that India can join East Asia as a middle-income country."[5]

The India Brand Equity Foundation (IBEF) makes another case as to why ASEAN should interact more intensively with India:

> "One by one, ASEAN nations are increasingly realizing the merits of building bridges with Asia's second economic giant, India in order to reduce Chinese hegemony in the region. China's low-cost exports are hitting ASEAN's traditional export markets — and, increasingly, the ASEAN market themselves. For ASEAN countries, competition is particularly acute in garments and textiles, machinery and electrical appliances and other manufactured goods and, in some cases, footwear. Foreign direct investments are also flooding into China, while the flow into ASEAN has slowed markedly. To counter this problem, ASEAN nations believe that India can act as a suitable business buffer in the region, and create more trade and investment leverage."[6]

Since 1992, there have been a slew of agreements between ASEAN and India.

- In 1992, India became a "sectoral dialogue partner" with ASEAN in terms of the trade, tourism, and science and technology sectors.
- India was invited by ASEAN to become a full dialogue partner in 1995 during the 5th ASEAN summit in Bangkok.
- India was invited in 1996 to become a member of the ASEAN Regional Forum (ARF).
- Agreed to ASEAN on enhancing close economic cooperation and to work toward India — ASEAN Regional Trade and Investment Area (RTIA) as a long-term objective.
- India signed a free trade agreement (FTA) with Thailand in 2003 and under the terms of the agreement, 84 items could be imported from

---

[5] Quoted in Bansal, R (2004). The Monday interview: Goh Chok Tong (12 July 2004), *Financial Express*.
[6] India Brand Equity Foundation (2004). *Look East, Look West: A Bridge Across Asia*. http://www.ibef.org/artdisplay.aspx?cat_id=402&art_id=4291

Thailand at 50 percent of the duty prevailing in India. This agreement was in fact exploited by a number of companies which routed their products to India via Thailand and took advantage of the lower custom duties. Table 1 shows Thailand's exports to India increased from $380 million in 2003 to $1.2 billion 2006.

- In 2003, India signed a Comprehensive Economic Cooperation Agreement with Singapore with the objective to "to strengthen and enhance the economic, trade and investment cooperation".[7]
- Probably the most important agreement that was signed between India and ASEAN has been the "Framework Agreement of Comprehensive Economic Cooperation" that was signed in Bali in 2003.

The objectives of the agreement, as per the framework,[8] are:

- Strengthen and enhance economic, trade, and investment cooperation between the parties.
- Progressively liberalize and promote trade in goods and services as well as create a transparent, liberal, and facilitative investment regime.
- Explore new areas and develop appropriate measures for closer economic cooperation between the parties.
- Facilitate the more effective economic integration of the new ASEAN Member States and bridge the development gap among the Parties.

The framework document says: "The Parties agree to enter into negotiations in order to establish an India–ASEAN regional trade and investment area (RTIA), which includes a free trade area (FTA) in goods, services and investment, and to strengthen and enhance economic cooperation." Some of the measures that it proposes are:

- Progressive elimination of tariffs and non-tariff barriers in substantially all trade in goods.
- Progressive liberalization of trade in services with substantial sectoral coverage.
- Establishment of a liberal and competitive investment regime that facilitates and promotes investment within the India–ASEAN RTIA.

Tables 1 and 2 show the level of growth of trade between India and ASEAN countries and what it shows is the building of a considerable relationship between India and ASEAN countries. The growth in both merchandise

---

[7] The full agreement is available at http://commerce.nic.in/ceca/toc.htm
[8] The full framework agreement is available at http://www.aseansec.org/15278.htm

Table 1. Imports to India from select ASEAN countries (US$ millions) (1992–2006).

	Brunei	Indonesia	Malaysia	Philippines	Singapore	Thailand	Vietnam	Total	% of Indian imports
1992	0.11	65.86	228.19	31.54	307.65	48.6	34.45	716.4	3.7
1993	0	56.41	381.7	9.2	594.57	54.85	57.01	1,153.74	5.6
1994	0	119.52	249.16	5.94	626.11	57.15	43.79	1,101.67	4.7
1995	0.12	322.31	490.21	11.78	899.95	171.65	44.08	1,940.1	6.8
1996	0.04	461.83	904.08	21.5	1,115.15	169.95	15.51	2,688.06	7.3
1997	0.03	599.16	1,042.24	16.46	1,064.21	197.36	1.7	2,921.16	7.5
1998	0.02	732.51	1,180.32	27.77	1,199.33	233.6	8.74	3,382.29	8.1
1999	0.05	828.92	1,610.38	37.25	1,383.85	273.05	9.14	4,142.64	9.8
2000	0.11	959.96	2,026.49	56.31	1,536.28	328.17	11.54	4,918.86	9.9
2001	0.15	904.42	1,151.6	62.97	1,435.68	314.97	12.35	3,882.14	7.8
2002	0.36	1,039.91	1,136.92	95.13	1,307.98	424.35	18.97	4,023.62	7.8
2003	0.32	1,383.59	1,468.31	124.01	1,437.64	379.75	29.24	4,822.86	7.8
2004	0.34	2,123.52	2,047.96	122.19	2,086.8	609.47	38.24	7,028.52	9.0
2005	0.54	2,616.66	2,298.06	187.32	2,650.3	865.52	86.46	8,704.86	7.8
2006	0.88	2,933.08	2,388.23	201.05	3,229.83	1,201.57	130.45	10,085.09	7.1

Source: Centre for Monitoring the Indian Economy (CMIE).

Table 2.   Exports from India to select ASEAN countries (US$ millions) (1992–2006).

	Brunei	Indonesia	Malaysia	Philippines	Singapore	Thailand	Vietnam	Total	% of Indian exports
1992	0.7	149.54	203.87	64.73	391.11	200.09	13.01	1,023.05	5.7
1993	0.46	130.27	178.57	51.41	553.61	238.58	16.33	1,169.23	6.7
1994	0.43	234.68	247.03	58.18	751.16	356.09	27.98	1,675.55	7.5
1995	2.4	277.77	286.57	99.45	770.5	406.7	58.59	1,901.98	7.2
1996	7.26	663.4	393.75	144.45	902.98	473.63	124.55	2,710.02	8.5
1997	6.04	592.34	531.58	183.8	978.29	447.45	118.17	2,857.67	8.5
1998	2.26	437.78	490.49	239.01	780.65	344.9	126.76	2,421.85	6.9
1999	3.26	185.23	321.63	118.71	517.33	320.92	125.4	1,592.48	4.8
2000	1.3	325.1	447.23	143.68	669.81	449.92	154.55	2,191.59	6.0
2001	3.32	394.87	601.1	201.63	862.41	528.69	224.96	2,816.98	6.4
2002	2.87	535.3	776	248.53	975.21	635.02	218.82	3,391.75	7.7
2003	4.46	827.69	750.85	472.93	1,424.38	712.6	338.06	4,530.97	8.6
2004	4.59	1,127.98	893.38	321.75	2,126.29	832.26	410.72	5,716.97	9.0
2005	5.06	1,332.05	1,083.61	412.06	3,998.97	901.02	555.73	8,288.5	9.9
2006	42.89	1,370.32	1,151.4	489.89	5,569.02	1,062.1	687.11	10,372.73	10.1

Source: Centre for Monitoring the Indian Economy (CMIE).

imports from and merchandise exports to the main ASEAN countries has been fairly phenomenal. Table 1 shows the imports from the main ASEAN countries to India. These exports have grown from a mere $716 million in 1992 to an amazingly large $10.08 billion in 2006. Exports from India shows the same story; growing from US$1.02 billion in 1992 to $10.37 billion in 2006. Exports from India to the main ASEAN countries accounted for 10 percent of total Indian merchandise exports. India is becoming increasingly linked to ASEAN's production networks especially in the more knowledge services parts of the value-added chain. Other areas of economic cooperation in science and technology, information technology (IT), human resource development (HRD), and transport and infrastructure have also intensified. While cross-border linkages in these areas are not always easy to quantify, they are no less important than the more quantifiable aspects of economic interactions.[9]

Conclusion

While "Asian economic regionalism" has been a topic of long-standing debate in academic and policy arenas, there has been a particular heightening of interest in the subject over the last few years. This is due to a number of reasons. The first is the contagious effects of the Asian economic crisis of 1997–1998, along with the perceived inadequate responses to the crisis by multilateral agencies and extra-regional economic powers like the United States and the European Union. The second is some notable external developments in regionalism, including hesitant moves to create a Free Trade Area of the Americas (FTAA), and, more importantly, the enlargement of the European Union and the successful launch of the euro. The third is the rapid and sustained growth in, and consequent economic emergence of, China and India, and the realization that these two emerging Asian giants have been altering the dynamics of the global economy and will continue to do so for some time to come.[10] The broadening and deepening of bilateral economic and strategic links between China and India that has been taking place in the last few years has the potential to dramatically alter the Asian landscape both economically and strategically over the medium and longer-terms. Yet, this growth story in bilateral linkages has gone virtually unnoticed in other parts of Asia, including Southeast Asia.

---

[9] See Sen, R, MG Asher and RS Rajan (2004). ASEAN–India economic relations: Current status and future prospects. *Economic and Political Weekly*, 3296–3307.

[10] For instance, see Wilson and Purushothaman, *op. cit.*

While everyone would recognize the infeasibility of including all the 40-plus "Asian" members of the Asian Development Bank (ADB) or the United Nations Economic and Social Commission for Asia and the Pacific (UN-Escap), even something narrower like the 22-member Asian Cooperation Dialogue (ACD) Forum inspired by the former Thai prime minister, Thaksin Shinawatra, may be too broad. As has been made apparent by the Asia Pacific Economic Cooperation (APEC) Forum, an overly broad-based membership will make any sort of Asian economic alliance far too unwieldy and ineffective, as well as being susceptible to the "convoy problem" in which progress of the economic alliance is limited by the least willing member.

ASEAN has outlined three criteria as necessary conditions for attaining membership to the newly created East Asian Summit (EAS). First, the candidate country must have substantive relations with ASEAN. Second, it must be a full dialogue partner with ASEAN. Third, it must be a signatory to ASEAN's Treaty of Amity and Cooperation (TAC). In addition to the three North Asian countries, China, Japan, and Korea (which together with ASEAN constitute the ASEAN Plus Three or APT framework), India too was invited to the inaugural EAS held in Kuala Lumpur in December 2005, as were New Zealand and Australia.

Going forward it is important to keep in mind that attempts to exclude important Asian players in any alliance could lead the spurned parties to take defensive or reactionary strategies whereby they attempt to create their own intra- or extra-regional groups. This in turn could spawn a number of cross-memberships between alliances, giving rise to a highly complex, and rather untidy, patchwork quilt of ineffectual and competing alliances in Asia.[11] The inability to develop a cohesive Pan-Asian alliance will always limit the potential influence Asia might have in global affairs — compared to Europe, for instance — despite the shifting of economic gravity to the region. Europe has been able to shed the Cold War-induced estrangements, tensions and biases, and is consciously building a "New Europe" by expanding membership eastwards. Can Asia similarly rise to the challenge and look forward with foresight and optimism rather than be held hostage to the past? The need of the hour in Asia is credible and visionary statesmanship to drive the process. As Asher and Sen (2005) write:

"The time has come for Asia to put behind the cold war mindset and its institutions. It is essential that all major Asian economies are represented in the

---

[11] For instance, see Rajan, RS (2005). Asian economic cooperation and integration: Sequencing of financial, trade and monetary regionalism. In *Asian Economic Cooperation and Integration: Progress, Prospects and Challenges*, Manila: ADB, pp. 77–92.

post-cold war New Asia. As observed by India's Prime Minister Dr. Manmohan Singh, bringing together all major Asian countries in Asian Economic community would constitute an 'Arc of Advantage, across which there would be large scale movement of goods, services, people, capital, ideas and creativity'."[12]

[12] Asher, MG and R Sen (2005). India–East Asia integration: A win–win for asia, *Discussion Paper No. 91/2005*, RIS, Delhi.

Chapter 17

Going It Alone: Singapore's Trade Strategy*

(With Rahul Sen)

Introduction

While Singapore recovered smartly from the 1998 East Asian financial crisis, its growth prospects were adversely affected because of the downturn in the global electronics cycle as well as the general deterioration in the external environment (particularly the sharp slowdown in the United States in the early 2000s and recession in Japan). Given the country's heavy dependence on international trade, the Singapore economy suffered a fairly acute economic contraction in 2001; the worst in 30 years. Its impact on rising rates of redundancies, bankruptcies, financial and asset markets, consumer and business sentiment, and the like, were quite devastating.[1]

It is against this rather bleak background that Singapore adopted its twin strategy of going it alone and increasing integration with Asia's emerging giants such as China and India. It attempted to aggressively source preferential trade accords ("free trade agreements" or FTAs in common parlance) with a number of countries in Asia and elsewhere. Singapore established its first bilateral trade agreement with New Zealand in 2001 (termed the Agreement between New Zealand and Singapore on a Closer Economic Partnership or ANZSEP). Since then it has negotiated similar bilateral trade and economic cooperation pacts with Japan, United States, Australia, European Free Trade Association or EFTA (which consists of Iceland, Liechtenstein, Norway, and Switzerland), Australia, Hashemite Kingdom of Jordan, India, Korea, Panama, and also a plurilateral agreement termed as the Trans-Pacific Strategic Economic Partnership (involving New Zealand, Chile, and Brunei). The city-state is in

---

* This chapter draws on Rajan, RS and R Sen (2005). Dancing with the dragon and the elephant: Singapore's trade integration with Asian giants China and India gathers pace. *Business Times* (Singapore), August.
[1] See Rajan, RS (2003). Introduction and overview: Sustaining competitiveness in the new global economy. In *Sustaining Competitiveness in the New Global Economy: A Case Study of Singapore*, RS Rajan (ed.), Cheltenham: Edward Elgar.

the process of negotiating bilateral pacts with Canada, Mexico, China, Pakistan, Peru, Ukraine, and the Gulf Cooperation Council (GCC). Besides this, Singapore is involved in ASEAN-wide regional negotiations with China, Korea, Japan, India, Australia, and New Zealand, with a goods trade pact being already in force between ASEAN–China and ASEAN–Korea.

That said, preferential trade agreements are not an entirely new component of Singapore's commercial trade strategy which in turn is the cornerstone of the city-state's larger international economic policy. While being among the most ardent of supporters of the global trading system, Singapore has actively pursued a second track to liberalization via the regional route in the 1980s and 1990s. Regionalism has hitherto involved both the Southeast Asian region via the 10-member ASEAN (Association of Southeast Asian Nations) grouping and the larger Asia and Pacific region via the 21-member APEC (Asia Pacific Economic Cooperation) grouping. However, the crisis and structural changes within ASEAN appear to have held up the pace if not commitment by some of the ASEAN members to trade liberalization and seem to have sapped the organization's collective economic strength, while APEC has become unwieldy and appears ill-equipped to handle substantive trade and investment liberalization issues effectively. Accordingly, Singapore policy-makers have underscored the need to explore alternative liberalization paths. Sourcing of trade pacts on a bilateral basis — bilateralism for short — has become an integral part of Singapore's new commercial trade strategy.[2]

A Going-It-Alone Trading Strategy for Singapore

Singapore's choice of partners as part of its trade strategy of bilateralism may be broadly divided into two groups. The first group, which includes the United States and Japan, are major established trading partners, constituting some one-third of the city-state's total merchandise trade. These economic giants are also major investors in the city-state as they are in Southeast Asia at large. Bilateral trade accords with these two economies are best seen as a formalization of the *de facto* extensive and deep linkages that already exist. Entering into broad-ranging trade agreements with them is not only a means by which Singapore might gain greater market access (with Japan in particular) but is also a way of avoiding the possible imposition of protectionist measures in the future (with regard to the United States in particular), as well

---

[2] For a detailed discussion of Singapore's trade policy, see Rajan, RS and R Sen (2002). Singapore's new commercial trade strategy: Examining the pros and cons of bilateralism. In *Singapore Perspectives 2002*, Chang, LL (ed.), Singapore: Times Academic Press.

as managing future trade tensions, including establishing orderly dispute settlement mechanisms. Being among the first few countries to establish trade accords with these two and other economically significant economies also ensures that Singapore is not discriminated *ex post* in the event that its "trade competitors" form such pacts with third countries.

There are further reasons why Singapore's bilateral trade initiatives with the United States and Japan are especially noteworthy. While the United States has signed a series of bilateral agreements with Canada, Israel, Mexico and Jordan, the Singapore–United States trade pact is the first of its kind that the United States has signed with an Asian economy. The Singapore–Japan trade pact, which was recently reviewed and upgraded to include new provisions, is interpreted by some as an important signal of Japan's weakening adherence to nondiscriminatory multilateralism, not unlike the shift in the trade policy stance by the United States in the 1980s which led to the global proliferation of regional trade agreements. The consequence of Japan's shift from a sole emphasis on the multilateral trading route ought not to be understated. Japan has hitherto been among the staunchest amongst multilateral countries and has long resisted alternative routes to trade liberalization. In addition, rightly or wrongly, the Singapore–Japan trade accord was viewed as a precursor to the formation of an East Asia-wide FTA between economies in Southeast Asia plus Japan, Korea, and China (ASEAN plus Three or APT), and possibly extended to India, Australia, and New Zealand.[3]

The second group of countries with which Singapore formalized trade accords, including Australia, New Zealand, Panama, Jordan, India, Korea, and the European Free Trade Association (EFTA) countries (Iceland, Liechtenstein, Norway and Switzerland), individually do not account for more than 3 percent of either Singapore's total exports, domestic exports, or total imports. Presumably the aim here is to seek out new markets in view of the seeming loss of growth momentum in Singapore's immediate neighbors. Indeed, concerns have sometimes been expressed that Southeast Asia has lost the dynamism and drive toward trade and investment liberalization and integration (which entails much more than intra-regional tariff elimination) that it had pre-crisis, and is seen by extra-regional foreign investors as the "less attractive cousin" of China and India.[4] Singapore policy-makers were therefore keen to ensure that international investors do not perceive it as being in the same boat as the rest of the region, i.e., Singapore remains on the radar screen of world investors even if Southeast Asia as a whole may not be. Conversely, it is plausible that Singapore could act as the "flag-bearer" for the region in that its

---

[3] ASEAN plus the six countries form the East Asia Summit (EAS) which is discussed in Chapter 18 of this Volume. Japan has recently floated a new regional trade and economic cooperation initiative named Comprehensive Economic Partnership in East Asia that includes all the 16 EAS members.
[4] See Chapter 15 of this Volume for a discussion of the economic rise of China on ASEAN.

trade initiatives could help maintain global interest and draw extra-regional investments into Singapore and the Southeast Asian region as a whole as the crisis-hit regional economies gradually rebuild their financial and economic structures. The surge of recent bilateral trade pact initiatives by Singapore is also interpreted as a means of prompting other ASEAN/APEC member economies to hasten the process of regional and unilateral liberalization.

Singapore's Economic Partnerships with China and India

Singapore's policy-makers have repeatedly emphasized that being a highly open economy, the city-state's growth prospects critically depend on it being cognizant of and extremely responsive to the challenges and opportunities posed by changing economic and business events and conditions regionally and globally. One of the most significant events in recent times has been the ongoing rapid integration with the world economy of China and India, the world's second and fourth largest economies in Purchasing Power Parity (PPP) terms, respectively and the rapid growth rates in the two economies (Fig. 1).[5]

   In an attempt to gain a first mover advantage, Singapore has been aggressively strengthening its economic partnerships with both the rapidly growing Asian giants. Between 2000 and 2006, while Singapore's total global merchandise trade (exports plus imports) nearly doubled from US$271 billion to $513 billion, its bilateral merchandise trade with China increased between four and five times from US$12–13 billion to US$54 billion during the same period, and that with India tripled from slightly less than US$4 billion to over

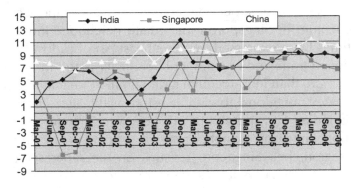

Fig. 1. Quarterly GDP growth rates of China, India, and Singapore (percent) (Q1 2001–Q4 2006).

Source: Bloomberg.

---

[5] Figure 1 also makes apparent that Singapore's growth rates have picked up considerably since mid-2005.

Table 1. Singapore's total bilateral merchandise trade (US$ billions) (2000–2006).

	Domestic exports	Re-exports	Total exports	Total imports	Total bilateral trade
2000	78.59	58.91	137.50	134.24	271.75
2001	65.98	55.46	121.45	115.71	237.16
2002	66.95	58.53	125.48	116.73	242.21
2003	86.42	73.49	159.91	136.22	296.13
2004	106.96	92.22	199.18	174.06	373.23
2005	124.44	105.03	229.48	199.88	429.36
2006	143.88	129.30	273.18	239.90	513.09

Source: *Yearbook of Statistics*, Singapore and Bloomberg.

US$12.5 billion. Consequently, China's share of Singapore's total trade increased from 4.6 percent in 2000 to 10.5 percent in 2006, while India's share increased from 1.4 percent to 2.4 percent during the same time period (Tables 1–3). China moved from being the city-state's 10th largest trade partner in 1994 to the fourth largest by 2004,[6] while India rose from a more modest 18th position in 1994 to 14th position by 2004, However, Singapore's merchandise trade with India has been on a particularly rapid ascent in recent times. While Singapore has enjoyed a sustained bilateral surplus in its trade with India over this period, it has generally experienced a trade deficit with China over the same period. However, it is imperative to keep in mind that, unlike a country's aggregate trade balance which is a reflection of its net national savings and investment position, bilateral trade balances have little if any macroeconomic implications or interpretations (though they may at times have political repercussions, as exemplified by the United States–China trade row).

Moving away from broad aggregates, Singapore's domestic exports to both countries have been dominated by electronic products, parts, components, and accessories (PCAs) as well as oil-related exports, which largely consist of refined petroleum products. Electronic products and PCAs and oil have constituted about a half or more of Singapore's total domestic exports to both China and India. Domestic exports in turn have made up about 38 percent of Singapore's exports to China and 33 percent to India in 2006 (Table 4). Table 4 also shows that both countries are well above the Singapore average with the rest of the world. However, while the proportion of re-exports in Singapore's total exports to India has remained more or less stable during the entire decade, it has been gradually increasing in the case of Singapore's exports to China.

---

[6] This is clear from the latest data on bilateral trade published in the *Yearbook of Statistics*, Singapore, 2005.

Table 2. Trade with China (US$ billions) (2000–2006).

	Domestic exports to China	Percentage of total domestic exports	Total exports to China	Percentage of total exports	Imports from China	Percentage of total imports	Total bilateral trade	Percentage of total bilateral trade
2000	2.34	3.0	5.37	3.9	7.10	5.3	12.46	4.6
2001	2.71	4.1	5.31	4.4	7.18	6.2	12.49	5.3
2002	3.50	5.2	6.88	5.5	8.89	7.6	15.77	6.5
2003	4.79	5.5	10.13	6.3	11.07	8.1	21.20	7.2
2004	7.00	6.5	15.43	7.7	16.26	9.3	31.69	8.5
2005	8.99	7.2	19.73	8.6	20.49	10.3	40.23	9.4
2006	10.21	7.1	26.65	9.8	27.38	11.4	54.03	10.5

Source: Yearbook of Statistics, Singapore and Bloomberg.

Table 3.   Trade with India (US$ billions) (2000–2006).

	Domestic exports to India	Percentage of total domestic exports	Total exports to India	Percentage of total exports	Imports from India	Percentage of total imports	Total bilateral trade	Percentage of total bilateral trade
2000	0.93	1.2	2.79	2.0	1.07	0.8	3.86	1.4
2001	0.94	1.4	2.71	2.2	1.12	1.0	3.83	1.6
2002	0.96	1.4	2.64	2.1	1.16	1.0	3.80	1.6
2003	1.31	1.5	3.09	1.9	1.44	1.1	4.53	1.5
2004	1.76	1.6	4.19	2.1	2.80	1.6	6.98	1.9
2005	2.19	1.8	5.89	2.6	4.07	2.0	9.96	2.3
2006	2.58	1.8	7.71	2.8	4.90	2.0	12.62	2.5

Source: Yearbook of Statistics, Singapore and Bloomberg.

Table 4. Domestic exports as a percentage of total exports (2000–2006).

	Total domestic exports as percentage of total exports	Domestic exports to China as percentage of total exports to China	Domestic exports to india as percentage of total exports to India
2000	57.2	43.7	33.3
2001	54.3	51.1	34.5
2002	53.4	50.9	36.2
2003	54.0	47.3	42.3
2004	53.7	45.4	42.1
2005	54.2	45.6	37.3
2006	52.7	38.3	33.4

Source: Yearbook of Statistics, Singapore and Bloomberg.

Electronic products and PCAs also occupy prominence in Singapore's imports from China, indicating a significant proportion of intra-industry trade taking place between the two countries. This is not surprising as both countries are integral parts of the regional value-added network in East Asia. India, which has traditionally not been a part of this network, does not yet have that high concentration of electronic products and PCAs among its major products of imports by Singapore. However, as the Indian economy globalizes further and fosters its latent comparative advantage in manufacturing (which it is rapidly doing), one can expect intra-industry trade in electronic PCAs to also become more prominent in Singapore–India bilateral trade.[7]

An important caveat is in order. The foregoing observations pertain only to merchandise trade for which detailed data are available. As such, the data above significantly understates the increasing role of offshoring activities and integration of service functions in manufacturing activities of Singapore involving China and India. As is well known, Singapore is also a major player in international trade in commercial services, while China and India too are major exporters of certain services. In particular, while China has achieved global comparative advantage in trade in travel and tourism services, India has gained the same in communication and computer-related as well as professional business services over the past decade.

In the area of tourism, China and India have rapidly become among Singapore's top visitor-generating markets. Between 1994 and 2006, visitors from China to Singapore grew from just over 164,900 to about almost 1.03 million, while those from India grew from about 173,800 to almost 650,000 over the same period (Table 5). In 2003, China was the highest

---

[7] See Chapter 12 of this Volume for a discussion of trade in PCAs in East Asia.

Table 5. Visitor arrivals into Singapore from China and India (millions of people) (1994–2006).

	China	India	Total
1994	0.16	0.17	6.90
1999	0.37	0.29	6.96
2000	0.43	0.35	7.69
2001	0.50	0.34	7.52
2002	0.67	0.38	7.57
2003	0.57	0.31	6.13
2004	0.88	0.47	8.33
2005	0.86	0.58	8.94
2006	1.03	0.65	9.75

Source: *Yearbook of Statistics*, Singapore and Bloomberg.

non-ASEAN visitor-generating market for Singapore, while India was the fifth largest (after Japan, Australia, and the United Kingdom). Somewhat less well known is the fact that Indian tourists were the third highest spender on a per-day basis in Singapore in 2002 (only after Japanese and Italian tourists).

Visitor flows from India can be expected to be further spurred with the introduction of international flights by private Indian airlines, as well as by increases in the number of direct flights from Singapore to new destinations in India (viz. Amritsar and Ahmedabad). The same is true for China. Liberalization of air services will also facilitate more intensified business interactions and people-to-people contact, which is an important catalyst for enhancing bilateral trade. Paradoxically for Singapore, however, intensified travel and people-to-people contact between China and India — which is rapidly occurring — significantly diminishes the value of Singapore as an intermediary or middleman between its two giant Asian neighbors.

While data are unavailable on the other types of bilateral services, anecdotal evidence indicates that the linkages are getting stronger. While trade and investments between Singapore and China have been well documented, two recent examples in the Indian context is Singtel's equity partnership with Bharti telecom in India, wherein the former has raised its equity stake in its joint venture company Bharti Televentures from 28 percent to over 30 percent in May 2005, and the acquisition of a 37.5 percent equity stake in 2006 by DBS Bank, Singapore in Cholamandalam Investment and Finance Co. Ltd., a non-bank financial firm in India specializing in consumer finance.

Trade in goods and services has been promoted by enhanced cross-border capital flows. Given China's relatively underdeveloped financial system, the bulk of foreign investment flows from Singapore (and elsewhere) into China have been forged via foreign direct investment (FDI) (Table 6). In contrast,

Table 6. Stock of Singapore's direct investment by destination (Singapore $ billions) (2000–2004).

	Total direct investment	China	Mauritius
2000	98.29	15.71	4.92
2001	133.61	15.72	3.78
2002	148.92	18.05	5.42
2003	155.68	19.82	5.99
2004	173.81	20.91	9.20

Source: *Yearbook of Statistics*, Singapore.

Note: Mauritius is used as a proxy for investment in India. India has a double-taxation treaty with Mauritius (it has no income tax) and all or nearly all of FDI to India are routed through Mauritius. FDI data in India always shows Mauritius as the highest investor of FDI in India.

portfolio flows and Foreign Institutional Investments (FIIs) are significant channels of fund inflows in India. Thus, Singapore government's holding company, Temasek Holdings, which established an office in Mumbai, is already one of the top private equity investors in India. Temasek has acquired stakes in a number of notable Indian companies and appears to be keen on doing much more in India in the near future.

Bilateral Trade Agreements

As a core member of ASEAN, Singapore has been involved in negotiating FTAs with both China and India. The ASEAN–China and ASEAN–India FTAs are expected to be fully implemented within a decade, at least with the more advanced ASEAN members.

Singapore and China agreed to launch negotiations for a bilateral FTA on 25 August 2006, at the 3rd Joint Council for Bilateral Cooperation (JCBC) meeting held in Beijing. The negotiations are envisaged to yield a comprehensive agreement, extending beyond trade in goods, and will include trade in services, investments, and other areas. The idea is also to inject additional momentum into the establishment of the ASEAN–China Free Trade Area (ACFTA) within a few years.[8]

Singapore has concurrently engaged India bilaterally through the Comprehensive Economic Cooperation Agreement or CECA which was signed by Prime Ministers Manmohan Singh and Lee Hsien Loong on 29 June 2005.

---

[8] For a discussion of the origins of the ACFTA, see Lijun, S (2003). China–ASEAN free trade area: Origins, developments and strategic motivations. *ISEAS Working Paper in International Politics & Security Issues*, 1. For a more recent discussion on the impact of ACFTA on ASEAN, see Tongzon, JL (2005). ASEAN–China free trade area: A bane or boon for ASEAN countries? *The World Economy*, 28, 191–210.

The agreement, being comprehensive in scope (so-called "integrated package"), covers partial trade liberalization (on the Indian side), investment promotion, facilitation, and protection and the agreement to negotiate mutual recognition of qualifications in services for five professions. Further, the CECA also includes a double taxation avoidance agreement, as well as agreements for closer cooperation in a broad range of areas such as education, e-commerce, science and technology, the media and intellectual property, and provisions pertaining to temporary movement of natural professionals.

The rationale for a Singapore–India CECA has been aptly summarized in a Morgan Stanley report[9]:

> "We believe that enhanced Singapore-India economic relations based on the CECA are built on an aim to spur on the unannounced four-pronged economic and geopolitical strategy adopted by the Singapore government in recent years. The economic strategy emphasizes building a large and profitable external economy, maintaining a large manufacturing-technology sector, developing enhanced new high value-add services, globalizing Singapore and Southeast Asia economies and leveraging its enhanced economic relationship with the West, India and China to position Singapore as the global business place in Asia."

The agreement took effect from 1 August 2005 and is anticipated to facilitate the growing *de facto* economic integration between Singapore and India over the coming years. Singapore is very keen on investing in India in the telecom, banking, automobiles, pharmaceuticals, and energy sectors, and the Indian government expects FDI inflows from Singapore to shoot up significantly.[10] A study by the Associated Chambers of Commerce and Industry of India (Assocham) estimates that Singapore's cumulative investments in India, which is around US$3 billion, could go up to US$5 billion by 2010 and to US$10 billion by 2015 as a result of the CECA. It is also estimated by the same study that the CECA will pave the way for bilateral trade between Singapore and India to touch US$50 billion by 2010 against the volume of about US$12 billion in 2006.[11] However, it remains to be seen if and to what extent businesses from both sides actually utilize this agreement. While India is keen on signing more bilateral agreements with other ASEAN countries such as Malaysia and Thailand, India needs to view such bilateral and regional FTAs strictly as complements rather than substitutes to a more generalized liberalization with the rest of the world. This is particularly so as

---

[9] Lian, D (2005). Singapore's Indian niche. *Morgan Stanley Equity Research*, 12 August.

[10] Thomas, JJ (2005). India–Singapore CECA: A step towards Asian integration? *ISAS Insights No. 06*. Singapore: Institute of South Asian Studies.

[11] See The Associated Chambers of Commerce and Industry of India (Assocham) study on "India–Singapore Comprehensive Economic Co-operation Agreement: A Pathfinder for the India–Asean FTA", 2005.

FTAs do not offer a significant scope for domestic reforms, and leads to partial liberalization that is not uniformly welfare-enhancing for all sections of the population. For a largely and significantly agrarian economy like India, it is therefore imperative that it simultaneously continues along its path of unilateral liberalization with the rest of the world in a calibrated and judicious manner, in order to be globally competitive, and benefit from free trade.

Conclusion: Areas of Concern with Trade Agreements[12]

Bilateral trade accords, particularly the recent ones Singapore is involved in, go well beyond just merchandise trade liberalization, also encompassing liberalization of services trade and other "behind the border" impediments to trade and investment flows. In other words, they include trade and investment facilitation measures such as investment protection, harmonization and mutual recognition of standards and certification, protection of intellectual property rights, opening of government procurement markets, streamlining and harmonization of customs procedures, and the development of dispute-settlement procedures. Such trade accords which focus on "deep" integration could help establish a precedent or benchmark for multilateral trade negotiations. Simultaneously, to the extent that contracting parties to a trade accord agree to move beyond their respective WTO commitments, there may be a demonstration effect that motivates future rounds of broader multilateral negotiations under the auspices of the WTO.

It is commonly noted that since Singapore has one of the most liberal trade and investment regimes in the world with near-zero tariff rates on most goods (and limited non-tariff barriers), the scope for trade diversion (i.e., replacement of lower cost suppliers from non-member countries) from Singapore's vantage point is quite small. Nonetheless, it would be wrong to conclude that there are no ill effects whatsoever.

An important issue of concern is to what extent the various bilateral, sub-regional, and transnational arrangements might contradict each other and if and how such contradictions will be overcome. Only time will tell. What can be said is that the proliferation of a number of overlapping trade agreements raises many technical problems with regard to the implementation of special provisions or rules of origin (ROOs) which are meant to prevent goods being re-exported from/circumvented through the lower tariff country to the higher tariff one (i.e., trade deflection). Even with a single FTA, a concern is that ROOs with a particular country, say the United States, may be sufficiently prohibitive so as to induce Singapore exporters to source their inputs from

---

[12] Some of the arguments made here were initially discussed in Rajan, RS and R Sen, *ibid.*

the United States than some other developing country in Asia (such as Korea, for instance). In other words, the United States exports its external tariffs to Singapore. This appears to have been the case with NAFTA where the United States negotiated a ROO on Mexican assemblers of automobiles. ROOs also give rise to significant costs due to the need for administrative surveillance and implementation. In practice, ROOs are particularly complex — they are almost 200 pages in case of NAFTA and 80 pages of small print in the case of the European Union's agreement with Poland — as they have to take into account tariffs on imported intermediate goods used in products produced within the FTA.

The book-keeping and related costs escalate sharply as production gets more integrated internationally (what Jagdish Bhagwati has colorfully termed the "spaghetti-bowl" phenomenon) and countries get involved with an increasing number of separate but overlapping FTAs. However, whether such a spaghetti-bowl practically emerges in the Singapore and broader regional context would depend to a large extent on the utilization of these FTAs and their impact in the business world. It has been recently estimated that the ASEAN Free Trade Agreement (AFTA), ASEAN's first regional FTA, which has one of the simplest ROOs for tariff preferences, has remained grossly under-utilized at about 5 percent of total trade, with many exporters preferring to pay the MFN tariffs instead.[13] The observation raises concerns regarding the implementation of FTAs, and the degree of implementation integrity that Singapore's trading partners adhere to in ensuring that businesses find it cost-effective in utilizing FTAs for trading and investment purposes.

Academic and policy interests in bilateral and plurilateral trade arrange-ments have been preoccupied by the question as to whether they are "stum-bling" or "building" blocs toward multilateral liberalization. It is clear that the Singapore policy-makers are of the opinion that FTAs are building blocs and complementary to rules-based multilateralism. In other words, bilateral-ism is seen as being "WTO-Plus" rather than a substitute for the WTO. Singapore's policy-makers have made concerted attempts to reaffirm the pri-macy of the multilateral trading system. While constant strong support for multilateralism and the WTO as the bedrock of the world's trading system is undoubtedly of importance, the GATT/WTO rules regarding FTAs (which are aimed at ensuring that the rights of third parties are not compromised) remain highly vague and loose. The wordings of the GATT/WTO rules are open to a variety of interpretations and, for all intents and purposes, are ineffective. What can be said, however, is that time and efforts spent on

---

[13] Sen, R (2006). Bilateral trade and economic cooperation agreements in ASEAN: Evolution, characteris-tics, and implications for Asian economic integration. Paper circulated for discussion at the *2006 Program of Seminars at the IMF-World Bank Meetings*, September 16–18, Institute of Policy Studies (IPS), Singapore. Subsequently published as *ISEAS Working Paper in Economics and Finance*, 1, 2007.

negotiating and implementing a series of bilateral and plurilateral trade accords may divert scarce resources from the multilateral trade rounds. Potentially more important than the direct impact of this "scarce negotiator resources argument" to Singapore is the fact that, by being involved in a number of trade agreements, Singapore must accept at least partial responsibility for diverting attention of trade partners away from multilateral negotiations. For instance, the US Trade Representative (USTR) paying more attention to a number of bilaterals may mean much less attention at the margin, being paid to the WTO.

While some Southeast Asian neighbors greeted the initial response to Singapore's bilateral trade strategy with much skepticism and even irritation, this view has significantly softened in recent times. Indeed, countries such as Malaysia, Thailand, the Philippines, and recently Indonesia are now emulating the Singapore strategy of bilateralism. In fact, in the haste to negotiate as many FTAs as possible, they are ignoring important domestic economic reforms which are critical for their growth prospects and to sustain competitiveness. For most of these developing and middle- and low-income ASEAN members, it is important to understand that the engine of liberalization and regulatory reform has to be home-driven, with FTAs playing at best a supportive role.[14] In the meantime, Singapore remains steadfast in its goal of negotiating new trade pacts, as evidenced by the official web site that is dedicated to FTAs:

> "Free Trade Agreements (FTAs) are superhighways that connect Singapore with key economies in North & South America, Europe, Asia and the Middle East. Global trading routes become congested as competition grows, but our businesses will enjoy first-mover advantage through FTAs. Goods and services flow more freely; economic integration deepens; the seeds of overseas partnerships take root."[15]

---

[14] Sally, R and R Sen (2005). Whither trade policies in Southeast Asia? The wider Asian and global context. *ASEAN Economic Bulletin*, 22, 92–115.
[15] See http://www.iesingapore.gov.sg/wps/portal/FTA.

Chapter 18

ASEAN Economic Integration: Taking Care of Business*

Introduction

Regional economic integration is certainly the flavor of the day — not just regional economic *cooperation* but actually regional economic *integration*. A succinct explanation of the difference between the both as well as what regional integration means is as follows:

> "It is important to distinguish regional cooperation from regional integration. Regional cooperation refers to policy measures jointly undertaken by a group of countries typically located within a geographic area, to achieve a level of welfare that is higher than what is possible when compared to pursuing such a goal unilaterally. Some regional initiatives are intended to facilitate or enhance economic integration, while others are not. Regional integration, on the other hand, is *de facto* integration of economies within a geographic region. It may be market-driven integration, that is, there is no explicit agreement or coordinated action among countries within a region to integrate their economies; or policy-induced integration, that is, one that results from regional cooperation. Regional integration can vary in intensity. Full economic integration occurs when goods, services, and factors of production can flow freely and financial markets are unified among countries within a region."[1]

When one thinks about economic integration amongst countries in a particular region, the first thing that comes to mind is the European Union (EU). The 1957 Treaty of Rome marked the start of the economic integration of Europe — beginning with Western Europe but gradually extending eastwards. In the preamble, the first declaration by the signatories of the treaty reads "to lay the foundations of an ever closer union among the peoples of Europe, resolved to ensure the economic and social progress of their countries by

---

* This chapter draws on Rajan, RS. Taking stock of ASEAN economic integration (6 August 2004), *Business Times* (Singapore).
[1] Lamberte, MB (2005). An overview of economic cooperation and integration in Asia. In *Asian Economic Cooperation and Integration: Progress, Prospects, and Challenges*, Asian Development Bank.

common action to eliminate the barriers which divide Europe, affirming as the essential objective of their efforts the constant improvements of the living and working conditions of their peoples".[2]

Like the EU, the Association of Southeast Asian Nations (ASEAN), has also had the aspect of economic integration and cooperation embedded in their founding declaration. ASEAN was founded in 1967 with Indonesia, Malaysia, Philippines, Singapore, and Thailand as its founding members. The first summit was held in Bangkok and of the five objectives contained the "Bangkok Declaration", two of them are[3]:

- "(A desire) to establish a firm foundation for common action to promote regional cooperation in Southeast Asia in the spirit of equality and partnership and thereby contribute towards peace, progress and prosperity in the region".
- "(I)n an increasingly interdependent world, the cherished ideals of peace, freedom, social justice, and economic well-being are best attained by fostering good understanding, good neighborliness, and meaningful cooperation among the countries of the region already bound together by ties of history and culture".

Since its founding, the membership of ASEAN has been *widened* to include 10 countries in Southeast Asia (the initial five as well as Brunei, Cambodia, Laos, Myanmar, and Vietnam). Nevertheless, the aim of *deeper* ASEAN economic integration has remained unchanged; in fact it has been the bedrock of most ASEAN discussions. Developments in the external environment have worked in tandem to raise the awareness about the need to hasten the process of intra-ASEAN integration. These developments include: (a) the stalling of multilateral trade talks; (b) the economic emergence of China and India and concomitant concerns about loss of ASEAN's global competitiveness; and (c) the spate of new free trade pacts being negotiated in Asia and in particular, by ASEAN members themselves.[4]

While the overall economic effects of Asia's new wave of trade pacts remain uncertain, ASEAN is potentially well placed to reap the benefits of this new regionalism. The three largest countries in Asia, viz. China, India, and Japan, are due to fully implement trade pacts with ASEAN by 2010, 2012, and 2011, respectively. South Korea, Australia, and New Zealand have also been actively courted by ASEAN, as has the United States. Nonetheless, for ASEAN to capitalize fully on its *de facto* hub status, greater efforts need

---

[2] More information on the Treaty of Rome is available at http://europa.eu/scadplus/treaties/eec_en.htm

[3] "The ASEAN Declaration" also known as the "Bangkok Declaration" signed in Bangkok on 8 August 1967. Available at http://www.aseansec.org/1212.htm

[4] See Chapter 17 of this Volume.

to be expended to maintain cohesion and deepen intra-ASEAN integration. This chapter takes stock of the ongoing process of economic integration and addresses some of the challenges toward ASEAN economic integration.

A Brief History of ASEAN Economic Integration

Though the Bangkok ASEAN Declaration of 1967 laid out the case as well as the need for increased economic integration, not much was done in this area for a while. This lull in further negotiations resulted, perhaps, because of the war that took place in the region from the latter part of the 1960s to the mid-1970s. In 1976, the "ASEAN Concord" was signed in Bali and that declaration provides that "Member States shall cooperate in the field of trade in order to promote development and growth of new production and trade". In 1977, there was an agreement signed in Manila where members agreed to adopt various instruments on trade liberalization on a preferential basis. After the third summit meeting of the ASEAN heads of government in Manila in December 1987, ASEAN declared that "Member States shall strengthen intra-ASEAN economic cooperation to maximize the realization of the region's potential in trade and development".[5]

However, most of these agreements and declarations really did not amount to much action on the ground. The real breakthrough came in January 1992 when, in Singapore, six ASEAN member countries signed the Common Effective Preferential Tariff (CEPT) scheme for an ASEAN Free Trade Area (AFTA).[6] The aim of the CEPT scheme was to reduce tariff barriers to no more than 5 percent and completely eliminate quantitative restrictions as well as other non-tariff barriers within AFTA. An ASEAN note in 2003 said "The elimination of tariffs and non-tariff barriers among the ASEAN members has served as a catalyst for greater efficiency in production and long-term competitiveness. Moreover, the reduction of barriers to intra-regional trade gives ASEAN consumers a wider choice of better quality consumer products".[7] However, there were some exclusions in the list of goods. The same note goes on to say: "734 tariff lines in the General Exception List, representing about 1.09 percent of all tariff lines in ASEAN, are permanently excluded from the free trade area for reasons of national security, protection of human, animal or plant life and health, and of artistic, historic and archaeological value".

---

[5] "Manila Declaration" signed in Manila on 15 December 1987. Available at http://www.aseansec.org/5117.htm

[6] The 6 ASEAN countries or ASEAN 6 are Brunei, Indonesia, Malaysia, Philippines, Singapore, and Thailand. The other 4 members, Cambodia, Laos, Myanmar, and Vietnam joined later.

[7] Southeast Asia: A Free Trade Area. http://www.aseansec.org/viewpdf.asp?file=/pdf/afta.pdf

In 1997, in Kuala Lumpur, "Vision 2020" of ASEAN was released and on the subject of economic integration, it says "We resolve to chart a new direction towards the year 2020 called, 'ASEAN 2020: Partnership in Dynamic Development' which will forge closer economic integration within ASEAN". Finally in 2003, ASEAN countries signed the ASEAN Concord–2 and on the issue of setting up an ASEAN Economic Community, it says:

> "The ASEAN Economic Community is the realization of the end-goal of economic integration as outlined in the ASEAN Vision 2020, to create a stable, prosperous and highly competitive ASEAN economic region in which there is a free flow of goods, services, investment and a freer flow of capital, equitable economic development and reduced poverty and socio-economic disparities in year 2020."

Limited *de facto* Integration

Under the region's flagship trade initiative, viz. AFTA, the bulk of intra-ASEAN trade enjoys tariff rates between 0 and 5 percent (the newer members, Cambodia, Laos, Myanmar, and Vietnam, have been granted longer timetables to implement AFTA). While AFTA came into force earlier than originally planned (1 January 2002 for the original ASEAN members) and a target zero-tariff rate will be achieved by 2010 (2018 for the transition members), its impact has thus far proven to be rather disappointing. Even though AFTA 96 percent of all of ASEAN's trade now falls within the AFTA, there are wide differences among the ASEAN-6 members with respect to their commitments to tariff elimination under the CEPT scheme. Thus, while some of the ASEAN countries viz. Singapore has reduced most of its CEPT tariff rates to zero, others viz. Malaysia and Philippines have not yet fulfilled all their AFTA commitments, with some of the products still attracting high tariffs higher than those within the CEPT range of 0–5 percent. The newer members have been given a deadline till 2010 to comply with the AFTA commitments for tariff reduction.

Further, although AFTA is already implemented, costs of complying with the Rules of Origin (ROOs) to satisfy the criteria for preferential treatment are perceived to be quite high by the businessmen. A recent study estimates that current utilization rate of tariff concessions under the CEPT scheme is as low as 5 percent. This is largely due to lack of clear and transparent procedures as well as absence of credibility and mutual trust between the countries that provide and receive preferential tariff treatment under AFTA. Further, the margins of preference between the ASEAN-wide tariff rate (referred to as the "Common Effective Preferential" tariffs or CEPT) and those applied by ASEAN countries to imports from the rest of the world are rather low.[8] Further, AFTA is narrowly focused on reducing and eventually eliminating intra-ASEAN tariff barriers on merchandise trade. Non-tariff and other trade hindering barriers have not been adequately addressed by AFTA.

The data bears out the limited effectiveness of AFTA. First, intra-ASEAN trade has accounted for only about one-fifth of ASEAN's total trade, this share remained stagnant over the last decade (and much of the intra-ASEAN trade is due to Singapore), at the expense of its increasing trade linkages with the two Asian giants China and India. Intra-ASEAN trade is also far lower than other regional economic alliances such as the European Union (two-thirds) or the North American Free Trade Area (one half). Second, only a small proportion of the intra-ASEAN trade is conducted under the CEPT (45 percent of intra-ASEAN trade is in electrical and electronic parts and components broadly defined).[9]

In addition, little to no progress has been made in facilitating intra-ASEAN services trade (the ASEAN Framework on Services or AFAS has been largely ineffective). One of the prime reasons behind this has been political constraints, associated with the protectionist interests of those who might lose from reforms in AFAS. Further, there are significant constraints in the AFAS Framework itself that restrict speedy liberalization of regional service trade. A major constraint is the uneven levels of development among the ASEAN economies. As such, technical expertise in legal and sectoral aspects of services trade liberalization must be provided for new ASEAN members, many of whose service sectors are not even well developed. Second, there is a need to add credibility to the liberalization agenda under AFAS, by specifying coverage of sectors and detailed time lines for progressive liberalization. Analysts have argued that a multi-track approach may be suitable for sectors that are growing rapidly and are likely to be less affected by national interests. In this context, it is argued that AFAS should follow a negative-list approach than the currently existing positive list one, as it would allow greater coverage and transparency in negotiations, and assure service providers of fair and non-discriminatory treatment with respect to market access in all service sectors, unless specifically exempted. This would also allow greater consistency with the bilateral

---

[8] Drawing lessons from the CER grouping (consisting of Australia and New Zealand), it has been suggested that ASEAN members might consider a waiver of the rules or origin for those goods wherein the difference between the ASEAN member's MFN tariff rate is 5 percent or lesser, which could perhaps enhance the utilization of AFTA by exporters and importers. See Lloyd, P and P Smith (2006). Global economic challenges to ASEAN integration and competitiveness: A prospective look, *REPSF Project No. 05/004, Regional Economic Policy Support Facility (REPSF)* (September).

[9] For details see Austria, MS (2004). The pattern of Intra-ASEAN trade in priority goods sector, *REPSF Research Project No. 03/006* (August).

approach wherein most of ASEAN's services trade negotiations have been based on a negative list.[10]

Further, services trade liberalization would require ASEAN members to undertake domestic reforms, particularly on regulatory issues, in order to benefit from service trade liberalization. This is particularly so in case of the financial services sector, which has already suffered adversely in the crisis of 1997–1998. It would also require ASEAN economies to devise an adequate safeguard mechanism in order for policymakers to respond efficiently to possible negative effects on the domestic economy from such liberalization.

Besides the AFTA and AFAS initiatives that provide limited *de facto* building blocks for economic integration, there is also the ASEAN Investment Area (AIA) initiative that is force for the founding members of ASEAN and Brunei Darussalam and accords ASEAN investors preferential treatment with regard to market access and the granting of national treatment, for all sectors except for those deemed to be sensitive. The newer members of ASEAN, Cambodia, Laos, and Vietnam have until 1 January 2010 to implement AIA. However, as in case with other schemes for ASEAN economic integration, implementation of this scheme has been uneven among ASEAN members. Indeed, the framework of agreement of the AIA lacks substantive details, although being legally binding, as the implementation is left to the individual members. In addition, recent free trade pacts of ASEAN and its individual members with its extra-ASEAN trading partners have all committed to investment liberalization, which could render the AIA to be insignificant, unless steps are taken by ASEAN to build upon the AIA in order to develop a common framework for investment liberalization for investors from both inside and outside the region.[11] Further, there is also a need to harmonize the tax laws and regulation in ASEAN for investors to take advantage of it as a single market that integrates the capital with the goods and services market in the near future.[12]

ASEAN Competitiveness as seen by McKinsey

A McKinsey study estimate that manufacturing costs as well as logistics costs will decline as a result of full economic integration.[13] Their logic is that

---

[10] For a recent report on AFAS see Thanh, VT and P Bartlett (2006). Ten years of ASEAN framework agreement on services (AFAS): An assessment, *REPSF Project No. 05/004, Regional Economic Policy Support Facility (REPSF)* (July).

[11] For details see Hew, D *et al.* (2006). AIA-Plus: Building on free trade agreements (ASEAN and Five Dialogue Partners — CER, China, India, Japan, Korea), *REPSF Research Project No. 04/010* (December).

[12] For details see Farrow, I and S Jogarajan (2006). ASEAN Tax regimes and the integration of the priority sectors: Issues and options, *REPSF Project No. 05/005, Regional Economic Policy Support Facility (REPSF)* (October).

[13] See Schwarz, A and R Villiinger (2004). Integrating Southeast Asia's economies, *The McKinsey Quarterly*, No. 1.

Potential cost savings in electronics industry, index: cost before integration = 100

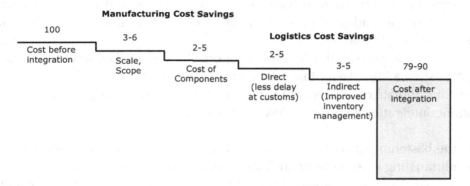

Fig. 1. Analysis by McKinsey on potential savings to the electronics industry in ASEAN if countries integrate.

Source: McKinsey & Co.

because there is a bigger consumer market, it reduces per-unit cost because of economies of scale. Then because of reduced customs duties, the manufacturers will benefit if they export goods to another country. All in all, they estimate that the costs of the electronic industry will reduce by some 10–20 percent. Figure 1 shows how the electronics industry in the ASEAN region could benefit from economic integration.

While the potential gains from integration within ASEAN are significant, another McKinsey Consulting report on ASEAN Competitiveness highlighted three significant concerns that investors have expressed about ASEAN[14]: (a) subscale and fragmented markets; (b) unnecessary costs due to different product standards and customs procedures; and (c) unpredictable policy implementation by ASEAN members, including the recent back-tracking by some countries on their respective liberalization commitments (e.g., Malaysia in the case of motor vehicles and parts, Indonesia in agricultural products, and Philippines in the case of petrochemical products).

In recognition of these concerns, at the Bali summit in October 2020, the 10 ASEAN leaders agreed to the goal of creating an ASEAN Economic Community (AEC) by 2020 (so-called "Bali Concord II"). The AEC, which was initially mooted by then Singapore Prime Minister Goh Chok Tong, is one pillar of the "ASEAN Community", the other two being political and security cooperation and socio-cultural cooperation. The primary

---

[14] The McKinsey report is titled "ASEAN Competitiveness Study" and was commissioned by the ASEAN Secretariat.

objective of the AEC is to deepen and accelerate intraregional economic integration by liberalizing trade, investment and skilled labor flows and addressing behind-the-border barriers thus creating a single production base and single market.[15]

As a follow-up to the McKinsey report, the ASEAN Economic Ministers established a High-Level Task Force (HLTF) on ASEAN economic integration. Specific initiatives suggested by the HLTF to advance the process of economic integration in the next few years include:

- the hastening of customs clearance and simplifying customs procedures;
- eliminating existing tariff and non-tariff barriers to trade;
- accelerating the implementation of the Mutual Recognition Arrangements (MRAs) for key sector such as electrical, electronic, and telecommunications equipment;
- harmonizing standards and technical regulations;
- creating a more effective ASEAN Dispute Settlement Mechanism (DSM); and
- fast-tracking of liberalization of 11 priority sectors. They are automotive, wood-based products, rubber-based products, textiles/apparels, agro-based products, fisheries, electronics, air travel, tourism, information and communications technologies (ICT), and healthcare.

Conclusion: Multi-Speed Approach within ASEAN

While ASEAN needs to focus specifically on making the region a seamless and enlarged production base, there remain a number of skeptics about the effectiveness of ASEAN as an economic entity (as opposed to a political one). For instance, the vast and growing income gaps and heterogeneity among the various members may well act as a road-block to deeper economic intra-ASEAN integration in the near term. They could also limit the ability of the association to develop a common strategy to deal with extra-regional countries. Indeed, while ASEAN as a group is engaged in

---

[15] There have been a number of papers on the ASEAN Economic Community. For instance, see Cuyvers, L, PD Lombaerde and S Verherstraeten (2005). From AFTA toward an ASEAN Economic Community … and beyond, *Discussion Paper No. 46*, Center for ASEAN Studies: Antwerp; Hew, D (2003). Towards an ASEAN Economic Community by 2020: Vision or reality? Viewpoints, Institute for South East Asian Studies (June 16). For a discussion of the ASEAN Economic Community and the newer members of ASEAN, see Thanh, VT (2006). Can the CLV effectively engage in the ASEAN integration? Paper for presentation at the Seminar Accelerating Development in the Mekong Region — The Role of Economic Integration, Siem Reap (26–27 June 2006).

negotiations with China and India, Thailand and Singapore — which are the two most enthusiastic liberalizers in ASEAN — are negotiating separate comprehensive agreements with these two countries as they are concerned about the slow pace of negotiations and implementation of ASEAN-wide agreements.

Apart from establishing trade pacts with third countries, Singapore and Thailand have recently formed a "Singapore–Thailand Enhanced Economic Relationship" (STEER). Among other things, the aim of the STEER is to act as a high level forum to intensify bilateral economic cooperation across various sectors (agriculture and food, life sciences, automotive parts and components and financial services). Other areas of cooperation include development of SMEs, customs cooperation, healthcare, spa services, tourism, transport logistics, financial services, ICT, and MRAs. In another substantive step in bilateral cooperation, Singapore has joined in the early harvest program initiated between Thailand and China in their bilateral FTA. The agreement will involve the three countries eliminating tariffs on all fruits and vegetables and came into effect on 1 January 2005.

Clearly, just as some ASEAN countries prefer to take a more graduated approach to liberalization (as they aim to balance domestic economic priorities and promote their external economic interests), Singapore and Thailand are fully justified to "go-it-alone" in pursuit of their respective national interests. Recognizing this reality of multi-speed integration among member countries, ASEAN leaders implicitly endorsed the "2 plus X" approach, whereby any two-member countries can choose to integrate certain sectors faster bilaterally if they so desire. (The "plus X" presumably refers to either other ASEAN members or Dialogue partners like China and India.)

Nonetheless, there are valid concerns that this multi-speed approach taken toward integration will further stratify ASEAN and undermine its ability to act as a unified hub as they outreach to the rest of the world. Indeed, ASEAN's first mover advantage in the FTA game may in fact be eroding. For instance, China and India are both now much more focused on opportunities for mutual rather than zero sum gains. There are signs of intensified business and economic interactions between these two Asian giants, as there are bilateral cultural and political ties. ASEAN's response to these and other dynamics in the global economy needs to be resolute; deeds and declarations will no longer suffice.

Table 1.   Intra-ASEAN exports of ASEAN 6 countries (US$ billions) (1996–2005).

	1996	2001	2002	2003	2004	2005
Brunei	0.4	0.8	0.7	0.6	0.9	1.5
Indonesia	8.3	9.5	9.9	10.7	13.0	15.8
Malaysia	22.7	21.0	22.1	24.6	31.8	36.7
Philippines	3.0	5.0	5.5	6.6	6.8	7.1
Singapore	34.4	32.9	34.0	36.0	43.5	71.9
Thailand	12.1	12.6	13.2	16.6	21.1	23.9
Total	80.8	81.8	85.8	97.2	116.8	155.1

Source: ASEAN Trade Statistics Database, ASEAN Statistical Pocketbook.

Table 2.   Intra-ASEAN imports of ASEAN 6 countries (US$ billions) (1996–2005).

	1996	2001	2002	2003	2004	2005
Brunei	2.8	0.5	0.6	0.6	0.6	0.7
Indonesia	5.5	5.7	7.0	8.0	11.7	17.3
Malaysia	14.7	15.3	17.3	20.1	26.2	29.1
Philippines	4.0	4.2	5.2	6.4	8.4	8.9
Singapore	27.4	29.0	30.5	31.2	37.4	52.2
Thailand	9.8	10.1	10.5	12.8	15.8	21.6
Total	64.2	66.0	72.0	81.2	101.2	132.1

Source: ASEAN Trade Statistics Database, ASEAN Statistical Pocketbook.

Table 3.   Intra-ASEAN exports as percentage of total exports (1996–2005).

	1996	2001	2002	2003	2004	2005
Brunei	17.9	21.9	25.4	19.7	17.1	24
Cambodia	—	4.9	4.8	4.8	3.2	4.7
Indonesia	15.4	16.9	17.4	17.6	18.2	18.5
Laos	—	—	—	71.0	84.2	84.8
Malaysia	30.6	23.9	23.7	24.8	25.1	26.1
Myanmar	—	42.9	49.8	68.6	74.2	49.9
Philippines	15.2	15.5	15.7	18.2	17.2	17.3
Singapore	29.3	27.0	27.2	25.0	24.3	31.3
Thailand	21.7	19.3	19.9	20.6	21.7	21.8
Vietnam	—	—	—	—	14.8	17.6
Total	25.0	22.3	22.6	22.9	22.5	25.3

Source: ASEAN Statistical Pocketbook.

Table 4.   Intra-ASEAN imports as percentage of total imports (1996–2005).

	1996	**2001**	**2002**	**2003**	**2004**	**2005**
Brunei	64.2	41.6	39.2	45.6	42.6	49.1
Cambodia	—	72.7	35.9	58.3	33.6	36.4
Indonesia	11.9	18.5	22.4	24.7	25.1	30
Laos	—	—	—	74.7	—	51.6
Malaysia	19.5	20.9	21.9	25.1	24.9	25.5
Myanmar	—	46.9	56.2	52.5	49.2	54.9
Philippines	14.1	14.1	15.6	17.1	19.0	18.7
Singapore	22.2	25.0	26.2	24.4	22.9	26.1
Thailand	13.5	16.2	16.8	16.7	16.6	18.3
Vietnam	—	—	—	—	24.2	27.4
Total	18.3	21.1	22.2	22.8	22.2	24.5

Source: ASEAN Statistical Pocketbook.

Chapter 19

Uncooperative Cooperation: The Saga of Economic Cooperation in South Asia

Introduction

There have been a number of studies showing the beneficial welfare effects of increased trade. Indeed, if there is any region that requires increased economic welfare, it is South Asia. Despite India's and South Asia's impressive growth performances over the last decade, the South Asian region is a comparatively troubled region. It has a very large population and is marked by deep poverty across large swathes of the population. It has been estimated that of every five people living in poverty in the world, one lives in South Asia. According to the UNDP's Human Development Report in 2006, all South Asian countries were poorly ranked — Sri Lanka at 93, followed by Maldives at 98, India at 126, Pakistan at 134, Bhutan at 135, Bangladesh at 137, Nepal at 138, while Afghanistan was not even ranked.[1]

As a means of improving the economic prospects of the region through greater cooperation and integration, the South Asian Association for Regional Cooperation (SAARC) was founded on 7 December 1985 in Dhaka, Bangladesh. The founding members were Bangladesh, Bhutan, India, Maldives, Nepal, Pakistan, and Sri Lanka. In 2007, the eighth member included into SAARC was Afghanistan. In 2007, China, Japan, United States, South Korea, and the European Union (EU) were granted observer status.[2] The official reason for the founding of SAARC is as follows:

> The idea of regional cooperation was first proposed through "a regional forum"
> by Bangladesh in 1980, with a view to holding periodic, regional-level

---

[1] The UNDP's *Human Development Report* is available at http://www.undp.org/.

[2] An older — predominantly South Asia-based — regional alliance is the Bangkok Agreement established in 1975 as an initiative of the United Nations Economic and Social Commission for Asia and the Pacific (UN-ESCAP). Initial membership involved seven countries, namely Bangladesh, India, Laos, Republic of Korea, Sri Lanka, Philippines, and Thailand. The Bangkok Agreement was renamed the Asia Pacific Trade Agreement (APTA) in 2005 and the current members are: Bangladesh, China, India, South Korea, Laos, and Sri Lanka. The UN-ESCAP acts as the secretariat for the Agreement. Another sub-regional grouping involving South Asia is the BIMSTEC which was formed in 1997 and whose members are Bangladesh, India, Sri Lanka, and Thailand. Myanmar joined the organization as a full member in 1997.

consultations among countries in South Asia on matters of mutual interest and possible cooperation in economic, social, cultural and other fields. The rationale was primarily predicated on the premise that regional experiences elsewhere in the globe had been highly successful and that the countries in the South Asian region would benefit enormously from such cooperation as it would strengthen their competitive position, both individually and as a group.[3]

The so-called "Dhaka Declaration" of 1985 was high on the language, noting that:

"(I)nherent logic strongly justified regional cooperation, particularly among South Asian countries, because the countries in the region enjoy geograph-ical contiguity, historical, social, cultural and ethnic affinities which would act as centripetal forces and thus, contribute substantively to facilitate coor-dination and to reducing of transaction costs."[4]

Despite this, no clear-cut goals were laid out on how to intensify economic cooperation within South Asia, and progress in regional cooperation — let alone integration — has been limited.[5]

Trade Agreements in South Asia

Economic cooperation and integration in South Asia largely rests on the SAARC Preferential Trading Arrangement (SAPTA) and the Agreement on South Asian Free Trade Area (SAFTA).

SAARC created an inter-governmental group to establish SAFTA in 1991. However, the agreement on SAPTA was only signed on 8 April 1993 in Dhaka. The preamble of the SAFTA agreement says that SAARC leaders were "convinced of the need to ... promote intraregional trade which presently constitutes a negligible share in the volume of the South Asian trade".[6] The SAPTA agreement came into operation in December 2005.[7] SAPTA was formed to deal with arrangements relating to tariffs, non-tariff measures, and direct trade measures. Since its inception, there have been four rounds of

---

[3] See http://www.saarc-sec.org/main.php?id=43&t=3.2.

[4] The Dhaka Declaration and the Joint press statement is available at http://www.saarc-sec.org/main.php?id=47&t=4.

[5] For a recent discussion of the status of regional integration in South Asia to date and factors that have hindered it, see Das, DK (2007). Integration of South Asian economies: An exercise in frustration? *Asian-Pacific Economic Literature*, 21, 55–68.

[6] The full SAPTA agreement is available on the SAARC Secretariat's website http://www.saarc-sec.org/old/freepubs/sapta.pdf.

[7] A South Asian Economic Union (SAEU) is to be formed on this basis by 2020.

Table 1. Number of products covered and the depth of preferential tariff concessions agreed to by SAARC member states in the first three rounds of trade negotiations under SAPTA.

Country	No. of products
Bangladesh	572
Bhutan	266
India	2402
Maldives	390
Nepal	425
Pakistan	685
Sri Lanka	211
Total	4951

Source: SAARC.

negotiations. Negotiations in the first two rounds were mostly about products. In the first round, 226 items were included in the list on which duties would be cut by 10–90 percent. In the second round, 1,871 items were added to that list. The third round of negotiations started in July 1997 and ended in November 1998. Negotiations were restricted to products but were on across-the-board basis. By the end of the third round, there were 4,951 items on the list. (Table 1 shows the country-by-country comparison of the number of products on the list and the depth of tariff concessions after the first three rounds of negotiations.) The fourth round of negotiations concluded in 2002, and by the end, there were more than 5,500 products in the list. However, this accounted for less than 10 percent of tradable goods.

The agreement on creating SAFTA was signed in January 2004 in Islamabad, Pakistan. It came into effect in January 2006 and is supposed to be completed by 2016. According to the agreement, the objectives of SAFTA[8] are:

- Eliminating barriers to trade in, and facilitating the cross-border movement of goods between the territories of the Contracting States.
- Promoting conditions of fair competition in the free trade area, and ensuring equitable benefits to all Contracting States, taking into account their respective levels and pattern of economic development.
- Creating effective mechanism for the implementation and application of this agreement, for its joint administration, and for the resolution of disputes.
- Establishing a framework for further regional cooperation to expand and enhance the mutual benefits of this agreement.

---

[8] Information on SAFTA can be found at http://www.saarc-sec.org/main.php?t=2.1.6.

Table 2.   Items in sensitive list in SAFTA.

Countries	No. of tariff lines	Percentage of total lines
Bangladesh	1,254	24.0
Bhutan	157	3.0
India	884	16.9
Maldives	671	12.8
Nepal	1,310	25.5
Pakistan	1,183	22.6
Sri Lanka	1,065	20.3
Total	6,524	

Source: SAARC and Ministry of Commerce, Pakistan.

For the purposes of the agreement, member countries were divided into LDCs or Least Developed Countries (Bangladesh, Bhutan, Nepal, and Maldives) and non-LDC's (India, Pakistan, and Sri Lanka). Afghanistan was not a member at the time of the signing of the agreement, but it comes under the category of LDC. Under Article 7 there are to be no tariff reductions on items in the sensitive list. (Table 2 shows the number of items per country that are on the sensitive list.) Non-LDCs are to be reduced to tariff levels of 0–5 percent for LDCs by 2009.[9] Tariff reductions by non-LDCs for non-LDCs will be done in two phases. In Phase 1 (2006–2008) existing tariff rates above 20 percent are to be reduced to 20 percent within 2 years and tariffs below 20 percent are to be reduced on a margin of preference basis of 10 percent per year. In Phase 2 (2008–2013) tariffs are to be reduced to 0–5 percent within 5 years. Tariff reductions by LDCs for all SAARC members will be done in two phases. In Phase 1 (2006–2008) the existing tariff rates above 30 percent are to be reduced to 30 percent within 2 years, and tariffs below 30 percent are to be reduced on a margin of preference basis of 5 percent per year. In Phase 2 (2008–2016) tariffs are to be reduced to 0–5 percent within 8 years.

Limited *de facto* Integration in South Asia

The extent of actual regional economic cooperation in the SAARC region was very limited. This is apparent from Tables 3 and 4 which show the extent and share of intra-group exports and imports between 1980 and 2004. However, when SAARC is compared to groups such as ASEAN, Mercosur, and the

[9] The foregoing was based on information from the Pakistani Ministry of Commerce web site. Though the modalities of tariff reduction in Article 7 are given on the SAFTA agreement, the Pakistani ministry web site has given the dates while the SAARC agreement gives generic timelines. More information is available at http://www.commerce.gov.pk/SAFTA.asp.

Table 3. Intra-group exports (1980–2004).

Group	Partner	Unit	1980	1990	2000	2001	2002	2003	2004
EU 25	Intra-trade of group	Percentage	60.95	67.06	67.20	66.66	66.74	67.62	67.03
		US$ millions	483,141.17	1,022,932.49	1,618,916.24	1,623,481.21	1,732,013.22	2,101,502.80	2,440,655.08
	Total trade of group	US$ millions	792,712.26	1,525,304.91	2,409,034.52	2,435,510.92	2,595,201.65	3,107,931.08	3,641,258.54
EU 15	Intra-trade of group	Percentage	60.82	65.93	62.10	61.25	61.06	61.70	61.10
		US$ millions	456,856.66	981,259.50	1,420,089.62	1,408,991.03	1,491,271.79	1,796,301.01	2,080,118.35
	Total trade of group	US$ millions	751,159.30	1,488,360.33	2,286,914.86	2,300,350.88	2,442,277.40	2,911,168.00	3,404,526.60
Euro Zone	Intra-trade of group	Percentage	51.44	55.09	50.76	50.16	49.66	51.05	50.75
		US$ millions	306,472.86	669,970.68	946,890.55	954,330.82	1,006,698.50	1,244,221.73	1,465,792.18
	Total trade of group	US$ millions	595,827.60	1,216,163.03	1,865,487.96	1,902,661.88	2,027,114.10	2,437,389.30	2,888,330.60
MERCOSUR	Intra-trade of group	Percentage	11.60	8.86	20.00	17.11	11.47	11.94	12.04
		US$ millions	3,423.68	4,127.11	17,828.67	15,156.48	10,228.46	12,731.62	16,720.84
	Total trade of group	US$ millions	29,525.54	46,559.37	89,147.65	88,570.19	89,155.93	106,670.74	138,891.50
ASEAN	Intra-trade of group	Percentage	17.35	18.96	22.99	22.36	22.68	22.05	21.98
		US$ millions	12,413.45	27,364.76	98,059.83	86,331.38	91,764.66	100,716.82	125,531.24
	Total trade of group	US$ millions	71,538.73	144,365.28	426,486.69	386,129.91	404,615.55	456,875.17	571,090.49
SAARC	Intra-trade of group	Percentage	4.75	3.17	4.10	4.31	4.19	5.63	5.34
		US$ millions	612.67	862.96	2,593.37	2,826.68	2,997.97	4,773.32	5,919.36
	Total trade of group	US$ millions	12,887.67	27,229.44	63,294.57	65,598.11	71,490.36	84,767.39	110,884.70

Source: UNCTAD trade database.

Note: "Percentage" in the table means intra-group exports as a percentage of total exports for that particular group.

Table 4. Intra-group imports (1980–2004).

Group	Partner	Unit	1980	1990	2000	2001	2002	2003	2004
EU 25	Intra-trade of group	Percentage	54.16	64.27	62.09	62.34	63.51	64.52	64.41
	group	US$ millions	483,642.46	1,013,045.92	1,522,718.91	1,511,109.23	1,602,054.76	1,973,396.50	2,370,618.29
	Total trade of group	US$ millions	892,974.97	157,6147.04	2,452,523.16	2,423,886.95	2,522,475.33	3,058,679.85	3,680,757.92
EU 15	Intra-trade of group	Percentage	53.99	63.19	57.96	57.75	58.66	59.39	58.82
	group	US$ millions	455,666.59	972,452.20	1,328,018.34	1,299,639.84	1,368,237.68	1,674,189.02	1,986,487.45
	Total trade of group	US$ millions	843,943.08	1,538,963.90	2,291,359.60	2,250,503.10	2,332,531.80	2,818,913.50	3,377,092.50
Euro Zone	Intra-trade of group	Percentage	44.51	53.33	48.06	48.82	49.60	50.44	50.40
	group	US$ millions	301,513.74	658,744.89	883,300.46	888,360.86	933,320.67	1,157,976.57	1,386,185.22
	Total trade of group	US$ millions	677,412.78	1,235,197.90	1,837,910.30	1,819,852.00	1,881,564.80	2,295,684.80	2,750,611.70
MERCOSUR	Intra-trade of group	Percentage	8.27	14.21	19.75	18.62	17.19	19.11	18.22
	group	US$ millions	3,327.08	4,505.94	18,343.34	16,193.16	11,231.46	13,636.88	17,909.75
	Total trade of group	US$ millions	40,220.60	31,713.76	92,876.03	86,966.76	65,341.26	71,376.86	98,275.30
ASEAN	Intra-trade of group	Percentage	14.36	15.22	22.48	21.94	22.79	22.57	22.48
	group	US$ millions	9,264.49	24,845.63	82,929.86	74,119.70	80,892.37	88,144.94	114,359.77
	Total trade of group	US$ millions	64,537.45	163,243.28	368,965.85	337,808.39	355,017.31	390,616.04	508,679.29
SAARC	Intra-trade of group	Percentage	1.99	1.97	3.48	3.62	3.52	4.42	3.87
	group	US$ millions	493.75	755.69	2,717.54	3,083.22	3,274.64	4,463.77	5,637.56
	Total trade of group	US$ millions	24,810.94	38,391.42	78,193.06	85,158.12	92,956.52	101,083.91	145,618.15

Source: UNCTAD trade database.
Note: "Percentage" in the table means intra-group exports as a percentage of total exports for that particular group.

European Union (EU), it falls short both in terms of exports as well as imports. In 1980, the intra-trade exports as a percentage of total exports was a paltry 4.8 percent while it was 60.8 percent in the EU15 region and 17.4 percent in ASEAN. Over the years, that percentage has not increased much at all. In 2004, it was 5.3 percent, while it was 22.0 percent in ASEAN and 61.1 percent in EU15. Looking at the intra-group imports does not alter the picture by much. In 1980, intra-group imports as a percentage of total imports was negligible at 2.0 percent compared to 54.0 percent in the EU15, 14.4 percent in ASEAN, and 8.3 percent in Mercosur. In 2004, the share for SAARC was 3.9 percent compared to 58.8 percent in the EU15, 22.5 percent in ASEAN, and 18.2 percent in the Mercosur region.[10]

Another measure of regional integration is intra-regional FDI. According to the Asia Regional Integration Center of the Asian Development Bank, FDI between SAARC countries was an extremely low $11.0 million in 2002, $0.4 million in 2001, $9.4 million in 2000, and $8 million in 1999.[11] A recent study on bilateral FDI flows reports that annual intra-South Asian FDI flows averaged US$5.2 million between 1997 and 2000, and this number grew to $14.6 million between 2001 and 2005. This is comparable to an annual average of $1.7 billion for intra-ASEAN FDI flows between 1997 and 2000 and this grew to an annual average of $2.62 billion between 2001 and 2005.[12]

The low level of regional integration is also revealed in terms of the high number of items on the sensitive list, i.e., items that will never come under the purview of SAFTA and can still be subject to high tariffs (Table 2). Although Bhutan has the smallest number of sensitive list items, at only 3 percent of their tariff lines, it is not very significant as Bhutan has very few resources and its manufacturing facilities are highly dependent on India for inputs. Additionally, there is an India–Bhutan FTA already in existence. The most puzzling case is that of India which has 884 items on the sensitive list representing some 16 percent of its total tariff lines. In comparison, in the India–ASEAN FTA that is being negotiated, the number of items in the sensitive list was some 550 lines in 2006 and this is going to be brought down to around 350 in the near future.

In a 2006 report, the World Bank makes a blunt but accurate assessment of intra-South Asian integration when they noted:

"South Asia is the least integrated region in the world, where integration is measured by intraregional trade in goods, capital, and ideas. Intraregional trade as a share of total trade is the lowest for South Asia. There is little

---

[10] Of course, some of the trade between the South Asian nations (especially India–Pakistan) either goes unrecorded or is diverted via a third country (e.g., Dubai).
[11] ARIC Regional Indicators database http://aric.adb.org/indicator.php.
[12] See Hattari, R and RS Rajan (2007). Intra-Asian FDI flows: Trends, patterns and determinants. Mimeo ICRIER, New Delhi (April).

cross-border investment within South Asia. The flow of ideas, crudely measured by the cross-border movement of people, or the number of telephone
calls, or the purchase of technology and royalty payments, are all low for
South Asia. In South Asia, only 7 percent of international telephone calls
are regional, compared to 71 percent for East Asia. Poor connectivity,
cross-border conflicts, and concerns about security, have all contributed to
South Asia being the least integrated region in the world."[13]

Will SAFTA help rectify this? The above cited World Bank report *pours
cold water* on the supposed benefits of SAFTA and offers reasons as to why
an FTA among South Asian countries is not "economically attractive".[14] First,
the South Asian economies are relatively small in terms of GDP and trade
flows. Because of small per capita incomes, the aggregate economic size of
the region remains small. The South Asian region accounts for 1.1 percent of
world trade but that drops to 0.4 percent when India is excluded. Second,
despite the proposed tariff reductions, the level of protection among the
SAARC countries remains quite high especially among agricultural commodities. The third reason pertains to the selection of excluded sectors and
rules of origin in the sense that when countries get to choose sectors that can
be excluded from tariff preferences, domestic lobby groups could influence
policy-makers to exclude sectors that are less likely to be able to endure
competition from the union partners. In addition, the report observes:

> "(T)he case for the SAFTA on both economic and political grounds is not
> especially persuasive. Economically, the region is small in relations to the
> outside world and remains heavily protected. Prima facie, these features
> imply that trade preferences to regional partners will likely be trade divert-
> ing rather than trade creating….(T)he rules of origin and sectoral exceptions
> are more likely to restrict the expansion of intraregional trade in precisely
> those sectors in which the countries have comparative advantage; that is, the
> sectors in which trade creation is more likely."[15]

The report goes on to note that the movement toward SAFTA has arisen
primarily because of political reasons. As it notes:

> "First, with most countries in the world moving forward with more and more
> (F)TAs, there is a clear sense in the region that it may be falling behind in this
> race. In the absence of hardnosed economic analysis, the view that 'if all oth-
> ers are doing it, it must be good' dominates. Second, the region has definitely
> suffered from the trade diversion generated by the many (F)TAs in the Americas
> and the European Union and its neighbors. The leaders in the region may

---

[13] The World Bank (2006). South Asia growth and regional integration. Report No. 37858-SAS, December.
[14] *Ibid.*, Chapter 7.
[15] The World Bank (2006), *op. cit.*, pp. 136–137.

therefore see a strategic advantage in forging ahead with as many of their own (F)TAs as possible in response. Third, politicians do not seem to distinguish between discriminatory and nondiscriminatory liberalization as sharply as economists do. As a result they see bilateral agreements as one of the instruments of liberalizing trade. Sometimes they even see it as a superior instrument because it leads to reciprocal liberalization in the partner counties. Fourth, SAFTA is also seen as a vehicle of promoting better political ties among neighbors, especially India and Pakistan, which have had a long history of rivalry."[16]

Conclusion: SAARC and the Role of India

India dominates the South Asian region in every possible way. India encompasses around 72 percent of South Asia's land area, 78 percent of the GDP, and around 75 percent of the population of SAARC as a whole. It is the region's largest exporter and importer of goods and services in the region and the biggest FDI recipient in the region. India is also not overly dependent on the region. Tables 5 and 6 show India's exports to and imports from the region, and exports to SAARC countries accounted for some 5 percent of total exports in 2006 while imports were 1 percent less of the total imports in 2005.

While a pre-liberalization India may have warmed up to the idea of SAFTA, a post-liberalization India seems somewhat less interested in the initiative despite having signed on to SAFTA. Part of this has been due to the fact that India has had a bad experience with Pakistan on the issue of Most Favored Nation (MFN) status. MFN status broadly means that a country will not be treated worse than any other country. India granted Pakistan MFN status in 1995 but Pakistan has refused to reciprocate, citing the Kashmir issue. This was despite Pakistan's ratification of SAFTA. This in turn has significantly limited the scope for expansion of intra-regional trade.

In view of the above, India has instead found the bilateral route to be a more productive path of liberalization in South Asia. Thus, India signed the Indo-Sri Lanka Free Trade Agreement (ISFTA) on 28 December 1998 and the agreement entered into force from 1 March 2000. India also has separate trade agreements with Afghanistan, Bangladesh, Maldives, and Nepal.[17] More generally, as India started liberalizing the economy in mid-1991, it started to earnestly pursue a "Look East" stance which explicitly has as its goal, an intensified economic relationship with Southeast Asian and East Asian countries. Table 7 shows the exports of goods from India to ASEAN, China, and the United States, and the percentage of total exports, while Table 8

---

[16] The World Bank (2006), *op. cit.*, p. 141.
[17] For an inventory of India's current trade agreements, see http://commerce.nic.in/india_rta_main.htm.

Table 5. India's exports to SAARC countries (US$ millions) (1993–2006).

	Total exports	Bangladesh	Bhutan	Maldives	Nepal	Pakistan	Sri Lanka	SAARC	As % of total exports
1993	17,436.9	334.2	2.0	7.2	68.1	47.8	233.3	692.7	4.0
1994	22,213.0	429.7	9.9	7.9	98.0	64.0	287.7	897.3	4.0
1995	26,337.5	644.8	11.1	15.4	120.1	57.3	366.7	1,215.4	4.6
1996	31,841.9	1,050.6	17.2	15.7	160.3	76.9	401.9	1,722.7	5.4
1997	33,498.0	869.7	22.0	10.4	165.9	157.4	477.8	1,703.1	5.1
1998	35,048.7	787.4	13.3	8.8	170.3	143.3	489.8	1,612.9	4.6
1999	33,211.0	995.4	9.6	8.4	122.4	106.1	437.0	1,678.8	5.1
2000	36,759.5	636.9	7.6	7.3	151.4	93.1	499.8	1,396.1	3.8
2001	44,147.4	874.4	1.1	24.5	141.1	186.6	630.5	1,858.1	4.2
2002	43,957.5	1,005.2	7.6	27.0	215.1	144.4	632.8	2,032.1	4.6
2003	52,823.5	1,178.3	39.1	31.7	351.1	206.6	922.8	2,729.5	5.2
2004	63,886.5	1,741.9	89.6	42.4	669.8	287.1	1,320.1	4,150.9	6.5
2005	83,501.6	1,630.5	84.6	47.6	742.8	520.8	1,412.6	4,438.9	5.3
2006	103,085.6	1,632.2	99.1	67.2	859.3	681.8	2,018.2	5,357.7	5.2

Source: Centre for Monitoring the Indian Economy (CMIE).
Note: The years here mean financial years. For example, 2006 would mean April 2005 to March 2006.

Table 6. India's imports from SAARC countries (US$ millions) (1993–2006).

	Total imports	Bangladesh	Bhutan	Maldives	Nepal	Pakistan	Sri Lanka	SAARC	As % of total imports
1993	20,582.8	11.4	1.1	0.1	23.3	122.0	12.9	170.9	0.8
1994	23,304.9	17.9	3.0	0.3	28.9	43.5	20.0	113.6	0.5
1995	28,662.2	38.2	18.3	0.2	36.6	52.8	30.7	176.8	0.6
1996	36,730.0	86.0	34.8	0.2	49.2	45.2	41.4	256.8	0.7
1997	39,165.5	62.3	33.8	0.2	64.1	36.2	45.2	241.8	0.6
1998	41,534.6	50.9	13.5	0.2	95.3	44.5	30.2	234.6	0.6
1999	42,379.2	62.4	6.1	0.1	144.8	214.4	37.7	465.5	1.1
2000	49,798.6	78.3	18.0	0.4	188.9	68.3	44.3	398.1	0.8
2001	50,056.3	74.0	21.0	0.1	231.1	64.1	44.8	435.1	0.9
2002	51,566.7	59.3	24.0	0.4	357.0	65.0	67.6	573.2	1.1
2003	61,533.3	62.2	32.2	0.3	282.3	44.9	91.0	513.0	0.8
2004	78,202.9	77.7	52.4	0.4	286.2	57.7	194.9	669.3	0.9
2005	111,471.5	59.4	71.0	0.6	345.7	94.9	378.2	949.8	0.9
2006	143,408.5	118.7	88.8	2.0	379.9	177.5	571.6	1338.5	0.9

Source: Centre for Monitoring the Indian Economy (CMIE).

Note: The years here mean financial years. For example, 2006 would mean April 2005 to March 2006.

Table 7. India's exports to other countries/regions (US$ millions) (1993–2006).

	Total exports of India	ASEAN	As % of total exports	China	As % of total exports	US	As % of total exports
1993	17,436.9	1,169.23	6.7	132.89	0.8	3,307.34	19.0
1994	22,213.0	1,675.55	7.5	278.77	1.3	3,994.87	18.0
1995	26,337.5	1,901.98	7.2	254.3	1.0	5,022.08	19.1
1996	31,841.9	2,710.02	8.5	333.2	1.0	5,528.67	17.4
1997	33,498.0	2,857.67	8.5	615.32	1.8	6,560.95	19.6
1998	35,048.7	2,421.85	6.9	718.94	2.1	6,809.44	19.4
1999	33,211.0	1,592.48	4.8	427.06	1.3	7,198.03	21.7
2000	36,759.5	2,191.59	6.0	539.41	1.5	8,393.85	22.8
2001	44,147.4	2,816.98	6.4	830.03	1.9	9,251.55	21.0
2002	43,957.5	3,391.75	7.7	954.79	2.2	8,538.75	19.4
2003	52,823.5	4,530.97	8.6	1,979.38	3.7	10,917.3	20.7
2004	63,886.5	5,716.97	8.9	2,957.11	4.6	11,497.9	18.0
2005	83,501.6	8,288.5	9.9	5,613.56	6.7	13,760.1	16.5
2006	103,085.6	10,372.73	10.1	6,720.16	6.5	17,201	16.7

Source: Centre for Monitoring the Indian Economy (CMIE).

Note: The years here mean financial years. For example, 2006 would mean April 2005 to March 2006.
ASEAN numbers do not include Cambodia, Laos, and Myanmar.

Table 8. India's imports from other countries/regions (US$ millions) (1993–2006).

	Total imports to India	ASEAN	As % of total imports	China	As % of total imports	US	As % of total imports
1993	20,582.8	1,153.74	5.6	118.51	0.6	2,019.81	9.8
1994	23,304.9	1,101.67	4.7	301.58	1.3	2,738.81	11.8
1995	28,662.2	1,940.1	6.8	761.04	2.7	2,906.53	10.1
1996	36,730.0	2,688.06	7.3	813.19	2.2	3,866.98	10.5
1997	39,165.5	2,921.16	7.5	757.55	1.9	3,689	9.4
1998	41,534.6	3,382.29	8.1	1,120.7	2.7	3,721.36	9.0
1999	42,379.2	4,142.64	9.8	1,096.47	2.6	3,639.37	8.6
2000	49,798.6	4,918.86	9.9	1,288.27	2.6	3,568.3	7.2
2001	50,056.3	3,882.14	7.8	1,494.92	3.0	2,844.37	5.7
2002	51,566.7	4,023.62	7.8	2,042.47	4.0	3,159.02	6.1
2003	61,533.3	4,822.86	7.8	2,797.55	4.5	4,452.34	7.2
2004	78,202.9	7,028.52	9.0	4,056	5.2	5,038.29	6.4
2005	111,471.5	8,704.86	7.8	7,095.06	6.4	6,998.47	6.3
2006	143,408.5	10,085.09	7.0	10,737.92	7.5	7,776.83	5.4

Source: Centre for Monitoring the Indian Economy (CMIE).

Note: The years here mean financial years. For example, 2006 would mean April 2005 to March 2006. ASEAN numbers do not include Cambodia, Laos, and Myanmar.

shows the same for imports. Examination of these tables clearly shows an increased partnership in terms of trade with ASEAN and China.[18] To supplement this increased partnership, India is negotiating an FTA with ASEAN, has an FTA with Thailand since 2001, a Comprehensive Economic Cooperation Agreement (CECA) with Singapore since 2005, and is looking to sign bilaterals with other Southeast Asian nations.[19] All of these suggest that India is slowly breaking away from its South Asian moorings and moving East.

The success of SAARC going forward is directly dependent on the extent of interest that its largest member decides to take in it which in turn depends on the India–Pakistan rivalry. While India may have been interested in the concept of SAARC in the mid-1980s as well as into the 1990s, its interest has certainly waned in the 2000s. The expansion of SAARC to allow for the observer status of the countries like Japan, China, and Korea may help to reinvigorate the alliance, though one will have to wait and see.

[18] Also see Kelly, D and RS Rajan (2006). Introduction to managing globalisation: Lessons from China and India. In *Managing Globalisation: Lessons from China and India.* D Kelly, RS Rajan and G Goh (eds.), Singapore: World Scientific, Chapter 1.
[19] See Chapter 17 of this Volume.

Chapter 20

Monetary and Financial Cooperation in Asia: More than Just Buzzwords?*

Introduction

There are a number of factors that have motivated monetary and financial regionalism and cooperation in Asia. First was the body blow that the region received from the financial crisis of 1997–1998 and the perceived inadequate response to it from extra-regional players. Second are the ongoing concerns about continued under-representation of Asia in IMF quota distribution and Asia's apparent lack of voice in international monetary affairs, along with the belief that Asia has ample resources for regional self-help.[1] Third have been external developments in regionalism, particularly the deepening and broadening of the European Union (EU). To be sure, many economists have remained circumspect about the potential benefits of deeper monetary integration in Asia (do the microeconomic benefits outweigh the macroeconomic costs arising from loss of monetary policy sovereignty?), and there are signs of emerging tensions within the EU regarding the net benefits of a single currency. Nevertheless, there is no doubting the inspiration that many Asian policy-makers have drawn from the deepening and broadening of European regionalism, especially in the monetary and financial areas. Fourth has been the growing *de facto* economic interdependence (so-called "market-driven regionalism") as well as the regional nature of spillovers ("contagion").[2]

---

* This chapter draws on Rajan, RS (2006). Monetary and financial cooperation in Asia: emerging trends and prospects. *Discussion Paper No.107*. New Delhi: Research and Information System for Developing Countries (RIS).

[1] See Henning, R (2005). Systemic contextualism and financial regionalism: The case of East Asia. mimeo (August). For a recent discussion of IMF Quota formulas and shares, see Cooper, RN and T Truman (2007). The IMF Quota formula: Linchpin of fund reform. *Policy Brief No. 07-01*, Washington, DC: Peterson Institute; and Mirakhor, A and I Zaidi (2006). Rethinking the governance of the international monetary fund. *IMF Working Paper No. WP/06/273*, December.

[2] For a discussion of the definitions, types and channels of contagion, see Rajan, RS (2003). Safeguarding against capital account crises: Unilateral, regional and multilateral options for East Asia. In *Financial Governance in East Asia*, de Brouwer, G (ed.), pp. 239–63. London: Routledge.

This chapter also takes stock of the recent ongoing monetary and financial regionalism in Asia, paying specific attention to the Chiang Mai initiative (CMI) as well as the Asian Bond Fund (ABF) initiative. The chapter also discusses next steps that might be taken to enhance monetary and financial regionalism in Asia, including issues surrounding the Asian Currency Unit (ACU).[4]

Monetary Regionalism in Asia: Chiang-Mai Initiative (CMI)

It has long been recognized that inadequate liquidity can threaten the stability of international financial regimes.[5] Illiquidity can create crises even when economic fundamentals are sound, or it can make a bad situation worse when the fundamentals are weak. Moreover, once it becomes a problem, illiquidity further undermines the confidence of international capital markets. Capital outflows increase, thereby reducing liquidity still further. The speed and intensity of economic adjustment following a crisis is largely

---

[3] For a discussion of capital account crisis and the IMF's role in managing them, see Ghosh, A, T Lane, M Schulze-Ghattas, A Bulír, J Hamann and A Mourmouras (2002). IMF-supported programs in capital account crises. *IMF Occasional Paper No. 210*, February.

[4] The acronym ACU is actually already used in Asia — the "Asian Clearing Union" has been in existence since December 1974 and is based in Tehran, Iran. This ACU was an initiative of the Bangkok-based UN-ESCAP aimed at developing a region-wide system for clearing payments among members. The current members are Bangladesh, Bhutan, India, Iran, Nepal, Pakistan, Sri Lanka, and Myanmar (Burma).

[5] See Bird, G and RS Rajan (2002). The evolving Asian financial architecture. *Essays in International Economics No. 26* (February), Princeton University.

dictated by the scarcity of liquidity; it is the extreme shortage of liquidity that called for rapid adjustment in East Asia in 1998.[6]

Having appreciated the importance of ensuring adequate liquidity as a safeguard against future financial crises, many Asian countries consciously attempted to build up reserves immediately after the crisis, partly as a precautionary motive.[7] Nonetheless, the region's reserve accumulation (so-called "floating with a life-jacket") is costly on many fronts since the countries are effectively swapping high-yielding domestic assets for lower yielding foreign ones. In view of this, it is recognized that countries need to buttress their own reserve holdings with external liquidity arrangements. The need to provide adequate liquidity to help forestall a crisis in a distressed economy and prevent its spread to other countries took center stage in the reform of the financial architecture immediately after the crisis.

The International Monetary Fund's (IMF) response was to create the Contingent Credit Line (CCL). "The CCL was conceived as a precautionary line of defense to help protect countries pursuing strong policies in the event of a balance of payments need arising from the spread of financial crises".[8] The idea here was to establish a precautionary line of credit for countries with "sound" policies that might be affected by contagion from a crisis and to finance this from outside the Fund's quota-based resources by new arrangements to borrow (NAB). The negotiation of conditionality with potential users of the CCL would therefore take place before the country needed to draw on liquidity from the Fund. But no country negotiated a CCL. Consequently, the facility underwent a major review and partial overhaul, and was eventually shut down. The CCL has not been replaced by another similar liquidity facility and the international financial architecture has made limited progress in the area of liquidity enhancement as a financial safeguard.

Against this background, and in recognition that financial stability has the characteristics of a regional public good, it is understandable that Asian countries have been eager to promote regional monetary cooperation. The CMI has taken center stage in this regard. The CMI is a network of swap arrangements which was agreed among ASEAN plus Three (APT) countries in

---

[6] For instance, the East Asian process of "V-shaped" adjustment was not very different from the stylized patterns of previous currency crisis episodes in developing countries. See Eichengreen, B and A Rose (2001). To defend or not to defend? That is the question. mimeo (February). However, the degree of initial contraction and subsequent recovery was far greater in East Asia, attributable to the severe liquidity crisis that was triggered by investors' panic. See Rajan, RS and R Siregar (2001). Private capital flows in East Asia: Boom, bust and beyond. In *Financial Markets and Policies in East Asia*, G de Brouwer (ed.), pp. 47–81. London: Routledge.

[7] See Chapter 1 of this Volume.

[8] See IMF (2001). *Annual Report 2001*. Washington, DC: IMF (September).

May 2000.[9] It is important to keep in mind that the CMI was not envisaged to be either a mechanism for inappropriate currency pegging in the region or a mechanism for managing a crisis after it erupts. Rather, it is primarily aimed at preventing a crisis from erupting in the first instance.

The CMI has two components, viz. (a) ASEAN swap arrangement (ASA) which was expanded from five to ten countries, and from US$ 200 million to US$1 billion and increased again to US$2 billion;[10] and (b) networks of bilateral swap arrangements (BSAs) among the three North Asian countries (Japan, China, Korea) and one of the three and one of the ASEAN countries (Fig. 1).[11] The expanded ASA is to be made available for two years and is renewable upon mutual agreement of the members. Each member is allowed to draw a maximum of twice its commitment from the facility for a period of up to six months

Network of Bilateral Swap Arrangements (BSAs) under the Chiang Mai Initiative (CMI)   (after inurement of the 3rd BSA between Japan and Thailand)

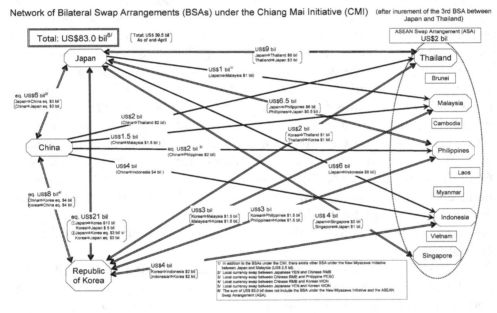

Fig. 1.   The Chiang Mai initiative: Progress to date (as of May 2006).

Source: Ministry of Finance, Japan web site.

---

[9] The 10 ASEAN countries are Indonesia, Malaysia, Philippines, Singapore, Thailand, and Brunei Darussalam, as well as the newer/transition members, viz. Cambodia, Laos, Myanmar, Vietnam, Timor-Leste (formerly East Timor).

[10] There are also a series of repurchase agreements (repos) that allow ASEAN members with collateral such as US Treasury bills to swap them for hard currency (usually US dollars) and then repurchase them at a later date.

[11] For more details on the CMI and monetary regionalism in Asia more generally, see Henning, *op. cit.*, and Park, YC (2004). Beyond the Chiang Mai initiative: Prospects for regional financial and monetary integration in East Asia. Paper prepared for meeting on G-24, September.

with the possibility of a further extension of six more months at most. The basic characteristics of the BSAs are as follows. Twenty percent of the liquidity can be drawn automatically without conditionality for 630 days (90 days, renewable seven times). Interest paid is LIBOR +1.5 percent for first 180 days, rising by 50 basis points for each renewal to a maximum of LIBOR +3 percent. Importantly, the swap providing countries form their own individual opinions on the potential swap recipient. Drawing of more than 20 percent regional liquidity requires the country to come under IMF conditionality.

The CMI is an important step in Asian monetary regionalism as it is the first time regional countries have pre-committed resources as a means of regional financial safeguard. However, it clearly remains a work in progress. A number of important details remain to be worked out if the CMI is to be an effective liquidity enhancing measure. First is the inadequate size especially of the liquid component. For instance, the current aggregate size of $75 billion among all 13 APT countries (Fig. 1) pales in comparison to the crisis packages offered to Korea, Indonesia, and Thailand in 1997–1998. Second is the issue of how coordination between potential creditor countries is to be done. For instance, is the bilateral arrangement subject to regional approval? How is borrowing/lending to be distributed? Both these questions lead on to the key issue of how to regionalize (though more commonly referred to as "multilateralize") the CMI, which is a series of bilateral and rather uncoordinated swaps. In fact in the Joint Ministerial Statement of 8th APT's Finance Ministers' Meeting in Istanbul in May 2005, there was an agreement to re-evaluate the process/possibility of regionalizing the arrangements.[12] As part of this there was an agreement to look into developing a collective mechanism to activate the swaps. There was also recognition of the need to improve on and link surveillance more closely and effectively to the CMI. Other issues relating to the CMI include raising the non-IMF-linked share (what type of independent conditionality with teeth?) and making transparent and automatic the condition for withdrawal, and there is a need for further augmentation of the CMI in terms of expanding the size of the CMI and enlarging it to include other Asian countries. As two observers of the CMI have pointed out:[13]

"Another issue is where India, Australia, and New Zealand (the later two are in the Asia-Pacific grouping) stand in this. ASEAN has already entered into a framework agreement with India on a comprehensive economic partnership. China has entered into arrangements with India, New Zealand and Australia,

---

[12] See "The Joint Ministerial Statement of the 8th ASEAN+3 Finance Ministers' Meeting" (Istanbul, 4 May 2005) (http://www.aseansec.org/17448.htm).

[13] Dayantra-Banda, OG and J Whalley (2007). Regional monetary arrangements in ASEAN+3 as insurance through reserve accumulation and swaps. *Working Paper No. 22*, Centre for International Governance Innovation, p. 41. The authors also broach the important issue of regional leadership.

and Japan also has regional arrangements with these countries. Some initial negotiations for a free trade area between ASEAN, Australia, and New Zealand have also begun. These three countries have increasingly more open economies, and their links with East Asia are likely to expand over time. These economies have been increasingly integrating with East Asia. Including them in East Asian regional forums and arrangements expands the set of developed and fast growing economies with well-functioning economic and financial systems and markets. Nonetheless, attempts are underway to include India, New Zealand and Australia in the ongoing East Asian policy dialogue on economic cooperation. In 2005, the ASEAN+3 countries agreed to pursue the evolution of the ASEAN+3 Summit into an East Asian Summit by the participation of ASEAN, Japan, China, Korea, India, Australia, and New Zealand. The possibility of ASEAN+6 monetary cooperation can thus not be ruled out."

Over time, consideration should be given to transforming the CMI into a regional reserve pooling mechanism.[14] A regional reserve pool could involve three tiers of liquidity. The first tier is owned reserves which offers the highest degree of liquidity and have zero conditionality but is costly. The second tier is subdivided into a country's own reserves placed with regional pool and other members' reserves with the pool. The third tier is conventional IMF lending. With such a structure, the degree of liquidity could be inversely related to the degree of conditionality. Overall though, it warrants repeating that effective deepening of regional monetary integration will not happen until there is a considerable strengthening of the regional surveillance mechanism with well worked out surveillance and policy conditionality.[15]

Financial Regionalism in Asia: Asia Bond Fund (ABF)

The financial crisis of 1997–1998 also made apparent significant gaps and weaknesses in East Asia's financial sectors. While the regional economies are taking noteworthy steps to strengthen, upgrade, and integrate their financial

---

[14] As recommended by Rajan, RS and R Siregar (2004). Centralized reserve pooling for the ASEAN plus three (APT) countries. In *Monetary and Financial Cooperation in East Asia*. pp. 285–330. Palgrave-McMillan Press for the Asian Development Bank. and Rajan, RS, R Siregar and G Bird (2005). The precautionary demand for reserve holdings in Asia: Examining the case for a regional reserve pool. *Asia-Pacific Journal of Economics and Business*, 5, 21–39.

[15] As noted by Dayantra-Banda and Whalley (2007), *op. cit.*,

"The system at present is aimed at insurance rather than achieving wider monetary and financial development and the current system does not require a single regional monetary authority. If monetary cooperation in ASEAN+3 is to take on a wider form, a system of simultaneous monetary development involving a common exchange rate policy, a single monetary authority, and deeper financial market development are necessary foundations. Seemingly, a single monetary authority is needed to ultimately complete the monetary integration process in the region, but many problems confront the emergence of that authority." (p. 44)

systems, the contagious nature of the 1997–1998 crisis has led many observers and policy-makers to the view that there are positive externalities from cooperating to strengthen their individual financial sectors, to develop regional financial markets, and to diversify their financial structures away from bank-based systems to bond markets. What is wrong with Asia's continued heavy dependence on bank lending as a source of private market financing?

Bond financing is considered a relatively more stable source of debt financing as bank loans are primarily illiquid, fixed-price assets in the sense that the interest rate — which is the price of the loan — does not vary much on the basis of changing market circumstances. Thus, almost all the adjustments have to take place via rises and falls in the quantity of bank lending, which in turn leads to sharp booms and busts in bank flows.[16] These sudden reversals in bank flows had calamitous and long-lasting effects on the domestic financial systems in the East Asian economies in 1997–1998. The World Bank has also acknowledged the importance of bond markets compared to bank lending, noting:[17]

> "(c)ompared to the bank market, bond markets offers some advantages in terms of longer maturities, tradability, and back-weighted repayment structures that help support equity returns (p. 157)."[18]

In this regard, there have been two main initiatives underway in East Asia. One is the ABF established by the 11 members of the Executives' Meeting of East Asia-Pacific Central Bank (EMEAP),[19] and the other is the Asian Bond Market Initiative (ABMI) by APT economies.[20] The latter which was endorsed at the ASEAN+3 Finance Ministers Meeting (AFMM) in Manila in August 2003,

---

[16] For instance, see Ito, T and YC Park (eds.) (2004). *Developing Asian Bond Markets*, Canberra: Asia Pacific Press; and Eichengreen, B and P Luengnaruemitchai (2005). Why doesn't Asia have bigger bond markets? *Working Paper No.10576*, NBER. For an overview of Asian bond markets, see Hamada, K, SC Jeon and JW Ryou (2004). Asian bonds markets: Issues, prospects and tasks for cooperation. Paper prepared for the *Korea and the World Economy III Conference*, July 3–4.

[17] World Bank (2004). *Global Development Finance*. New York: Oxford University Press.

[18] According to one study, bank-based financial systems tend to be relatively more crisis-prone, and financial systems that are more bond financed-based tend to be associated with higher growth whether or not there is a crisis. See Arteta, CO (2005). Does bond market development help reduce the cost of crises? Evidence from developing countries. Mimeo (April).

[19] The EMEAP "is a cooperative organization of central banks and monetary authorities (hereinafter simply referred to as central banks) in the East Asia and Pacific region. Its primary objective is to strengthen the cooperative relationship among its members. It comprises the central banks of 11 economies: Reserve Bank of Australia, People's Bank of China, Hong Kong Monetary Authority, Bank Indonesia, Bank of Japan, Bank of Korea, Bank Negara Malaysia, Reserve Bank of New Zealand, Bangko Sentral ng Pilipinas, Monetary Authority of Singapore, and Bank of Thailand". See http://www.emeap.org/.

[20] More information on all these and other initiatives is available on the portal created and maintained by the Asian Development Bank (ADB) http://asianbondsonline.adb.org/.

focuses primarily on developing efficient bond markets in Asia to enable the private and public sectors to raise and invest long-term capital. The activities of ABMI are primarily concentrated on facilitating access to the market through a wider variety of issuers and enhancing market infrastructure to foster bond markets in Asia.

The focus of the remainder of this section is specifically on ABF which was established on 2 June 2003. The first stage of the ABF essentially involved the regional governments voluntarily contributing about 1 percent each of their reserves to a fund dedicated to purchasing regional sovereign and semi-sovereign bonds denominated in US dollars. The initial size of the ABF was about US$1 billion and the fund has been passively managed by the investment management unit of the Swiss-based BIS. The mandate is to invest in bonds in eight of the eleven member countries of EMEAP, the developed countries of Australia, New Zealand, and Japan solely being lenders to the ABF. In a noteworthy next step, the ABF 2 (second stage of the ABF) was established in December 2004. The quantum of funds involved was doubled in magnitude (US$2 billion), and its mandate is to invest in selected domestic currency sovereign and quasi-sovereign bonds in the eight countries.

More specifically, the ABF 2 comprises two components (US$1 billion each): (a) a Pan-Asian Bond Index Fund (PAIF) and (b) a Fund of Bond Funds (FoBF). The PAIF is a single bond fund, while the FoBF is a two-layered structure with a parent fund investing in eight single market sub-funds (Fig. 2). The International Index Company (IIC), a joint venture between ABN Amro, JP Morgan, and Morgan Stanley (iBoxx ABF), has created the benchmark indices for all nine funds. The funds will be passively managed to match the benchmark index. The seed money for single bond funds has been divided on pre-determined criteria and local fund managers have been appointed to manage the respective funds.

The specific criteria for market weights in each sub-fund (and distribution within PAIF) are based on: (a) the size of the local market; (b) the turnover ratio in that market; (c) the sovereign credit rating; and (d) a market openness factor. The market weights will be reviewed annually, with market openness being a particularly important factor in the allocation of weights.[21] The parent fund is limited to investments by EMEAP member central banks only. While the initial phase of PAIF was confined to investments by EMEAP central banks only (US$1 billion), it was opened up to investments by other retail investors in Phase 2.

In broad terms, the objectives of the ABF are fourfold: First, to diversify debt financing from bank lending to bond financing by developing regional

---

[21] Ma, G and EM Remolona (2005). Opening markets through a regional bond fund: Lessons from ABF2. *BIS Quarterly Review*, June, 81–92.

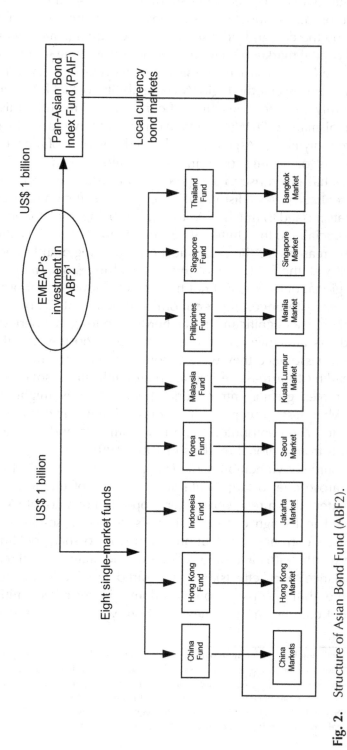

Fig. 2. Structure of Asian Bond Fund (ABF2).

Source: Ma, G and EM Remolona (2005). Opening markets through a regional bond fund: Lessons from ABF2. *BIS Quarterly Review*, June, 86.

financial/capital markets by reducing supply-side constraints and introducing low cost products and by raising investor awareness and broaden investor base on the demand side; secondly, to encourage a convergence in financial and capital market policies as well as accelerating improvements in the financial market infrastructure; thirdly, to recycle regional funds intraregionally and also reduce the region's vulnerability to "fickle" international investors; fourthly, to lessen the extent of currency and maturity mismatches (i.e., "double mismatches"). We elaborate on the latter two objectives below.

As is commonly noted, Asia as a whole holds the bulk of the world's savings. The excess of savings over investment along with quasi-managed exchange rates has given rise to a large current account and an overall balance of payment surpluses. Historically, the lack of sufficiently liquid financial instruments has led to much of Asia's savings being re-channeled outside the region, especially to the United States. In relation to this, it is often noted that one of the reasons for the intensification of the regional financial crisis of 1997–1998 was the fickleness of international investors, many of whom were extra-regional ones who did not have much knowledge about regional economies or differences in economic fundamentals between the economies. There was significant "panic herding" during that period as international creditors and investors chose to reduce exposures to all regional economies *en masse* once they were spooked by the crisis in Thailand and Indonesia, leading to a massive international bank run. Insofar as the ABF proposal promotes greater intraregional financing, this might make the region somewhat less susceptible to extra-regional "investor ignorance" which is said to have contributed to an indiscriminate and disorderly withdrawal of funds from regional markets in 1997–1998.

Another source of vulnerability made apparent by the 1997–1998 financial debacle arose due to large-scale accumulation of uncovered external debt. To the extent that a relatively larger proportion of a country's liabilities is denominated in foreign currency vis-à-vis its assets (so-called "liability dollarization"), a currency devaluation could lead to sharp declines in the country's net worth, with calamitous effects on the financial and real sectors (so-called "balance sheet" effects).[22] On the part of the developing Asia-Pacific economies, the ability to issue bonds in domestic currencies mitigates the concerns about currency mismatches (i.e., borrowing and interest payments

---

[22] The macroeconomic implications of these balance sheet effects have been explored by Rajan, RS and M Parulkar (2007). Real sector shocks and monetary policy responses in a financially vulnerable emerging economy. Forthcoming in *Emerging Markets Trade and Finance*; Rajan, RS (2007). Managing new style currency crises: The swan diagram revisited. *Journal of International Development*, 19, 583–606; and Bird, G and RS Rajan (2006). Does devaluation lead to economic recovery or economic contraction? Examining the analytical issues with reference to Thailand. *Journal of International Development*, 16, 141–156.

in foreign currency but assets and revenue streams in local currency) which in turn could negatively impact the project's solvency in the event of a currency devaluation.[23] Thus, while the ABF 1 was solely focused on foreign currency bonds, the ABF 2 is notable in that it involves transacting solely in local currency bonds.

While the ABF is a welcome move for regional financial cooperation, it is important not to oversell the initiative. Why? First and foremost is the quantum of funding available. The current US$2 billion funding of ABF 2 is a drop in the bucket relative to the region's aggregate reserve holdings or infrastructural financing requirements. Second, if the supply of good quality sovereigns and quasi-sovereign paper is limited (which appears to be the case) it could merely crowd out private bond purchases, hence leading to no new net financing.[24] This in turn implies the need to support "public providers of infrastructure services in achieving commercial standards of creditworthiness to access capital markets on a sustainable basis over the long term".[25]

Moving forward, the Asian countries need to persist with the attempts to develop well-functioning financial markets and institutions. In particular, countries need to deepen and upgrade national and regional government and corporate bond markets as a means of reducing the region's heavy reliance on banks. Greater attention needs to be given to lowering transactions costs in regional financial markets. In this regard it is important to note that discussions have been underway in the region about the possible creation of regional financial infrastructure (clearing and settlements systems, credit agency) as well as harmonization of withholding tax policies and capital account policies.

Masahiro Kawai, the Dean of the Asian Development Bank Institute (ADBI) in Tokyo, made the following observations in a speech on Asian bond market development[26]:

"Challenges in bond markets are many and, for this reason, a more focused approach would be helpful. It would be useful to focus on developing a

---

[23] It is important to ask the question as to why some countries are not able to borrow overseas in domestic currencies (so-called "Original Sin" hypothesis) *a la* Hausmann, R, U Panizza and E Stein (2000). Why do countries float the way they float? *Working Paper No. 418*, Inter-American Development Bank. Logically, if there is a significant risk premium imposed on a certain currency and if interest rates are "sufficiently" high, there will always be some potential borrowers. While this is true, the concern is that a potential solvency risk will merely be converted to a liquidity risk (to the extent that revenues in the event of a negative shock are not sufficiently high to meet the high interest payments). See Jeanne, O (2000). Foreign currency debt and the global financial architecture. *European Economic Review*, 44, 719–727.

[24] For a more detailed and forceful critique of such regional bond initiatives, see Eichengreen, B (2004). Financial development in Asia: The way forward. mimeo (January).

[25] See World Bank, *op. cit.*

[26] Kawai, M (2007). Asian bond market development: Progress, prospects and challenges. Keynote speech delivered at *High Yield Debt Summit, Asia 2007* (Singapore: May 16–17), p. 10.

liquid corporate bond market. Broadening the issuer base can help address the shortage of corporate investment paper in Asia but it is not the whole answer. Enabling environments need to be created for corporate bond market development through removal of regulatory, legal, tax and other impediments. Market infrastructure needs to be improved through the creation of efficient settlement systems directly linked to fixed-income exchanges and through the development of hedging instruments and derivatives markets. Corporate governance of firms should be strengthened through better accounting standards and disclosure requirements so that corporate issuers are subject to sufficient checks and balances."

While the ABF initiatives are modest steps in the right direction, it is important that it be expanded in size and membership. With regard to the latter, not all the ASEAN countries are part of EMEAP, and neither is India. These countries are therefore exclude from the ABF. Expansion of financial (and monetary) regionalism to include all members of ASEAN is justified by the fact that the APT countries as well as India, Australia, and New Zealand are founding members of the East Asian Summit (EAS).[27]

Conclusion: The Asian Currency Unit (ACU)

In addition to the CMI and ABF initiatives, a recent suggestion has been floated for an Asia Basket Currency (ABC) Initiative. The basic idea is that while the ABF merely purchases and holds on to sovereign and quasi-sovereign bonds, the ABC corporation would also create and issue basket currency bonds (weighted combination of regional currencies of the underlying national bonds) backed by regional sovereign bonds. If successful, the ABC could provide a fillip for the eventual creation of an Asian Currency Unit (ACU).[28]

---

[27] For a discussion of the EAS, see Chapter 16 of this Volume. Also see, Kumar, N (2005). Towards a broader Asian community: Agenda for the East Asia summit. *Discussion Paper No.100.* New Delhi: Research and Information System for Developing Countries (RIS).

[28] See Ito, T (2003). The ABC of Asian bonds. Paper presented at the *Second PECC Finance Forum Conference* (Hua Hin, Thailand: July 8–9). In the 8th APT Finance Ministerial Meeting in Istanbul in May 2005, the joint statement made reference to Asian currency basket bonds:

> "We will continue and expedite our efforts in undertaking a wide variety of studies and implementing various effective measures under the ABMI working groups....(W)e will introduce a roadmap that proposes gathering and sharing information in an integrated manner on bond market development and on our related efforts with the regular self-assessment conducted by member countries. The possible issuance of Asian currency-basket bonds could be explored under the auspices of the roadmap. We also agreed to embark the study of Asian Bond Standards to explore the development of international bond markets in Asia through tailoring necessary infrastructure and setting the procedure entrusted by global issuers and investors."

See "The Joint Ministerial Statement of the 8th ASEAN+3 Finance Ministers' Meeting" (Istanbul: 4 May 2005) (http://www.aseansec.org/17448.htm).

In a general sense the ACU is a weighted average of regional currencies *a la* the European Currency Unit (ECU).[29] At the microlevel the rationale for an ACU is to afford the opportunity for regional economic agents to invoice regional financial and trade transactions in the ACU, hence reducing the region's dependence on the US dollar and other external currencies. If successful, intra-regional intermediation of savings may be promoted, in the process possibly reducing the region's exposure to external shocks as discussed previously. However, in reality, it is unlikely that the ACU will be used on a widespread basis for some time to come.

The experience of Europe is instructive in this regard. The initial creation of the ECU in 1974–1975 did not lead to a widespread use of the unit. Even in the 1990s, until the actual creation of the euro, the vast majority of intra-European financial and trade transactions were not in ECUs but in US dollars primarily and other sovereign national European currencies. So it is not just the creation that is important, but there also has to be a coordinated agreement by regional bodies to start transacting in the new unit, failing which no one will want to take the first step.[30] The ACU has a better chance for success (in terms of becoming a significant regional vehicle currency) if a larger set of countries is included in the basket. In this regard it is imperative that the ACU be broadened from the proposed APT countries to also include India, Australia, and New Zealand (the other members of the EAS) all of which have significant financial market depth.

It has also been suggested that the ACU could be used as a means of enhancing *internal* exchange rate stability if the regional central banks begin to stabilize their respective currencies to the regional unit (i.e., helping reduce the possibility of regional competitive devaluations). The notion of stabilization vis-à-vis an internal basket *a la* Europe's Exchange Rate Mechanism (ERM) is distinct from stabilization vis-à-vis an external unit which would require that the ACU in turn be pegged in some way to external currencies such as the US dollar or euro, or some weighted average thereof. Of course, internal stability does not require the latter and in fact may exacerbate external currency stability. This may happen if regional countries substitute the use of external currencies for the ACU, hence being

---

[29] It is expected that the weights will be determined on the basis of regional country GDP and trade shares, with China, Japan, and Korea expected to dominate the weighting scheme. For an initial attempt at computing such a weighting scheme (which may not necessarily be the weights used by the ADB), see Ogawa, E and J Shimizu (2005). A deviation measurement for coordinated exchange rate policies in East Asia. *Discussion Paper No. 05-E-017*, REITI. Also see: http://www.rieti.go.jp/en/rieti_report/069.html.

[30] This inertial effect of existing currencies (i.e., advantage of incumbency) is based on the concept of "network externalities" or "lock in" effects, whereby there are limited incentives for economic agents to unilaterally take on a new currency (particularly for invoicing transactions). The network aspects of the internal currency status have been analyzed theoretically by Matsuyama, K, N Kiyotaki and A Matsui (1993). Toward a theory of international currency. *Review of Economic Studies*, 60, 283–307.

less concerned about fluctuations of their currencies relative to the external currencies. Conversely, effective external stability requires internal stability in the sense that if regional central banks do not explicitly or implicitly manage their currencies to the ACU, it is irrelevant whether the ACU *per se* is managed against the external currencies, as the proposed ACU will remain purely a theoretical construct. Indeed, the stated aim of the ADB at this stage is for the ACU to serve mainly as a means of benchmarking the extent of currency movements/deviations. As the ADB president, Haruhiko Kuroda noted:

> "The ACU ... could be used to monitor the stability of participating currencies and would tangibly demonstrate the need for greater exchange rate coordination. What Asia needs here is basically an exchange rate that is flexible toward the rest of the world but relatively stable within the region."[31]

Focusing on the notion of stabilization vis-à-vis an internal basket (i.e., regional currencies benchmarking movements to the ACU) while the potential microeconomic benefits noted above do not require internal stabilization, the latter could promote the more widespread use of the ACU. This is so as the regional central banks will automatically begin to use the ACU more extensively as a reserve and possibly even intervention currency, thus providing an additional inducement for private agents to intensify the use of the unit in invoicing and transactions.

Needless to say, the long-term viability of internal stabilization in an era of open capital markets requires there be an enhancement of regional surveillance, a degree of policy coordination, and an augmentation of regional liquidity arrangements. Nonetheless, given the divergence in economic and institutional structures in the region, absent macroeconomic policy coordination and mechanisms for automatic intra-regional fiscal transfers, any attempt at formal exchange rate coordination — let alone a full-fledged monetary union — is far too risky and premature and will likely be a failure, setting back prospects for other forms of economic integration.

---

[31] Kuroda, H (2005). Towards a borderless Asia: A perspective on Asian economic integration. Speech by Asian Development Bank (ADB) President at the Emerging Markets Forum (Oxford: 10 December).

Index

Agreement on South Asian Free Trade Area (SAFTA) 230–232, 235–237
ASEAN 69, 87, 88, 90, 91, 93, 94, 134, 140, 146, 175–189, 193, 195–201, 204–206, 211–213, 215–227, 232–235, 237, 240–242, 246–249, 254
ASEAN Economic Community (AEC) 220, 223, 224
ASEAN Free Trade Area (AFTA) 146, 186, 212, 215, 219–222, 224
ASEAN Investment Area (AIA) 146, 222
ASEAN Plus Three (APT) 201, 205, 245, 247–249, 254, 255
ASEAN swap arrangement (ASA) 246
ASEAN–China Free Trade Area (ACFTA) 186, 188, 212
Asia Basket Currency (ABC) Initiative 254
Asia Pacific Economic Cooperation (APEC) Forum 147, 201, 206
Asia vii, xi, xii, 3–8, 11–13, 17, 21, 23, 33–35, 37, 38, 43–46, 48, 51, 55, 57, 61, 65–71, 74, 75, 81, 87–96, 98, 99, 112, 113, 115–117, 125, 128, 134, 135, 139, 140, 142–147, 152, 158, 159, 163, 169, 171, 172, 175, 176, 180, 182, 184–186, 188, 189, 191, 193, 195, 196, 200–205, 210, 213, 215–219, 222, 229, 230, 232, 235–237, 243–250, 252–256
Asian Bond Fund (ABF) 35, 244, 248–254
Asian Bond Market Initiative (ABMI) 249, 250, 254

Asian Currency Unit (ACU) 244, 254–256
Asian Development Bank (ADB) 35, 74, 95, 99, 100, 131, 140, 147, 176–179, 183, 187, 201, 217, 235, 248, 249, 253, 255, 256

Band-Basket-Crawl (BBC) 43, 58, 59
Bangalore 101, 102, 155, 159
Bangalored 159
Bangkok Declaration 218
Bank of Thailand 40, 41, 49, 249
Banking crisis 88
Basic balance 18, 20, 21
Big Bang 74
Bilateral Swap arrangements (BSAs) 246, 247
Brazil, Russia, India, and China (BRICs) 193
Bretton Woods 6–8, 26
Business process outsourcing (BPO) 149, 152, 154, 155, 158

Capital account 4, 5, 7, 34, 72, 73, 79, 80, 81, 91, 92, 98, 243, 244, 253
Capital account deregulation 72, 79, 80, 92
Capital controls 73, 77, 80, 82, 83, 96
Capital flows vii, 4, 8, 16, 18, 19, 23, 42, 43, 57, 70, 72, 73, 77, 78, 81–84, 87, 91–96, 113, 116–119, 126, 135, 211, 245
Carry trade 87, 95, 97, 98
Central banks 3, 6–8, 10–12, 19–21, 24–26, 28, 31–34, 37–39, 41, 42,

44–49, 57–59, 66, 78, 84, 97, 104,
106, 249, 250, 255, 256
Central Provident Fund (CPF)   60, 61
Chiang Mai Initiative (CMI)   13,
244–248, 254
Chilean-type reserve requirements   83
Chinese renminbi   29, 33, 34
Cold turkey   74
Common effective preferential tariffs
(CEPT)   219–221
Competitiveness   12, 17, 51–56,
60–62, 73, 119, 125, 128, 142,
145, 157, 166, 181, 203, 216, 218,
219, 221–223
Contagion   5, 243, 245
Contingent credit line (CCL)   81, 245
Core inflation   44, 45
Currency board arrangement (CBA)
60
Currency crisis   30, 80, 82, 88, 245
Current account   4–8, 11, 15, 16,
18, 20–23, 30, 87–91, 116,
176, 252

Demographics   157, 171, 194
Double mismatches   252
Dutch disease   119

East Asian Crisis   65, 74
East Asian Summit (EAS)   193, 201,
205, 248, 254, 255
Euro   13, 16, 25, 27–30, 32–35,
57, 97, 200, 233,
234, 255
European Currency Unit (ECU)   27,
255
European Union (EU)   32, 33, 58, 95,
111, 147, 177, 196, 200, 215,
217, 218, 221, 229, 232–234,
236, 243
Executives' Meeting of East Asia-Pacific
Central Bank (EMEAP)   96,
249–251, 254
Exorbitant privilege   29, 34

FDI incentives   135, 136
Financial account   6, 18
Financial incentives   132–135
Fiscal/Tax incentives   132
Foreign aid   15, 85, 86, 111–113, 119
Foreign bank entry   xi, 65, 66, 70–75
Foreign direct investment (FDI)   vii, 9,
18, 20–22, 58, 61, 66, 69, 72, 92,
94–96, 107, 113, 115, 116, 118,
125–132, 134–137, 143, 144, 146,
147, 159, 168, 170–172, 175, 176,
182, 184–187, 194, 196, 211–213,
235, 237
Foreign exchange reserves (See
Reserves)   3–5, 9, 25, 27, 31, 32,
35, 103, 104, 106–108, 176

General Agreement on Trade in
Services (GATS)   73, 151
Global imbalances   xi, 3, 7, 23

Headline inflation   44

India–ASEAN Regional Trade and
Investment Area (RTIA)   196, 197
Indian rupee   29, 102, 106, 107
India-Singapore Comprehensive
Economic Cooperation Agreement
(CECA)   197, 212, 213, 242
Indo-Sri Lanka Free Trade Agreement
(ISFTA)   237
Infant industry argument   71, 131
Inflation targeting   37–49
Infrastructure in India   9, 99–101
International currency tax   81, 83
International liquidity   81
International Management
Development (IMD)   52–55
International Monetary Fund (IMF)
4–6, 22, 27, 28, 31, 38, 42, 45, 59,
65, 69–71, 73, 79, 81, 88–90, 92,
93, 96, 97, 119, 121, 126, 132,
134, 151, 152, 159, 172, 215,
243–245, 247, 248

Internationalization of the financial
    sector   66, 72
Investment promotion   127–131, 136,
    137, 213
Investment Promotion Agency (IPA)
    128, 129
IT/ITES industry   152, 153, 155, 157

Japanese yen   16, 27, 97

"Kaleidoscope" or "Knife-edge"
    comparative advantage   145, 181
KISS principle   45
Knowledge Process Outsourcing (KPO)
    154, 155

Lender of last resort (LOLR)   32, 47,
    70
Liability dollarization   252
LTCM Crisis 98

Mercantilism   xi, 3, 6, 7
Monetary Authority of Singapore (MAS)
    58–60, 249
Monetary policy rules (MPRs)   42,
    45, 59
Monetary regionalism   201, 244, 246,
    247, 254
Monetary sterilization   11, 48
Multifiber Arrangement (MFA)   167,
    181

Network externalities   30, 255
Nominal effective exchange rate
    (NEER)   55–57, 59, 60
North American Free Trade Agreement
    (NAFTA)   175, 215

Offshore currency trading   81
Offshoring   140, 149–152, 156, 210
Outsourcing   vii, 139, 140, 142, 144,
    149–152, 154–159, 166
Overseas Development Assistance
    (ODA)   111–113, 116, 118

Parts, components and accessories
    (PCAs)   139, 142, 143, 149, 180,
    207, 210
People's Bank of China (PBOC)   9,
    20, 58, 249
Pound sterling   25, 27
Production fragmentation   140, 146
Production sharing (see Production
    fragmentation)   139–142, 144,
    145–147, 149, 156, 180, 181
Prudence   xi, 3, 5, 6
Public–Private Partnerships (PPPs)
    102, 108, 110
Purchasing Power Parity (PPP)   28, 35,
    44, 175, 206

Real effective exchange rate (REER)
    17, 55–57, 59
Real exchange rate   12, 17, 44, 45,
    51, 55, 83, 119
Regional Trade Agreement (RTA)   146,
    205, 237
Remittances   111, 113–121
Reserve Bank of India (RBI)   11, 12,
    57, 103, 106, 107
Reserve currency   10, 20, 24–26, 28,
    30–34
Reserves   3–13, 17, 19–35, 38, 46,
    48, 57, 65, 68, 77, 81, 83, 87, 90,
    91, 93–96, 99, 103, 104, 106–108,
    176, 245, 247–249, 250, 253
Rules of Origin (ROOs)   214, 215,
    220, 236
Russian Crisis 98

SAARC Preferential Trading
    Arrangement (SAPTA)   230, 231
Savings glut   23
Singapore   viii, xi, xii, 3, 8, 10, 15,
    37, 43, 51–61, 65, 69, 71, 81, 87,
    88, 95, 99, 100, 107, 111, 118,
    128, 130, 134, 135, 140, 142, 145,
    149, 151, 157, 175, 178, 179, 182,
    183, 187–189, 193, 195–199,

203–221, 223, 225–227, 242, 246, 249, 251, 253
Singapore–Thailand Enhanced Economic Relationship (STEER)   225
South Asian Association for Regional Cooperation (SAARC)   229–239, 242
Spaghetti bowl phenomenon   215
Special Economic Zones (SEZs)   172, 173
Special Purpose Vehicle (SPVs)   9, 10, 104–106, 108
Sterilization (see monetary sterilization)   4, 11, 12, 48

Tobin tax   xi, 77, 78, 81–85
Transnational corporations (TNCs)   126, 127, 141, 142, 144, 145, 185

Treaty of Amity and Cooperation (TAC)   201

US dollar   xi, xii, 3, 4, 6, 7, 10, 11, 13, 16–18, 21, 23–27, 30, 32, 38, 49, 57, 59, 60, 95, 142, 150, 246, 250, 255
US dollar standard   26, 30, 32

World Bank   5, 8, 28, 29, 45, 46, 69, 70, 83, 87, 89, 91, 92, 94, 99, 100, 108, 109, 112–120, 129, 132, 140, 142, 143, 168, 176, 187, 215, 235–237, 249, 253
World Economic Forum (WEF)   52–55
World Trade Organization (WTO) Agreement   69

Zero interest rate policy (ZIRP)   97, 98